Professionals under Pressure

GW01250081

CARE & WELFARE

Care and welfare are changing rapidly in contemporary welfare states. The Care & Welfare series publishes studies on changing relationships between citizens and professionals, on care and welfare governance, on identity politics in the context of these welfare state transformations, and on ethical topics. It will inspire the international academic and political debate by developing and reflecting upon theories of (health) care and welfare through detailed national case studies and/or international comparisons. This series will offer new insights into the interdisciplinary theory of care and welfare and its practices.

SERIES EDITORS

Jan Willem Duyvendak, University of Amsterdam
Trudie Knijn, Utrecht University
Monique Kremer, Netherlands Scientific Council for Government Policy
  (Wetenschappelijke Raad voor het Regeringsbeleid – WRR)
Margo Trappenburg, Utrecht University, Erasmus University Rotterdam

PREVIOUSLY PUBLISHED

Willem Duyvendak, Trudie Knijn and Monique Kremer (eds.): *Policy, People, and the New Professional. De-professionalisation and Re-professionalisation in Care and Welfare*, 2006 (ISBN 978 90 5356 885 9)
Ine Van Hoyweghen: *Risks in the Making. Travels in Life Insurance and Genetics*, 2007 (ISBN 978 90 5356 927 6)
Anne-Mei The: *In Death's Waiting Room. Living and Dying with Dementia in a Multicultural Society*, 2008 (ISBN 978 90 5356 077 8)
Barbara Da Roit: *Strategies of Care. Changing Elderly Care in Italy and the Netherlands*, 2010 (ISBN 978 90 8964 224 0)
Janet Newman and Evelien Tonkens: *Participation, Responsibility and Choice. Summoning the Active Citizen in Western European Welfare States*, 2011 (ISBN 978 90 8964 275 2)
Patricia C. Henderson: *AIDS, Intimacy and Care in Rural KwaZulu-Natal. A Kinship of Bones*, 2011 (ISBN 978 90 8964 359 9)
Jeannette Pols: *Care at a Distance. On the Closeness of Technology*, 2012 (ISBN 978 90 8964 397 1)

PROFESSIONALS UNDER PRESSURE

The Reconfiguration of Professional
Work in Changing Public Services

Edited by
Mirko Noordegraaf
Bram Steijn

AMSTERDAM UNIVERSITY PRESS

Cover illustration: iStockphoto

Cover design: Sabine Mannel, NEON graphic design company, Amsterdam
Lay-out: JAPES, Amsterdam

ISBN   978 90 8964 509 8
e-ISBN   978 90 4851 830 2 (pdf)
e-ISBN   978 90 4851 831 9 (ePub)
NUR   756

Contents

Preface

Since the turn of the century, there has been a renewed interest in the classic theme of professionalism, with particular emphasis on public professionalism. Growing public and political concerns over the state of public service delivery – whether in policing, health care, education or welfare – have fueled debates about the pressures professionals face and the problems with professional service delivery that are the result of these pressures. Professionals, it is argued, face the burdens of business-like managers, experience a lack of occupational recognition, are subjected to excessive monitoring and accountability demands, and have lost their professional autonomies. Generally, this worrisome state is linked to the rise of managerialism. The increasing reliance on business-like management and performance measurement in public domains has harmed professional practices and values. Although many academics sketch refined pictures of pressured professionals, many of them reiterate worries and many also blame managerialism.

This book goes beyond worries and explanations that focus on such managerialism alone. On the basis of theoretical and empirical insights into sectors like health care, social welfare, education and policing, the authors show that professional work is not always burdened, that professionals have great leeway in coping with change, and that changes come from much more than mere managerialism. Changes in and around public services are induced by societal changes – new technologies, ICT, complex problems, distributed knowledge, demanding citizens. The extent to which they affect professional practices depends on the policy sector and organizations, and on the abilities of professionals to cope with pressures. Therefore, instead of getting rid of manageralism in order to *restore* public professionalism, this book stresses the importance of the *reconfiguration* of public professionalism. Contemporary service delivery calls for new professional skills and standards in order to maintain certain occupational autonomies and values, but at the same time modernize professional ways of working.

The book is the result of the Dutch collaborative research colloquium 'Professionals under pressure' (PuP) – started in 2006 and relabeled in 2012 'Reframing Public Professionalism' (RPP) – linked to research networks and projects abroad. It brings together Dutch scholars, who often also participate in international networks on professionalism, health care, education, and social work. International scholars, who have been visitors to the research colloquium, have contributed as well, especially Prof. Stephen Ackroyd and Prof. Janet Newman, both from the UK. We thank all authors for their cooperation and valuable contributions, and we thank all those colleagues who have more indirectly contributed to this volume. Special thanks also to the Netherlands Institute of Government (NIG) which has supported the colloquium, also financially. Finally, we thank David Schelfhout for his professional (!) editorial support.

Contrary to managerial times that call for immediate results, this book took quite some time, and 'the final touches' took more time than expected. However, time – including delay – is often crucial for improving performances and quality. We are certain that it brought this product to a higher level.

Mirko Noordegraaf and Bram Steijn
Utrecht and Rotterdam, October 2012

1 Introduction

Mirko Noordegraaf & Bram Steijn

Public service professionals 'under attack'?

There are many forms of public service delivery – providing healthcare, policing, educating children, assisting unemployed citizens in finding work – and in many ways, these services depend on professional workers. Policemen, medical doctors, nurses, teachers and welfare workers deliver services to clients. Although there are many types of professionals and it is difficult to define professionalism in clear and consistent ways, public service professionals have a few things in common. They primarily deal with clients – as cases, often complex cases – but they also serve public goals, such as safety, public health and employment. This case treatment is regulated by many rules and standards and to some or a large extent, these rules and standards are set by the occupational fields to which professional workers belong. The more standards are set by these occupational fields, the stronger these professionals are, also as far as autonomies and powers are concerned. This has always been legitimated by the fact that traditional professional rules and standards both concern case treatment, as well as wider public service ethics (e.g. Wilensky 1964; Freidson 2001). Professional fields not only establish bodies of knowledge and expertise in order to regulate complex case treatment; they also develop shared service orientations, in order to treat cases rightly and serve society ethically and justly. Professional associations secure both technical and ethical regulation.

Despite these clear features, public professionalism has always been a slippery concept, and increasingly, public professionalism seems to be under attack. To begin with, the value of functionalist readings of professionalism and professional strength is increasingly criticized. Professional regulation guarantees neither effective case treatment, nor societal gains. In fact, according to critical and political readings, (public) professionalism has mainly been a self-serving project, advancing the interests of professional workers themselves, instead of clients and society at large. Furthermore, there has been an uneasy relationship between professionalism and organizational contexts. Although contradictions between professionals and organizational action are logical and perhaps even desirable, they are contested as well. Most professional public service delivery occurs within bureaucratic and organizational systems. Clarke and Newman (1997) speak of bureau-professional regimes. Lately, these regimes are being reconfigured. Due to massive managerial reform programs, aimed at Western welfare state restructuring, the rationalization of service organizations and the improvement of service performances, professionalism is considered to be disciplined by managerial and market logics. Authors speak about 'troubled times' (Gleeson & Knigths 2006), 'attacks' on professionalism (Ackroyd 1996), 'deprofessionalization' (Broadbent et al. 1997) and 'persecuted professionals' (Farrell & Morris 1999). They stress the well-documented fact that our society increasingly distrusts professionals, that professionals are drawn into managerialized organizations, and that their professional autonomies and powers are far from secure.

These attacks and pressures that come from different directions, from above, beneath and sideways, are of course felt at and around workfloors where professionals do their work. No wonder that professionals and their associations (and others) have started to express worries and have voiced complaints about the state of affairs in public service delivery. This takes many different guises, and is framed and qualified differently, but the general thrust is clear. The parties involved stress the 'burdens' of professional work, the 'obligations' placed on professionals, and the 'demands' that policy-makers and others develop. Professionals are burdened by 'bureaucratic' systems, obliged to be loyal to 'meaningless' performance regimes, and forced to spend 'valuable work time' on administrative work instead of their 'real work', i.e. treating patients, educating children or arresting criminals.

Pressures: Where do they come from?

In short, when it comes to the state of professionalism in public services, such as police forces, immigration offices, welfare organizations, schools, hospitals, and the like, there seem to be many *pressures* on professional work and professionals *feel pressured*. Moreover, it is not only assumed or observed that there *are* pressures; many generally assume that these pressures are *caused by* managerialist reforms and that they are *problematic*, especially for professionals themselves. When people – politicians, administrators, experts, opinion leaders, professionals themselves – speak about public professionals, their line of reasoning can be summarized as follows (e.g. Noordegraaf 2008; De Bruijn 2010; De Bruijn & Noordegraaf 2010):

Public and non-profit organizations like police organizations, healthcare institutions and schools implement certain policies and to accomplish this they have professional workers who interact with clients and render services. These professionals, such as policemen, medical doctors, and teachers, are trained members of certain well-established and (partly) protected occupations. But they have been encapsulated by businesslike regimes, bureaucratic standards, and market pressures, which harm professional motivation, values and service delivery. Politicians want well-designed and (cost) controlled service systems, with appropriate incentives. Managers – especially those with MBA backgrounds – have turned their backs on workfloors and primarily opt for economies of scale, productivity, efficiency, and transparency. 'Clashes' between professionals and managers must be reduced by reducing the number of managers, and by 'setting professionals free'. Politics must be reinvented; politicians must set appropriate parameters for implementation and they must guard the autonomies of professionals.

Although there could be some truth in these argumentative steps, they must be handled with care (see e.g. Kuhlmann & Saks 2008; Muzio & Kirkpatrick 2011; Noordegraaf 2011; Faulconbridge & Muzio 2012). Although professionals might encounter the 'burdens of bureaucracy', it is questionable *whether these burdens have grown dramatically, where they come from, whether politicians and managers can be blamed, and what they mean, also in the longer term.* Pressures might also come from non-organizational or non-managerial sources, in fact, they might come from changing professional work and work forces themselves (e.g. Noordegraaf 2011). Moreover, pressures might not automatically create burdened professionals, as pressures – seen as new circumstances – might also offer new opportunities for professional services to innovate or be effective in new ways. Finally, there might be good reasons to renew professional work as well as work conditions, even if professionals feel burdened. All in all, an alternative reasoning might go like this:

Public and non-profit organizations still have professional workers, but the nature of their work is changing. Professionals are still operative, but the boundaries of professionalism have become less self-evident and inter-professional struggles have increased. Public and non-profit managers might act forcefully, but these managers are also subjected to pressures, i.e. bigger forces that come from elsewhere – politics, policy-makers and the media. Politicians and policy-makers want better and more efficient services, not only because of declining budgets, but also because of a perceived lack of quality. This is enhanced by the media, which tend to stress service failures. These forces are not merely intentional; they have a lot to do with changing demographic, socio-economic and cultural patterns. Professional services are unavoidably changing in nature, because clients have become assertive and demanding; because social norms – such as respect – have been changing; because means have become scarce, not only financial means but also human resources; because technologies have progressed; because risks have been mounting and because expertise has become contested. Pressures on professional work represent pressures on professional services, which represent political struggles over the nature, content and limits of service delivery.

In such lines of reasoning, bigger societal forces are stressed and practical questions about pressured professionals and their day-to-day experiences are turned into more fundamental questions about societal changes, ambiguous service settings and shifting forms of professionalism. 'Pressures' on professional work are not taken literally – they become a *symbol* of searches for new service settlements (compare Noordegraaf 2011; Faulconbridge & Muzio 2012).

Although more balanced approaches to professional work have been presented earlier (e.g. Exworthy & Halford 1999; Leicht & Fennell 1997, 2001; Farrell & Morris 2003; Kirkpatrick et al. 2005; Evetts 2006; Duyvendak et al. 2006; Noordegraaf 2007, 2011; Waring & Currie 2009; Faulconbridge & Muzio 2012), analyses of professionals, professional work and professionalism can be improved further. We need research that is both empirical as well as theory-driven, including research that explores what *really happens* on workfloors but also stresses bigger analytical themes that lie behind perceived problems. We have to understand shifting *control logics* in more refined ways, including research that focuses more on relations between professionals and others (also managers) and less on either professionals or isolated professional work practices, as well as research that highlights new and emerging organizational dimensions of professional service delivery.

This book contributes to the debate about pressured professionals by bringing together insights from Dutch scholars – these are all members of the so-called NIG Research Colloquium 'Professionals under pressure'[1] – it addresses more fundamental questions than normally can be found in practices and debates throughout the Western world. This is illustrated by the fact that two chapters are written by UK experts (Janet Newman and Stephen Ackroyd) who place Dutch debates and findings into an international comparative perspective. Against this background, the book tries to understand:

> 'what is really happening' in and around public service delivery, by analyzing 1) to what extent, how and why professionals are pressured, 2) how and why forms of professional control are changing, and 3) how and why new forms of organized professionalism are enacted.

MIRKO NOORDEGRAAF & BRAM STEIJN

Pressured professionals in the Netherlands

The book's Dutch 'bias' is valuable for scholars of other countries because there seems to be a Dutch case when it comes to pressured professionals. In the Netherlands, public and political debates on professionalism have increased exponentially since the turn of the century. This seems to be related to certain political events, such as the rise (and fall) of former politician Fortuyn and the subsequent reconfiguration of the political landscape (Noordegraaf 2008). Especially since 2003, when the Christian-Democrats (CDA) returned to political power, connected to the rise of Fortuyn's political movement, the Dutch orientation towards public professionalism was reversed rather radically. Backed by opinion leaders (Gabriel van den Brink, Thijs Jansen, Evelien Tonkens, Jos Van der Lans, Ad Verbrugge, March Chavannes, and others) as well as expert judgments and reports (e.g. RMO 2002; Van den Brink et al. 2005; Jansen et al. 2009) and certain 'movements' (e.g. Beroepseer.nl, also strongly linked to Christian-Democratic spheres), public and political opinion turned professionals into 'victims', who were 'constrained' and 'encapsulated'. They had to be 'freed'. Managers, on the other hand, were 'guilty' of constraining professionals, and their managerial worlds – with excessive 'layers' of managers and much 'overhead' – had to be eliminated as much as possible.

Other political parties readjusted their opinions on public service delivery, sometimes quite drastically. The liberal party, for example, started to blame managers for harming public services, whereas before 'management' was seen as the solution. In addition, certain authoritative studies (e.g. WRR 2004) were drawn into the new *pro-professional* public service ethos. Professional logics, with their emphasis on clients, quality and craftsmanship were seen as being weakened, whereas bureaucratic and managerial logics were seen as becoming hegemonic. The consequences were clear; we had to 'get rid of managers', as one former political executive said (a former Minister of Education); the value of honest professional work and 'real' professionalism had to be re-acknowledged.

Later on, these general turn-around tendencies were reinforced by subsequent political and public debates, which focused on specific service sectors. Backed by a continuous stream of reports – coming from political parties, but also from government ministries and advisory councils – and by specific 'incidents' in and around public services, service 'problems' were discussed in terms of 'over-bureaucratized' and 'overburdened' service organizations. Policemen were presented as 'alienated', teachers as being part of 'anonymous educational factories', and home care workers as 'time controlled' and 'Tayloristic' factory workers. Although attention for the 'growing number of' medical errors, incidents in youth care, and the like, did not eliminate the need for better management completely, they signaled the 'worrying' state of affairs, if not 'crisis' in and around public service delivery. In 2012, one of the leading Dutch newspapers (*de Volkskrant*, 28 January 2012) concluded that the 'divide between craftsmen and managers' was the most fundamental division in Dutch society.

All of this resulted in political attempts to 'rescue' social services, such as programs for 'reducing burdens', projects for generating 'professional freedom', and rules for stopping 'scaling up' and 'managerializing' professional services. It also resulted in much academic attention being paid to public professionals. More than ever, and perhaps more than elsewhere – at least in relative terms – Dutch scholars are actively studying public services, professionalism and professional practices. There is a wealth of research projects, reports and results, carried out by all kinds of researchers. This book profits from this. It brings together various researchers who have studied public professionals over the past few years. Some were visible in the fierce and rather 'black and white' Dutch public debate, but others were less visible and have mainly emphasized the nuances and intricacies of (changing) public professionalism.

Set-up of the book

The book starts with chapters by two prominent UK scholars. Stephen Ackroyd's chapter tells the story of forty years of (UK) research on professional occupations in several sectors. In a way, the main argument of this chapter fits the line of reasoning that was developed above: pressures on professionals must be problematized. Economic circumstances, organizational settings and management practices are important factors. The chapter also contextualizes public professional work (and compares it with professional work in the private sector) and puts changing manager-professional relations into a broader societal context, including the evolution of capitalism. In contrast, Janet Newman's chapter is more analytical and less tied to specific sectors and countries. It places 'new' pressures on professionals within the knowledge/power knot perspective developed by Clarke and Newman (2009). One of her arguments is that professionals are not just passive victims of reform but have an active role in shaping not only large-scale reform programs but also specific spaces of agency. Many of the subsequent chapters will refer to the analytical framework of Newman's chapter.

These subsequent Dutch-authored chapters are clustered into the following three parts:
- *Part I: Professionals and pressures*: How do reforms affect professional work and work settings; which bureaucratic burdens arise; how do professionals cope?
- *Part II: Professional practices and control*: Which changes in organizational control and governance systems can be traced; what are the consequences for professional autonomy and loyalties?

MIRKO NOORDEGRAAF & BRAM STEIJN

– *Part III: Organizing professionalism*: How do service managers respond to changes; which organizational structures arise; how do rules and standards change in order to accommodate changing professionalism?

Part I: Professionals and pressures

In chapter 4, Peter Hupe and Theo van der Krogt conceptually refine understandings of professional work, first by elaborating the notion of professionals, next by exploring the notion of pressures, and finally by emphasizing various coping strategies of professionals that might be applied when they face pressures. They go beyond black and white images of professionals and pressured professionals, and sketch a realistic picture of the complexities of professional work spheres.

In chapter 5, Romke van der Veen, also highlights these complexities, by focusing on healthcare and on the ways in which healthcare professionals are disciplined by new performance-based regimes. He distinguishes between professional autonomies and discretionary spaces and concludes that a loss of (institutional) autonomy does not imply a loss of (individual) decision spaces.

In chapter 6, Arie-Jan Kwak focuses on legal spheres, and like Van der Veen he shows that judges and accountants do not immediately experience a loss of professionalism as a result of managerial reform. But, more fundamentally, their work *is* transformed. He stresses the ideological sides of professional work and shows how longings for objectivity are more than managerial in the so-called 'age of expertise'; in fact, they are at the (societal) heart of legal work.

Part II: Professional practices and control

In chapter 7, Amanda Smullen returns to healthcare (mental heathcare) and like Kwak she analyzes ideological transitions in professional work, but she does so by analyzing how control is exerted. She focuses on the Dutch diagnosis-related treatment system that was introduced to finance and govern healthcare, including mental health care. She explains how this system was resisted but also how resistance is overcome by shifts in medical paradigms. In mental healthcare, biomedical psychiatry becomes more dominant.

In chapter 8, Lars Tummers, Bram Steijn and Victor Bekkers focus on policy control and analyze whether and how professionals are subjected to policy ideas and reforms. They use the term policy alienation to understand professional responses and especially show the importance of policy meaning (and meaninglessness). When policies have no meaning for professionals, professional workers feel alienated.

In chapter 9, Gjalt de Graaf and Zeger van der Wal also focus on relations between professionals and other actors, in this case professional administrators and organizational actors. They study these relations in terms of loyalties and mainly show varieties in professional administrative loyalties; different groups of workers develop different loyalties.

In chapter 10, Evelien Tonkens, Marc Hoitink and Huub Gulikers shift attention to external relations between professional workers and clients, and wonder whether new control logics appear at the edges of service organizations. Instead of assuming a market-based logic, with customers and preferences, they view changing relations as democratizing relations; professionals might contribute to the empowerment of citizens.

Part III: Organizing professionalism

In chapter 11, Mirjan Oude Vrielink and Jeroen van Bockel study bureaucratic burdens and administrative regulations, and wonder whether all 'burdens' and 'regulations' are in fact burdens and regulations. They especially show that professionalism and bureaucracy are not antithetical; they presuppose each other. Professionalism is also built upon rules and regulations, although professionals tend to organize these rules and regulations themselves.

In chapter 12, Rik van Berkel and Paul van der Aa focus on welfare agencies and welfare workers. They study how new welfare professionals – i.e. activation workers – are forced to become more professional, but they work in strong organizational contexts and they lack professional fields that regulate their professionalism.

In chapter 13, Martijn van der Meulen and Mirko Noordegraaf focus more on organizational contexts and analyze whether and how public managers – especially police chiefs – become professional managers. Contemporary professionalization does not only concern new modes of regulating professional fields, nor new types of work within organized policy implementation, such as welfare work; it also concerns the joint endeavour to improve management and to create professional managers. This is far from easy. Despite attractive yardsticks, such as leadership, public managers compete over legitimate definitions and forms of managerial professionalism.

In the final chapter 14, we will draw conclusions. On the basis of all of these chapters we reframe public professionalism from a socio-political perspective and we stress the relevance of *reconfigured* public professionalism that represents the changing nature of professional public services.

Note

1. See http://www.uu.nl/faculty/leg/NL/organisatie/departementen/departementbestuursenorganisatiewetenschap/onderzoek/publicmanagement/Re-

framingprofessionalism/Pages/default.aspx. The book builds upon other Colloquium initiatives, such as yearly NIG Conference workshops (November 2007, 2008, 2009), regular Colloquium meetings, and special issues of the Dutch journals *Bestuurskunde* (2007, no. 4) and *TvA* (2012, no. 3) that focus on the clash between professionalism and managerism.

References

Ackroyd, S. (1996). Organizations contra organizations: Professions and organizational change in the United Kingdom. *Organization Studies, 17*(4), 599-621.

Brink, G. van den, Jansen, Th., & Pessers, D. (2005). *Beroeps(z)eer. Waarom Nederland niet goed werkt.* Amsterdam: Boom.

Broadbent, J., Dietrich, M., & Roberts, J. (1997). *The end of the professions? The restructuring of professional work.* New York: Routledge.

Clarke, J., & Newman, J. (1997). The managerial state: Power, politics and ideology in the remaking of social welfare. London: Sage Publications.

Clarke, J., & Newman, J. (2009). Elusive Publics: knowledge, power and public service reform. In S. Gewirtz, P. Mahony, I. Hextall & A. Cribb (Eds.), *Changing Teacher Professionalism: international challenges, trends and ways forward.* London: Routledge.

De Bruijn, H. (2010). *Managing Professionals.* London: Routledge.

De Bruijn, H., & Noordegraaf, M. (2010). Professionals versus managers? De onvermijdelijkheid van nieuwe professionele praktijken [Professionals versus managers? The inevitability of new professional practices]. *Bestuurskunde, 3,* 6-20.

Duyvendak, J.W., Knijn, T., & Kremer, M. (2006). *Policy, people, and the new professional: De-professionalisation and re-professionalisation in care and welfare.* Amsterdam: Amsterdam University Press.

Evetts, J. (2006). Introduction: Trust and professionalism: Challenges and occupational changes. *Current Sociology, 54*(4), 515.

Exworthy, M., & Halford, S. (Eds.). (1999). *Professionals and the new managerialism in the public sector.* Buckingham: Open University Press.

Farrell, C.M., & Morris, J. (1999). Professional perceptions of bureaucratic change in the public sector: GPs, headteachers and social workers. *Public Money and Management, 19*(4), 31-36.

Farrell, C.M., & Morris, J. (2003). The neo-bureaucratic state: Professionals, managers and professional managers in schools, general practices and social work. *Organization, 10*(1), 129-156.

Faulconbridge, J., & Muzio, D. (2012). Professions in a globalizing world: Towards a transnational sociology of the professions. *International Sociology, 27* (1), 136-152.

Freidson, E. (2001). *Professionalism: The third logic.* Cambridge: Polity.

Gleeson, D., & Knights, D. (2006). Challenging dualism: Public professionalism in 'Troubled' times. *Sociology, 40*(2), 277-295.

Jansen, Th., Van den Brink, G., & Kole, J. (2009). *Professional pride: A powerful force.* The Hague: Boom.

Kirkpatrick, I., Ackroyd, S., & Walker, R. (2005). *The new managerialism and public service professions.* Basingstoke: Palgrave Macmillan.

Kuhlmann, E., & Saks, M. (Eds.). (2008). *Rethinking professional governance: International directions in healthcare*. Bristol: Policy Press.

Leicht, K.T., & Fennell, M.L. (1997). The changing organizational context of professional work. *Annual Review of Sociology, 23,* 215-231.

Leicht, K.T., & Fennell, M.L. (2001). *Professional Work: A Sociological Approach.* Malden, MA: Blackwell Publishers.

Muzio, D., & Kirkpatrick, I. (2011). Introduction: Professions and organizations – a conceptual framework. *Current Sociology, 59*(4), 389-405.

Noordegraaf, M. (2007). From pure to hybrid professionalism: Present-day professionalism in ambiguous public domains. *Administration & Society, 39*(6), 761-785.

Noordegraaf, M. (2008). *Professioneel bestuur.* Den Haag: Lemma.

Noordegraaf, M. (2011). Risky business. How professionals and professional fields (must) deal with organizational issues. *Organization Studies, 32*(10), 1349-1371.

RMO (2002). *Bevrijdende kaders.* Den Haag: Raad voor Maatschappelijke Ontwikkeling.

Waring, J., & Currie, G. (2009). Managing expert knowledge: Organizational challenges and managerial futures for the UK medical profession. *Organization Studies, 30*(7), 755-778.

Wilensky, H.L. (1964). The professionalization of everyone? *American Journal of Sociology, 70*(2), 137-158.

WRR (2004). *Bewijzen van goede dienstverlening.* Amsterdam: Amsterdam University Press.

2 Professions, professionals and the 'new' government policies

A reflection on the last 30 years

Stephen Ackroyd

Introduction

This chapter offers an account of a body of research relating to professions and professionalism in the UK public sector which the author has undertaken with colleagues over a thirty-year period. At the start of this period, following the election of a Conservative government in 1979, there was the introduction of a distinctive new policy. A decisive break with the past, this policy was collectively identified as New Public Management (NPM) (Exworthy & Halford 1999; Ferlie & Fitzgerald 2000). The general direction of policy did not change much thereafter, despite changes of administration and the election to power of different parties (Ackroyd 1995a; Harrison 2002). NPM was extended and consolidated over the intervening years. Thus, the policies under consideration may hardly be considered as new in 2012 – as the parentheses around 'new' in the title here indicate. However, many observers are still thinking of these polices as new. NPM is still something distinctive – it has not been accepted as simply the way things now are.

This chapter makes an assessment of a particular body of academic research undertaken to assess the implementation of NPM policies. Doing this assessment in conjunction with work undertaken in the Netherlands will allow readers to assess how far there are similarities in research interests and outcomes between academic communities in adjacent countries. Britain, like the USA (together sometimes called 'Anglo Saxon' economies and countries), is often regarded as in the forefront of change; though whether this is really so and what constitutes being 'in the lead' or 'behind' are matters of controversy. Anyway, the chapter is written in the hope that the research reported (and particularly its lack of impact) will be of interest to scholars and professionals working on similar organisations but within a somewhat different institutional context. The conclusion will discuss why the outcome took the shape it did.

NPM entails the proposition, in itself relatively unobjectionable, that existing arrangements for the provision of social welfare are inefficient, and, to improve this, it is necessary to turn to management modelled on the private sector. Inevitably, however, achieving efficiency as defined by NPM, was not a simple change easily implemented that would quickly improve things. To be made to work, NPM brought along in its train other necessary changes, such as the commodification of services and marketization of their procurement; but this was unclear at the outset. However, it soon became clear, and from a relatively early point, that the introduction of NPM meant substantially displacing both the existing mode of provision (administration) and some existing practices of the occupations that provided services within this framework (the public sector professions). The research to be considered here may be understood as work that gradually uncovered the extent of the opposition between NPM and the professional ideals and modes of organizing central to public sector professions. The extent to which it is necessary and desirable to change the character of the public sector professions, therefore, is a key issue brought to the surface by this research.

British professions in their field

I shall begin by making some points about the field of professional work in Britain. A first point is that certain kinds of professional work are growing in importance and becoming more abundant.[1] Almost all the significant growth in the UK economy in the last thirty years has been concentrated in financial and business services (Ackroyd 2002, 2011). The majority of growth of employment in the UK is also concentrated in this sector, and while many of the jobs created are unskilled (call-centre workers for example) or de-skilled (bank tellers and data entry jobs), there are many new jobs which are both highly skilled and highly rewarded. Some of these are in occupations of recent development such as business consultants and business systems designers, financial analysts and advisers, fund managers, project managers, public relations workers, marketing and advertising employees.

These occupations hardly existed 100 years ago. All have developed strongly in the last three decades. Some are now very large. At a conservative estimate there are more than 100,000 business consultants in the UK (Clarke & Kipping 2012), or roughly as many as there are doctors. However, these new occupations are not organized in the manner of traditional professions. They lack independent and effective professional bodies that certify the competence of practitioners, for example. Only a few traditional professions have shown comparable growth to the new business-related occupations discussed above. However, there are two important exceptions: accountancy and the law. The legal profession has around 120,000 qualified practitioners (up nearly 30,000 (24%) since 2001). The great growth in the legal services has been in commercial law, so this is not an exception to the rule that the only area of employment growth has been in business services. We shall return to the consideration of the legal profession later in this chapter. However, the main growth profession in the UK in recent years has been accountancy – a business service par excellence. Today there are approaching 300,000 practising accountants in Britain (up nearly 80,000 (28%) since 2001), and the profession continues to grow at a phenomenal rate. The UK already has the highest number of accountants per capita of any country in the world; and there are more accountants in Britain than in the whole of the rest of the EU taken together.

In most other areas of professional employment, in contrast with professions providing business services, there is little growth,[2] and professions are under severe challenge. The Engineering Council, the professional association for all types of engineers in the UK, estimates there will be over 100,000 job losses in the next few years, and only a small fraction of these will be replaced by newly qualified recruits. Public sector professions are under an acute challenge. The number of teachers fell in 2011 by 10,000 and almost everywhere in the social services the growth in employment does not keep pace with client needs. One favoured procedure for the public sector professions is skill dilution – the recruitment of unqualified assistants instead of fully qualified professionals. The ratio of unqualified teaching assistants to qualified teachers in British schools, for example, is now 1:2; in nursing, the ratio of health care assistants to qualified nurses is roughly 3:4. More generally, the profession, as a distinctive occupational form, is under challenge in two ways. It is criticized ideologically for being an unnecessary restriction in labour markets, and acted against materially, in that policies designed to remove monopolies of provision have been widely instituted. Accountancy and law are also under challenge, of course, and almost everywhere even amongst the more powerful professions, significant concessions have been made by these occupations accepting reductions of their monopoly power. However, it is fairly clear the closer the work of a profession is to growing parts of the economy, the more likely their own growth will occur. Given the remoteness of the public sector professions from the growing points of the economy, the question arises whether public sector professions can survive long[3]; certainly, it seems unlikely in their traditional forms.

A background question of this chapter concerns how academics may produce research which has secure empirical grounding and yet has broad policy relevance. The scholarly community in which I have been working has certainly tried to do good, collectively based research that is policy relevant, but there has been little success in terms of its influence. More generally, the aim here is to give an account of the solution to the problems of generalization worked out with my colleagues, and to let the reader be the judge of its contribution.

The research work I was associated with moved from detailed studies of a particular service (nurses in the hospitals of the National Health Service – NHS) to the established division of labour amongst the clinicians (doctors, nurses and ancillary medical staff) and the impact on these roles of the first developments of New Public Management (NPM). Subsequently, after a lot of work in the NHS, in collaboration with colleagues, we made systematic comparisons between the health service and other UK social services. We developed a protocol for comparing changes in a range of different services and estimated the effects of NPM. Finally, again in collaboration with colleagues, comparisons of a sample of professions in the public and private sectors in the UK were made, nationally and internationally. This work had good empirical grounding and revealed important findings. Nevertheless, in common with earlier work it failed to produce results of interest to policy-makers.

Phase I (1985-1999) Nurses and the division of labour in NHS hospitals

Research in the public sector with which I was associated was, at different times in the 1980s, looking at a range of services, including education and the police (Ackroyd et al. 1989, 1992). But the service which absorbed me was National Health Hospitals (Soothill et al. 1992; Ackroyd 1987, 1992, 1995). Serious problems began to emerge in NHS hospitals in the UK from the middle of the 1980s, and have continued since with deepening crises. These centred on such things as the supply and the motivation of health professionals, questions about the cleanliness and safety of hospitals and the division of labour between occupations. There was more than a little complacent puzzlement on show at the time. Surely the NHS, particularly the hospital service, was the envy of the world? There surely could not be anything basically wrong with it?

The reforming government elected in 1979 took the view that there was a need to improve NHS hospitals in particular. Costs had spiralled upwards, and it was natural for this government to take the view that efficiency was lacking. There was a general need – allegedly – to modernize. Hence the new government soon commissioned the NHS Management Enquiry (1982), under the chairmanship of an executive in charge of a major supermarket chain. This committee lost no time recommending that, since there was no developed management in NHS hospitals, and no group uniquely responsible for management, the solution was to put effective managers in there (Griffiths 1983). Yet it is not obvious – as later studies of professional firms would show – that organizations with little management are therefore not efficient or effective.

Academics typically wanted to get to the seat of the problem and many of them, including the research teams with which I was associated, began in-depth research into nurses. Close colleagues at the time, Soothill and MacKay (MacKay 1989; Soothill et al. 1992) led detailed research into nurse recruitment – and found that nursing was no longer an attractive career for the rising generation of school leavers (Francis et al.

1992). Later, the motivation and morale of existing nurses was studied, and found to be at an all-time low. There were evidently problems in the division of labour amongst hospital staff emerging. In our work a picture of the traditional pattern of relationships in the NHS hospitals was charted (Ackroyd 1992). In the heyday of the NHS hospital service, the senior doctors had the most powerful occupation, and to all intents and purposes, controlled the service. They held a strategic position in the hospital management committees, had come to monopolize the consultative positions in the regional and national administrative structure, and basically fixed the budgets, determining how much was spent on each medical specialty.

A lack of willingness by doctors to limit their activities or to ration their spending was leading to more effective service by allowing new treatments. As professionals do everywhere, there was a tendency for senior doctors to explore state-of-the-art treatments which test the boundaries of knowledge and skill. But they also rack up costs, whilst the mundane but necessary standard treatments (hernias and hips) were neglected. Waiting lists for these treatments formed, whilst there were spiralling costs. There was increasing pressure on nurses and ancillary staff who were meeting patients. In effect, NHS hospitals had become the victims of their own success. The capacity to do more did not lead to the diminution of demand, as was once naively assumed. On the contrary, better services stimulated demand and made the need for rationing acute (Ackroyd & Bolton 1999). In the end the available resources were stretched too thinly in many areas of provision. There is no doubt that the situation was wasteful too, but the solution adopted, to introduce a new occupation, the NHS hospital managers, with the brief to 'take charge', was questioned by most academic observers (Griffiths 1983).

The continuing confrontation between new managers and senior clinicians stands out as perhaps the most challenging episode of continuing misunderstanding of low-level non-cooperation I have witnessed. Certainly it did not lead to greater efficiency in the medium term, it simply added greatly to the costs of running a less efficient service. Clinicians – especially in surgery – took issue with what they saw as interference with their clinical freedom to decide which patients to treat. Managers on their part could see more clearly where the failure to provide treatment was causing problems for patients and embarrassment for the hospital. The gap between viewpoints was only closed through innovation of new systems of classification for conditions and treatments and the adoption of new operating procedures. However, until these practical steps were taken, there was often a stalemate that was difficult to resolve. Since the development of these protocols was primarily the initiative of management and difficult to generalize across specialties, the increase in the size of the managerial cadre continued. However, leading-edge policy did change. By the beginning of the 1990s, commoditizing clinical procedures and directing clinicians' activities in the performance of them shifted to introducing competition between providers for the provision of standardized procedures. In NHS hospitals, this took the form of the introduction of quasi-markets for clinical services, in which newly created commissioning bodies were given the capacity to switch their expenditure between hospitals – moving in one direction or another based on price considerations. By this means it was attempted to discipline the doctors in the hospitals (Kitchener 1998).

The introduction of NPM into hospitals thus introduced a new role (health service manager) and logic of resource allocation (marketization). The allocation of money to different activities meant activities were differently resourced in different locations. Also, the discretionary allocation of funds is built into NPM. The capacity to push rewards in the direction of the responsive and effective and to deny them to the recalcitrant or inadequate was part of the managerial process. However, these different outcomes also indirectly encouraged staff who were able to move (typically those with good credentials and track records) to areas where there was less pressure on resources and more recognition of competence and seniority. Thus, NPM often introduced a new instability that was absent before: it actively helped to produce difference in the performance of institutions. This is one of the most compelling aspects of these NPM innovations which will be referred to again.

Phase II (1995-2005) Comparative studies of UK social services: Health, housing, education and social work

Most academics researching public sector services knew the changes being introduced by NPM were not confined to the particular services they happened to be studying; but such is the predisposition to become an expert in a particular field that generalizations were seldom made. Broadly based research was rare. By the end of the 1990s, however, a great deal of detailed research had been completed in different areas of public services and there was an obvious need to produce a general account of the effects of the NPM. True, new textbooks covering change in the public sector services had begun to appear (Clarke & Newman 1997), but several research groups were also formed to make the comparisons more systematic.

One group with which I was involved began in a modest way by considering the problems involved in comparing the measures taken to introduce NPM and the experiences and actions of professionals in response across a range of services. In order to make systematic comparisons between changes in different social services we found it essential to use a similar analytical framework. Therefore, a small number of members of my research community formed an alliance to produce comparable results across a significant range of social services. Initially there were four areas for comparative research in addition to the NHS hospitals – education in schools, local authority social workers, and public housing managers and supervisors. In the end there were two active researchers in addition to myself: Ian Kirkpatrick (at the time conducting research into UK social services) and Richard Walker (engaged in research into housing provision). The chief results were published in a jointly authored book (Kirkpatrick et al. 2005).

We pooled our efforts as researchers with a shared theoretical perspective and focused our research on the relationships between professional groups within the services. However, we did not rely on this general similarity, but drew up a protocol of research subjects to enable systematic comparisons between the services of interest. We then worked over our material retrospectively and prospectively. We reappraised the research record across different services (our own and that of others), and we used similar criteria for observation and data collection regarding current events and research work going forward. Then we swapped data sets and preliminary conclusions arising from each other's work of synthesis. New research was undertaken where there seemed to be key gaps in the research record. Above all, we discussed research results and common problems of interpretation. It is pleasing to note that our partially imposed similarity of outlook did not stop us coming to unexpected conclusions.

Central questions at this stage were whether NPM was being introduced in similar ways and whether it was having similar effects in all types of services and institutional contexts. Our general results were quite startling. We concluded that the effects of NPM were rather different in the three services we considered. In NHS hospitals it was evident there was strong and effective resistance to NPM because there were dense concentrations of professional employees who had control of key resources and could mount an effective response to initiatives. Professionals in the NHS often interpreted the intrusion of a new managerial cadre, not unrealistically, as a real threat to their de-facto control of their own work. In terms of their own understanding, senior doctors in particular had little to gain and much to lose from the changes being introduced. By contrast, less professionalized occupations in other services, such as public housing, saw more attraction in the introduction of NPM. This was because the scope for employing specialist management in these services was small. Senior housing professionals could see themselves taking up managerial functions and occupying managerial roles: this would not diminish their status, but, if anything, would enhance it.

Amongst housing officials, the introduction of NPM was therefore widely seen as an opportunity to advance their professional development project. Their idea of the appropriate way to respond to the requirement to reform met the government criteria of acceptability fairly well, and was generally approved. Before NPM, housing was the least professionalized of the services we considered, and the occupation offered little resistance to the role definitions implicit in the reforms. We inferred this was because the members of the occupation saw in the reforms ways of expanding the independence of the occupation and increasing its importance (Kirkpatrick et al. 2007).

In social work, however, there was more attachment to the idea of professional practice by qualified social workers, who sometimes saw this being potentially threatened by the intrusion of a more developed managerial function. Being more professionalized, social workers were more likely to be at odds with NPM, but some in the occupation were not wholly against incorporating a type of managerial activity. Social casework as such offers little scope for career development. Thus, for the senior staff of the profession it was often seen as a natural progression to adopt managerial activities. By the end of the first five years of reforms, even junior social workers began to see their work as tailoring packages of provision appropriate to the needs of their clients. Significant splits appeared between social workers strongly attached to a professional model of casework who tended to resist NPM and those seeing the role as orchestrating specialist services and interested in becoming managers, who did not. Those disposed to manage were probably in the majority and they more readily embraced a managerial role and adapted to NPM reforms. This redefined the main activity of the social worker away from casework with clients towards planner and supervisor of care packages originated by others including specialist subcontractors (Kirkpatrick and Ackroyd 2003a, 2003b).

It is not claimed that these reforms led to more efficiency, merely to acceptance. Our conclusions were that NPM invariably added to the number of activities being undertaken and to the costs of provision. However, to return to our main theme: what seemed to be crucial in deciding the response of occupations to NPM was the existing condition of the profession and how it perceived opportunities and threats constituted by the introduction of new policies. We conjectured that the more professionalized a service was the more likely practitioners were to perceive the new policies as a threat, and the more realistic they were in thinking like this. Now, the more resistance that was encountered to NPM, the more effort was put into making NPM reforms; but, despite sustained efforts, there was sometimes little success. We concluded that, ironical though it may be, the effectiveness of NPM reforms was often inversely proportional to the efforts put into securing them. However, although we made these points to funding bodies, our findings did not lead to any reduction in the efforts put into developing NPM, or to redefining the managerial role or rethinking the division of labour between managers and professionals. If policies did not seem to be working that showed that, in order to work, more manpower (more managers appointed) and money should be put into consolidating them. When the conclusion was unavoidable that reforms were not working, policies were not withdrawn; at best, there was a change of emphasis or direction.

STEPHEN ACKROYD

Also, as had been seen with the NHS, almost everywhere NPM introduced more instability into relationships within and between institutions. This began early. Some of the first moves made to institute NPM had the effect of reallocating resources. This occurred in two ways. Firstly, as conditions in some organizations improved, staff who were able to move would seek positions in improving institutions, but, at the same time, such mobility would, if it continued, decrease the prospects for the institutions being left. Thus, we observed increased mobility of staff away from weak and potentially failing schools and hospitals to more effective and successful ones. Better-qualified staff would find it easiest to move, concentrating well-qualified staff in strong institutions. Such processes were made worse by many schemes implementing NPM, because there were incentives allocated to institutions that did improve, either in the form of access to discretionary awards, or new freedoms from administrative constraint, or both. This encouraged further mobility. Once such a process of decline was in motion, it would be increasingly difficult for an institution to attract the best staff, or to reverse a deepening deterioration. While positive effects of cumulative improvement are just what managers seek to do to increase the performance of particular organizations, it does not seem to have been noticed that improving cycles are implicated in the causation of declining cycles.

In free market competition, of course, it is an expected event for a poorly managed and inefficient organization to fail. However, it is questionable if this is an acceptable outcome for a social service: if social problems are not dealt with, they remain a cost. Dysfunctional families continue to be a social cost over generations. It seems to have come as a surprise to many supporters of the management of public institutions that they would induce market relations, and an expected outcome from competition is that some will fail. For example, from the research we reviewed, the creation of well-run, semi-private public housing estates managed by housing associations was an achievement of a new, efficiently run form of housing management. This was on one side of the balance sheet. On the other side this achievement is balanced by the existence of 'sink estates' made up of the residual local authority housing in which dense concentrations of unemployed tenants lived and where there was associated concentrated social pathology, such as family dysfunction, alcoholism and crime. It seems increasingly clear that something similar was there in other areas of social provision touched by NPM, and certainly was present in all three areas we compared in this stage of our research.

There were many things that puzzled us as researchers. It seemed to us that our findings had relevance, but were ignored. The limited research that went into studying quasi-markets in the NHS, for example, showed they were costly to implement and did not work well in the allocation of resources (Kitchener 1998). Nevertheless, this finding was used as a reason for causing a great deal of additional money to be com-

mitted to make quasi-markets work. Academics who were not economists might well continue to be funded and their advice was received,
but it clearly was not acted upon. On the other hand, one estimate published recently suggested that the expenditure on consultants by the NHS
alone (2000-2005) was allegedly 100 times more than the total spent on
consultancy by the British manufacturing industry as a whole (Craig
2008; see also Craig & Brooks 2006).

Phase III (2000-2008) Comparative studies of public and private professions

It was clear from our work on public sector professions in the UK that
they were becoming increasingly subjected to externally imposed controls and their professional autonomy progressively cut back. As our
work developed, we found public sector services providers were increasingly subject to managerial surveillance and control through such things
as performance measures and their morale was generally low. Surpris-
ingly, this reaction did not diminish over time through inurement. Thus,
it is difficult to see what has happened as a triumph for rationality and
efficiency.

The root of the matter seemed to be the allegiance of public sector
employees to professional ideals, and particularly those of self-organiza-
tion and public service. The logic of managerialism was seen by many
(practitioners and, as time went on, academics) to be directly against
professional values and priorities, and that resistance was found to be
directly related to the strength of the professional organization of different occupations established this connection clearly. However, wherever
professional practices remained there was recurrent tension between
managerial priorities and procedures and professional ones – as in social
work and teaching. Indeed, even though public sector professionals are
increasingly employees subject to direction, they remain quite powerful;
in practice, they are capable of retaining quite a lot of control over their
own work in the workplace, and of using this control to limit encroach-
ment on their day-to-day activities.

Historically, medical doctors were almost the only occupation working
primarily in the public sector with any pretensions to being a well-devel-
oped profession. Not only did the doctors have a strong professional
body (BMA) many had also been self-employed. For much of the 20th
century, general medical practitioners (GPs) – now known as primary
care doctors – were partners in privately owned medical practices. This
continued to be true even after the formation of the NHS in the decades
following World War II, though the extent of this gradually reduced.
Similarly, hospital consultants long cherished their status as contractors
to (rather than employees of) the NHS; carefully preserving their ability
to be in private business as well as holding NHS clinics. They were origi-

STEPHEN ACKROYD

nally 'consultants to the NHS', and were paid fees for each consultation, but the extent of this too gradually declined. In recent years, both the small business GP and private consultant contractors in hospitals have greatly diminished in number. Also, in recent years the control over the profession by the BMA has been weakened in various ways (Bolton et al. 2011). In view of this background it is hardly surprising that doctors have resisted the imposition of management on them, and have not taken over managerial roles in large numbers. Instead, there has been a rise in the number of specialist managers, and new career paths have opened up for them.

There is controversy about the extent of this development, but it is unarguable that NPM reforms have called into being a new occupation – public sector manager. This occupation largely did not exist before. In other services than the NHS there are fewer such people, but whether they were recruited from existing professionals or are newly trained or come from the private sector is beside the point, the fact remains that much time and effort are being devoted to managerial activities that were not done before. Against this background about ten years ago, it became increasingly important to us as researchers to find out about the private sector professions, and discover the character and extent of managerial activities there. To what extent did private sector arrangements bear comparison with the situation now reached by public sector professionals? At this phase, research was initiated with studies of business consultants and systems specialists (Ackroyd et al. 2000), a database of consultancy companies in Britain was established, and a number of case studies of selected companies were undertaken. Research into legal firms was also initiated at this time.

In addition to interest in business consultancies, there was the attraction of being able to make systematic and explicit comparisons between the organizational structures and managerial roles found and those in the public sector services. It became clear at an early stage that, although in some ways business consultancy was a professional occupation, with high status members, high remuneration and an esoteric knowledge base, in key respects it is unlike traditional professions. The knowledge base does not belong to individual practitioners – unless they are very small firms – but is a property of the owning company. However, even with the largest consultancy companies a great deal of operating autonomy was extended to consultancy teams, provided they worked within the protocols provided for each contract. Managerial intrusion on practice was actually small and the numbers of specialist managers few.

When studies of legal firms were undertaken, their internal management was found to be in some ways much the same as found in consultancies. Legal firms were clearly organizations of professionals in the traditional sense: practitioners must undertake extended training periods and acquire legal qualifications and practising certificates. The hold of the professional body on recruitment to the legal profession may have been weakened in recent years, but the professional organization remains strong. In the legal firm, partnership remained and professionals seemed to us to be in control of their firms (Ackroyd & Muzio 2007; Muzio & Ackroyd 2008a). Despite the rapid growth in the size of legal firms in England – the largest of which have more than 1,000 partners – they remained with their traditional pattern of partnership governance. Although there had been the growth of internal hierarchy in such firms, with the numbers of grades of solicitors becoming greater, and the rise to full partner in a large firm becoming correspondingly more difficult, the legal firm was recognizably constructed around traditional professional values. Professionals worked as autonomous teams and directive management was largely absent.

Thus, despite claims that NPM would introduce efficient management to public services – like that found in the private sector – this was failing to emerge here. Amongst solicitor firms and business consultancies, management, measured in terms of the time and staff devoted to it, was much less than in the post-reform public sector services. The NHS hospitals had become greatly over-provided with managers by comparison with legal firms. In 2008, we calculated ratios of 1:5 for managers to service providers in the NHS hospitals compared to 1:30 or 50 in legal firms depending on firm size and configuration. This implied levels of self-management in commercial businesses comparable to the NHS – as it used to be before NPM. At the time, and still today, the theory of the development of professional businesses was dominated by archetype theory, which suggested the emergence of a new type of *managed* professional business (Hinings & Greenwood 1988; Greenwood & Hinings 1988; Greenwood et al. 1990).[4] If this was the case, the new type of business was surviving on remarkably little management. Either way, the extent of the managerial cadre in the public sector was disproportionately large (Kirkpatrick & Ackroyd 2003a; 2003b).

At the end of this stage of research we looked at a wide range of occupations and specialisms, and published a book comparing the different occupations – doctors, lawyers and business consultants – we had studied in depth. We also paid attention to hitherto unstudied segments of occupations already familiar to us but beyond our range. Thus, in addition to extending the range of our studies of lawyers (by looking at international firms as well as English ones, and in-house lawyers as well as professional firms) we drew on studies of doctors in US hospitals as well as our own. Additionally, we began to consider research into business consultants and some of the few occupations predominantly in the private sector now recognizably developing patterns of the traditional profession: project managers and human resource managers. We summed up some of this new work in another book (Muzio et al. 2008). Former colleagues and research partners have gone on to make extended studies of a range of occupations – including business consultants, doctors and nurses, lawyers and social workers (e.g. Bolton 2005; Dent & Kirkpatrick 2011; Muzio 2004).[5]

In summary, interesting things were indicated. One was that traditional forms of profession with little management can be effective. Legal firms – and the legal profession – have been growing at a phenomenal rate and the movement was led by world-class businesses still utilizing the partnership form. It is true that driving this development was the increasing demand for legal services especially from world commerce and the growth of the City of London as a financial centre.[6] As a result, the lawyers easily absorbed the impact of government policies aimed at limiting their power. On the other hand, what was at one time probably the most prestigious profession of all, medicine, has been badly affected by similar policies combined with the effects of NPM. It can be argued that doctors are being subjected to dilution as a result of government policy as well. Having lost control of medical student numbers and medical curricula in recent years, the number of doctors in training has increased by nearly 50% and the requirements of their education have been reduced (Tooke 2008). Also important was the finding that the 'new professions', such as management consultancy that had emerged in the private sector had evolved quite different ways of organizing and had a different structure to the patterns being imposed on public sector services. From this it seemed transparently clear that the aim of public sector reform was to target, weaken and, if possible, remove professional forms of organization, as much as it was about improving efficiency. Weakening and removing the professionally based services was a necessary preliminary to replacing them with commercially organized forms of provision.

Conclusion

The experience of many researchers in the UK public sector in the last 30 years is of a consistent commitment to change through the implementation of NPM. The standardization of procedures, and marketization of modes of provision, have been the targets of NPM and have been backed by successive governments and policy chiefs. The overall direction of reform has not changed regardsless of the political character of the government. And it is not only government that has been taking a similar point of view. The idea that the welfare state is a burden on the taxpayer and the (undeniably large) cost of it in monetary terms is what matters, has become the common refrain of many people and organizations. Furthermore these players have also promoted the questionable propositions that more management and private subcontracting are the only workable answers to the high costs of provision. These assumptions are accompaniments of NPM that have become widely accepted.

Thus there are many agencies surrounding public sector institutions with similar views. Here we must note the consultancy companies regularly used to evaluate existing service provision, and which often recommend private solutions to the problems they evaluate. Numerous advisers, public relations firms and professionals, lobbyists, pro-market think tanks and plain ideologists, consistently promote the proposition that markets and quasi-markets are the best mechanisms for providing public sector services. The revolving door, through which executives and advisers move into regulatory bodies, government itself and back into the private sector, has become a blur. These pressures are, little by little, making headway. The result is a series of small steps being taken towards a fully market-based mode of provision of services.

It can be plausibly argued that the real direction of public policy has never been fully declared, but this is partly because there has been no need to do so. There is a developmental logic involved in the movement towards privatization. Public policy in the UK has moved successively from introducing management and focusing on efficiency, through the rationalization and commodification of services to achieve this, and then on to the marketization of provision and, finally, to privatization. Nowadays, NPM features centrally the dismantlement and removal of public services in their traditional forms and replacement by privately provided services. The services which are allowed to continue may still be paid for by the taxpayer, but will, supposedly, no longer be a drain on taxation. They will not represent a lost opportunity for firms and other organizations. Privatization has been fully realized in some areas: we now have privately run schools (so-called 'free' schools), privately owned primary care medical services and privately run prisons, and there are many more examples where there have been private sector loans to public institutions (PFI) that will have to be repaid over long periods, placing a severe stain on the effectiveness of services far into the future.

There seems to be no limit to the extent of belief in marketization, however, and there is a constant disparagement of the existing provision of services particularly in education and social work. The NHS is usually exempt from direct criticism, but here again there is no commitment to indefinite public ownership of the service. The plan seems to be to make the NHS a public service in name only. Services will be provided by a range of private contractors, but the name NHS will be a 'kitemark of quality', i.e. NHS purchasers will try to ensure that only the best private contractors are utilized (Leys & Player 2012). The small steps towards marketized provision seldom appear significant enough to arouse large-scale opposition. Advocates of marketized provision generally do not then try to convince the public and the professionals of the appropriateness of their policies or try to show that reform of the public services was necessary; they have focused their attention instead on infiltrating and influencing policy-making centres.

STEPHEN ACKROYD

If this account is true, it does explain why academic researchers have had so little influence on public policy. Research that questioned the appropriateness of reform or suggested there was virtue in existing arrangements was not 'on message' and so was regarded as irrelevant. Government (and their advisers) had their own views of cause and effect, their own sources of information and, most important of all, their own ideas about what needed to be done. Ministerial 'research units' and private consultants were often cited as the source of research support for proposed reforms though it was sometimes difficult to see what the basis for their claims actually was. Contrary evidence and argument seemed to be consistently overlooked or devalued – at best its presenters were seen as poorly or inappropriately motivated. Non-compliant academic advisers, where they existed, were retired and/or replaced. However, the commissioning of new academic research into these questions was never stopped. Research funding is, of course, not directly controlled by government, funding being channelled through research councils on which academics themselves are strongly represented. Often however, funded research which took periods of months if not years to produce was usually simply too late to be influential, or, equally often, it was studiously overlooked.

The reforms of the social services we have been considering here can be seen as related to basic shifts in the composition of the economy, and the changed values and policies of the now ascendant finance capitalist interests in British society. The welfare state is a set of institutions that in the past effectively reduced conflict – actual and potential – by supplementing wages with public provision against unemployment, ill-health and social breakdown. It was functional for a society which depended for its prosperity on a largely compliant working class whose output was critical to wealth creation. The shift away from manufacturing and the huge growth of finance capitalism, however, have meant the 'corporatist' regulatory system of industrial capitalism is now largely redundant and can be safely dismantled.[7]

Public policy has in effect abetted the processes of growth and decline that economic change has set in motion. Those professions that are close to the epicentre of capitalist growth and development (business consultants, business services providers, commercial lawyers and accountants) have grown; whilst professions far from this have benefitted little, and indeed the attacks on them have been successful. Thus, the changes of policy we have been considering are not simply rational choices governed by the objective appraisal of options and the selection of the best, most efficient and least costly. We also have to ask for whom these changes will be better and least costly. Against the background of the rise of finance capital, the dramatic loss of influence of the traditional professions in the public services (including academia) and the rising tide of commercial organizations and new professionals advocating the benefits of market provision, are clearly revealed as ideological phenomena.

Notes

1. Here, as elsewhere in my work, I have observed a threefold distinction between types of professions. Strongly influenced by Johnson (1972), I draw distinctions between occupations that can or cannot certify the competency of their members, control the supply of qualified recruits as well as exert day-to-day control over conditions of work – amongst other things. The approach recognizes that the particular status of a profession is achieved through what are called collective mobility projects (Larsson 1977) and are active in developing their status, rewards and consolidating their jurisdictions (Abbott 1988), but are limited in the extent to which they can do this by features of their context. In the analysis of the professions the key capacity of these occupations is their ability to achieve complete or partial occupational control of access to labour markets or 'closure' as it is called by Raymond Murphy (1984) and whose mobility project is primarily geared to improve and enhance this. Crudely put, traditional professions control the access of new recruits to their profession, issue credentials and test competency, and so have some ability to discipline existing members. Newer professions, such as accountants and engineers, teachers and social workers, are mostly salaried employees, who provide credentials and licence their members to practise, typically do not own or control their employing organization, though may have some considerable de facto control over day-to-day work. These weaker professions are called organizational professions because they are dependent on employment within organisations. Finally there are newer occupations – most of those formed in the last century – that have no strong and independent professional bodies, and do not issue credentials or license practice. These occupations do not exert external nor internal closure for themselves. If practitioners enjoy superior conditions of work it is because they are employed by powerful organizations. They are therefore organized on a quite different principle than collegiate and organizational professions (which are collectively 'traditional professions'). My thesis is that skilled work is increasingly organized in the manner of this third or organizational type of profession and the old-style professions (either collegiate or corporate) are under attack and often in decline.
2. An important exception here is medicine, where there has been the deliberate expansion of student numbers. The case of the doctors will be considered later in the chapter.
3. There has been a sharp reversal of the historical fortunes of the professions in this respect. Perkin argued persuasively (1989) that the professional pattern of organization constituted a distinctive logic of social provision (which he called 'the professional ideal'). According to Perkin, it came close to being the predominant mode of allocation by the 20th century. This was if anything consolidated down to 1970 or so, substantially occluding the alternative logic of the market which Perkin calls 'the entrepreneurial ideal'.

STEPHEN ACKROYD

4. There is no space for a detailed discussion of the qualities of archetype theory at this point, but suffice it to say we thought that much of the data from the British research projects available to us was not well-accounted for by these ideas.
5. There is an ongoing stream of research that has emanated from these beginnings. Several active former students are still working on the hospitals and different kinds of provision in the NHS. Colleagues are still working on lawyers and business consultants. There has also been some valuable general sociology created about the typical form of change processes.
6. English and American law are of course the basis of the emerging system of law used to frame the contracts used in the majority of international trade and business transactions.
7. During the period we have been examining here (1980-2010) there have been substantial changes in the distribution of wealth in the UK. During the 20th century inequality of income reached a peak in 1915, and, under pressure from social-democratic policies which included the redistributive contribution of the welfare state, was steadily eroded throughout the rest of the century until 1970 or so. Since 1975, the gains made in income equality have been largely reversed. The inequality of wealth distribution has now returned to its 1918 level in the UK.

References

Abbott, A. (1988). *The System of Professions*. Chicago: University of Chicago Press.

Ackroyd, S. (1987). *Report of the Exploratory Study of Nurse Morale in the Acute Unit of Lancaster District Health Authority*, Occasional Paper, Department of Behaviour in Organisations, University of Lancaster.

Ackroyd, S. (1992). Nurses and the Prospects for Participative Management the NHS. In C. Henry & K. Soothill (Eds.), *Themes and Perspectives in Nursing* (pp. 310-330). London: Chapman and Hall.

Ackroyd, S. (1995a). Management and the Professionals: Assessing the Impact of Thatcherism-Majorism on the British Public Services. *Work, Organisation and Economy Working Paper Series No. 24*, Department of Sociology, University of Stockholm, Sweden.

Ackroyd, S. (1995b). From Public Administration to Public Sector Management: A Consideration of Public Policy in the United Kingdom. *International Journal of Public Sector Management, 8*(2), 4-24.

Ackroyd, S. (1995c). Nurses, Management and Morale: A Diagnosis of Decline in the NHS Hospital Service. In L. MacKay et al. (Eds.), *Inter-Professional Relations in Health Care* (pp. 222-252). London: Edward Arnold.

Ackroyd, S. (1996). Organisation Contra Organisations: Professionals and Organisational Change in the United Kingdom. *Organization Studies, 17*(4), 599-622.

Ackroyd, S. (2002). *The Organization of Business*. Oxford: Oxford University Press

Ackroyd, S. (2011). Post-Bureaucratic Manufacturing? The Post-War Organization of Large British Manufacturing Firms. In S. Clegg, M. Harris & H. Hopfl (Eds.), *Managing Modernity: Post Bureaucracy?* (pp. 178-203). Oxford: Oxford University Press.

Ackroyd, S., & Bolton, S. (1999). It's not Taylorism: Mechanisms of Work Intensification in an NHS Hospital. *Work, Employment and Society, 13*(2), 369-387.

Ackroyd, S. & Bolton, S. (2001). Contemporary Research into the Management of Nurses. *International Journal of Public Sector Management, 15*(2), 98-106.

Ackroyd, S., Glover, I., & Currie, W. (2000). The Triumph of Hierarchies over Markets: Information System Specialists in the Current Context. In I. Glover & M. Hughes (Eds.), *Professions at Bay* (pp. 155-96). Aldershot: Avebury.

Ackroyd, S., Harper, R., Hughes, J., & Soothill, K. (1992). *Information Technology and Practical Police Work*. Milton Keynes: Open University Press.

Ackroyd, S., Hughes, J., & Soothill, K. (1989). Public Sector Services and their Management. *Journal of Management Studies, 26*(6). 602-619.

Ackroyd, S., & Muzio, D. (2007). The Reconstructed Professional Firm: Explaining Change in English Legal Practices. *Organisation Studies, 28*(5), 729-747.

Barry, J., Soothill, K., & Francis, B. (1989). Nursing the Statistics: A Demonstration Study of Nurse Turnover and Retention. *Journal of Advanced Nursing, 14* (7), 582-35.

Bolton, S., (2004). A Simple Matter of Control? NHS Hospital Nurses and New Management. *Journal of Management Studies, 41*(6), 317-333.

Bolton, S., Muzio, D., & Boyd-Quinn, C. (2011). Making Sense of Modern Medical Careers: The Case of the UK's National Health Service. *Sociology, 45*(4), 693-699.

Clarke, J., & Kipping, M. (Eds.) (2012). *The Oxford Handbook of Management Consulting*. Oxford: Oxford University Press.

Clarke, J., & Newman, J. (1997). *The Managerial State*. London: Sage.

Craig, D. (2008). *Squandered*. London: Constable.

Craig, D., & Brooks, R. (2006). *Plundering the Public Sector*. London: Constable.

Dent, M., & Kirkpatrick, I. (2011). Medical leadership and Management Reforms in Hospitals in England, Denmark, Netherlands and Kaiser Permanente. In C. Teelken, M. Dent & E. Ferlie (Eds.), *Leadership, Management, and the Professions in the Public Sector*. London: Routledge.

Exworthy, M., & Halford, S. (Eds.) (1999). *Professionals and the New Managerialism in the Public Sector*. Buckingham: Open University Press.

Ferlie, E., & Fitzgerald, L. (2000). *The Sustainability of the New Public Management in the UK: An Institutional Perspective*. Symposium paper, American Academy of Management, Toronto, August.

Francis, B., Peelo, M., & Soothill, K. (1992). NHS Nursing: Vocation, career or just a Job? In C. Henry & K. Soothill (Eds.), *Themes and Perspectives in Nursing* (pp.56-73). London: Chapman and Hall.

Greenwood, R., & Hinings, C.R. (1988). Organisational design types, tracks and the dynamics of strategic change. *Organisational Studies, 9*(3), 293-316.

Greenwood, R., Hinings, C.R., & Brown, J. (1990). 'P2-form' Strategic Management: Corporate practices in professional partnerships. *Academy of Management Journal, 33*(4), 725-755.

Griffiths Report (1983). NHS Management Inquiry. London: DHSS.

Harrison, S. (2002). New Labour, modernisation and the medical labour Process. *Journal of Social Policy, 31*(3), 465-485.

Hinings, C.R., & Greenwood, R. (1988). *The Dynamics of Strategic Change*. Basil Blackwell: Oxford.

Johnson, T. (1972). *Professions and Power*. London: Macmillan.

STEPHEN ACKROYD

Kirkpatrick, I. & Ackroyd, S. (2003a). Archetype Theory and the Changing Professional Organisation: A Critique and Alternative. *Organisation, 10*(4), 731-750.

Kirkpatrick, I., & Ackroyd, S. (2003b). Transforming the Professional Archetype: The New Managerialism in the UK Public Services. *Public Management Review, 5*(4), 509-529.

Kirkpatrick, I., Ackroyd, S., & Walker, R. (2005). *The New Managerialism and the Public Service Professions.* Basingstoke: Palgrave Macmillan.

Kirkpatrick, I., Ackroyd, S., & Walker, R. (2007). Public Management Reform in the UK and Its Consequences for Professional Organisation: A Comparative Analysis. *Public Administration, 85*(1), 9-27.

Kitchener, M. (1998). Quasi-Market Transformation: an Institutionalist Approach to Change in UK Hospitals. *Public Administration, 76,* 73-95.

Leys, C., & Player, S. (2012). *The Plot Against the NHS.* London: Merlin Press.

Larson, M.S. (1977). *The Rise of Professionalism: A Sociological Analysis.* London: University of California Press.

Mackay, L. (1989). *Nursing a Problem.* London: Open University Press.

Murphy, R. (1988). *Social Closure: The Theory of Monopolization and Exclusion.* Oxford: Clarendon Press.

Muzio, D. (2004). The Professional Project and the Contemporary Re-Organization of the Legal Profession in England and Wales. *International Journal of the Legal Profession, 11*(1-2), 33-51.

Muzio, D., & Ackroyd, S. (2008a). Introduction: Redirections in the Study of Expert Labour. In D. Muzio, S. Ackroyd & J.-F. Chanlat (Eds.), *Redirections in the Study of Expert Labour: Established Professions and New Occupations* (pp. 1-28). London: Palgrave.

Muzio, D., & Ackroyd, S. (2008b). Change in the Legal Profession: Professional Agency and the Legal Labour Process. In D. Muzio, S. Ackroyd & J.-F. Chanlat (Eds.), *Redirections in the Study of Expert Labour: Established Professions and New Occupations* (pp. 31-51). London: Palgrave.

Muzio, D., Ackroyd, S., & Chanlat, J.-F. (Eds.) (2008). *Redirections in the Study of Expert Labour: Established Professions and New Occupations.* London: Palgrave.

Muzio, D., Ackroyd, S., & Kirkpatrick, I. (2012). The Occupational and Organisational Development Project of Management Consultancy: Or Why Management Consultancy is not a Profession. In T. Clark & M. Kipping (Eds.), *The Oxford Handbook of Management Consulting.* Oxford: Oxford University Press.

Perkin, H. (1989). *The Rise of Professional Society: England Since 1880.* London: Routledge.

Sikka, P. (2009, 13 June). A Nation of Accountants. *The Guardian.*

Soothill, K., Barry, J., & Williams, C. (1992). Words and Actions: A Study of Nurse Wastage. *International Journal of Nursing Studies, 29*(2), 163-75.

Tooke, J. (2008). *Aspiring to Excellence: Findings of the Independent Enquiry into Modernising medical Careers.* London: Tavistock.

3 Professionals, power and the reform of public services

Janet Newman

Introduction

The role of 'public' professionals is one that has continually been contested. They are the bearers of forms of knowledge and expertise that the public value, but at the same time the public – in various manifestations – has often resisted or resented the power of professionals to make judgments about their lives and to broker access to the resources they need. It is professionals who are entrusted with the impossible job of reconciling 'needs' and 'wants' and of managing the relationship between the hopes and fears of those they serve. Professionals are also the carriers of all of the contradictions of 'modern' welfare states, embodying the dreams of equality and social justice while struggling with the realities of unruly populations, administrative recalcitrance and political game playing. It is no wonder, then, that professionals have always experienced themselves as under pressure. But of course the rewards can also be great. While such rewards are unevenly distributed across the hierarchical ordering of different professions, para-professions and support workers, they include for some relatively secure jobs with good pensions and rewarding work, not to mention the gratitude of clients and the respect of the wider society.

What, then, might be specific about the current period? To answer this question I want to do three things in this chapter. First, I want to explore issues of time – how can we understand the present? Can we see a gradual intensification of pressure over time, or is there something distinctive about the current challenges that produces a significant reordering of the meanings and practices of professional work: the places where it is carried out and the constraints professionals operate under? This inevitably raises questions of space in the sense of place – does national context make much difference? Second, I want to raise some questions about professionals as both the objects of change (being done to) and the subjects of change (actors reshaping welfare and service delivery). This opens out a second sense of space – the spaces within the welfare and public service system in which professionals act. In line with much of this volume I argue that professionals and professional work have tended to be the object of reform as modernizing welfare states have sought to challenge 'producer interests'. Professionals now operate under considerably greater constraint and scrutiny, and the 'knowledge-power knot' of expertise and authority has been loosened as a result of both occupational and social change. However professionals must also be viewed as agents, shaping change and leading – as well as sometimes resisting – reform. This takes me to my third argument: how to situate the analysis of changes to and within the professions in the context of wider debates about public governance. Here I suggest that theories of governance and of governmentality can, in their very different ways, offer helpful ways of analyzing 'professionals under pressure'.

Telling tales: Narratives of change

Diagnosing the contemporary inevitably means looking back over time. Was there ever a golden past of unconstrained and productive professional work in public arenas that has been forever ruptured by the forces of managerialism, consumerism and government regulation? I think this is a dangerous assumption. In looking back to the formative years of welfare states and expanding public sectors we can trace an uneven and incomplete postwar settlement[1] in which the public, professionals and some political parties were aligned in their investment in the 'good society' to come. The most attention has been focused on the disruptions to the political-economic settlement, and the challenges to the social democratic welfare state posed by the forces of neo-liberalism. However, as chapters in this volume recognize, we also need to pay attention to ruptures in the social settlement. To understand these we have to look back to the ways in which the postwar social settlement was partial and conditional. There were important exclusions, and from the 1970s onwards the women's movements, patient's movements and other groupings – many informed by the critiques of Illich and other voices (see chapter 5 – this volume) – began to challenge the paternalism and patriarchal practices of the professions. Such challenges continued, with disability movements, mental health service users, people with learning disabilities and others taking the stage in the late 20th century. Many of the current pressures faced by professionals flowed from such challenges; but it is important to recognize that they did not always come from 'outside'. Some radicals and activists themselves entered the professions and fought for change from within, often in alliance with social movements 'outside'. Current calls for democratization and choice (Tonkens et al., this volume) can be seen as continuing this tradition.

A narrative of change which views these recent challenges as assaulting a profession untouched by such claims over the last 50 years or so is, then, flawed. What matters, however, is not seeing such claims as simply emanating from groups and users: they are readily seized on by 'modernizing' politicians seeking to challenge professional power for a number of reasons: to win popular support by attacking what are presented as entrenched interests, to invoke greater citizen responsibility for functions previously viewed as the responsibility of the state, or to open up market logics in the name of 'choice'.[2] The political articulations between popular demands and modernizing logics differ considerably between countries. In Nordic welfare states there is still strong support for publicly funded welfare. However, in countries characterized by a stronger element of 'neo-liberal' reform, the political drivers of modernization have been relatively successful.

A rather different narrative of change and intensifying pressure concerns the ruptures to the organizational settlement. Public professions expanded in the growing bureaucracies of the welfare state, in which professional power was always constrained by and subject to logics deriving from administrative or bureaucratic imperatives. The alignment of professional and bureaucratic power, as Mintzberg argued, was always incomplete; the professional bureaucracy was an unstable form containing, one might suggest in hindsight, the seeds of its own demise, opening up the space for more managerial logics. The impact of these logics is powerfully revealed in the chapters that follow. I think, however, we need to be a little cautious about a narrative of the New Public Management sweeping all before it. NPM is not a singular entity but has come to stand for a range of reforms that are enacted and experienced very differently in different nations (Pollitt & Bouckaert 2004). It also changes over time. What began with principal-agent theory and purchaser/provider splits has evolved into highly sophisticated processes of outsourcing and commissioning, and the development of hybrid organizational forms that combine public and private authority in complex ways (Hansen & Salskov-Iversen 2008). These are no longer (if they ever were) the product of government dictate but are generated by organizational actors seeking survival and looking to maximize resource use in the context of global competition. In the UK public sector much professional work has been relocated to call centres in nations with cheaper labour or has been outsourced to multi-functional global companies. There has also been a growing market for companies supplying professional expertise to turn round 'failing' schools and hospitals; to provide professional workers from overseas to meet skill gaps or to work in 'unpopular' areas; or to meet fluctuating demands through agency work. These each offer new alignments between professional, managerial and market logics, and produce new kinds of organizational locations for professional work and of course new kinds of pressure – particularly those of managing personal risk and economic uncertainty. While driven by market opportunities and the search for profit, they cannot all be collapsed into a single entity of the NPM. Nor can the nation state any longer be viewed as the prime unit of analysis: transnational flows (of people, resources, ideas, policies) are as significant as national institutions.

What might this analysis offer in terms of the questions about change I set out in the Introduction? The first point to make is that the national context makes a difference, but only some difference. While the NPM is a transnational discourse, and while all mature welfare states are attempting to modernize in the face of what they view as globalizing pressures (not to mention the impact of the financial crisis of 2008), nations mobilize and enact change in different ways. Change will be managed and experienced differently in the Nordic nations; in the states based on 'pillarized' systems of social insurance; in the nations of Southern Europe; and in the accession countries of Central and Eastern Europe. I do not want to return to Esping-Andersen's typologies here, which are widely recognized to be deeply flawed. Even within the Nordic countries there is considerable diversity, and many nation states are marked by significant regional and national differences (e.g. regional in Italy; national within the UK). Nevertheless, some nations (France, Italy) are characterized by extensive popular resistance to neo-liberal reform, while in others (including the Netherlands and the UK) reform seems to have been easier. And the problems and pressures experienced by Central and Eastern European post-communist nations are clearly very different from those in the mature welfare states of Western Europe.

But in addition to national reform trajectories we also have to consider the impact of past colonial relationships and more recent patterns of migration on the flows (inwards and outwards) of professional workers and other occupational groups, especially care workers and support workers. Migrant workers – whether from former colonies, from Eastern Europe or from the global South – experience multiple forms of pressure, not only that of the work itself (often in the lowest paid and pressurized parts of welfare services) but also that of racism in the 'host' country. They may also be part of global care chains that require splitting one's emotional life between the care of service users and clients in the host country and that of family and dependents left for others to care for 'at home'. This reminds us of the difficulties of speaking of the professions as a cohesive entity; change will be experienced differently not only in different nations but in relation to different occupational groups (traditional professions, high and lower status welfare professions, para-professions, care workers and so on), and in relation to personal trajectories of change and mobility.

But is change intensifying? Are the pressures getting worse? My analysis suggests a conception of change based on notions of adaptability and fluidity – of people, markets, organizations – rather than a more linear conception of change. Certainly, change itself brings pressure, and the more change the more pressure. But what I have tried to suggest in this section is that an idealized image of professional work operating relatively free from pressure and constraint is based perhaps on a misremembering of the past.

We might distinguish here between the exacerbation of existing pressure (more clients, new social problems to be addressed, more difficult judgments as resources are stretched) and new kinds of pressure (more managerialism, greater scrutiny, the intensification of labour through the use of new technologies, more media scandals and higher visibility and risk). In order to tease out some of the different characteristics of new kinds of pressure (rather than simply bundling everything up as the NPM) I want, in the next section, to return to a model first developed by John Clarke and myself and elaborated in Clarke et al. (2007) and Clarke & Newman (2009).

Remaking professional work: Dismantling the knowledge-power knot?

Many of the pressures around public service professionalism have come to bear on – and are condensed in – what we have called the 'knowledge-power knot' (Clarke et al. 2007). The terminology here – linking knowledge and power in the image of a knot – is intended to convey a more tangled view of multiple threads, rather than a simple, stable and singular relationship between knowledge and power. In exploring different formations of power and their implications for public service professionalism we used the framing device of a diamond:

Figure 1 Framing knowledge-power knots

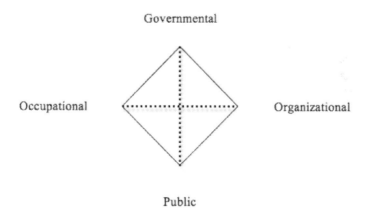

This offers a simple mapping of different pressures: the public places new expectations, government make new demands, organizations tighten managerial logics, occupations become more uncertain. But I want to focus not on what happens at the points of the diamond but on the lines that connect them: that is, on the constraints and spaces of agency produced as the relationships between different elements are remade. I do so selectively in order to highlight the most significant dynamics.

I want to start with *government-organizational* relationships. Governmental imperatives have typically searched for a new 'organizational settlement' based on fragmented and dispersed systems of providing services coordinated horizontally through competition or 'quasi-competition' (league tables, etc.) and connected vertically through principal-agent models of target setting and expanded scrutiny systems. Organizational imperatives are increasingly framed by these relationships, such that they become 'success' focused (Schram & Soss 2002). The management of performance (or at least the management of the representations of performance) is a key element in the organizational culture of public service provision (Clarke 2005). So too is increasing audit, regulation and scrutiny, each of which transfer some of the 'knowledge' in the knowledge power knot into new technologies that codify it into systems of 'best practice' against which performance can be judged.

But this does not mean that professionals are simply passive pawns in the face of new pressures. Two points are important here, both connecting *occupations* and *government*. First, it is the professions themselves which have often formulated the ideas of best practice that are subsequently rolled out in audit and inspection regimes. And many professionals, 'front-line' workers and publics tend to support greater regulation and inspection, aware not only of how awful bad practice was in some places in the past, but also wanting to defend services from low performing competitors. We have also seen some occupational groups trying to reposition themselves by laying claim to newly significant bodies of expertise – those of risk assessment, quality management, behaviour change. Evidence-based policy is a particularly contested area, with disputes around whose evidence counts and who can lay claim to it. Professionals complain about the constraints on discretion but also recognize that the 'evidence' of EBP can validate and defend the scientific knowledge basis of their work, using this to resist challenges to professional attacks (e.g. Newman & Nutley 2003 on the use of EBP by the then threatened probation service in the UK).

Second, professionals cannot simply be viewed as the implementers of government policy. As we showed in the 'Creating Citizen Consumers' project, policies are mediated and translated through professional discourses and adapted in the face of local priorities and needs. For example, professionals in health care translated the new discourses of choice in line with well established professional discourses on the need to offer patients a choice of treatments (rather than a choice of provider) and on the importance of greater involvement on the part of patients in decision-making – in order to produce better health outcomes rather than to 'modernize' services. Voice rather than choice was thus privileged. In social care professionals actively managed the imperatives to introduce individual budgets and/or direct payments, viewing these as more appropriate for some groups (e.g. young adults with physical disabilities) than others (frail older people, mental health service users) and

JANET NEWMAN

steering decision-making accordingly. Here consumerism was re-inflected as client 'empowerment'. We can thus see governmental discourses being translated through existing professional vocabularies (Newman & Vidler 2006; Kuhlmann & Newman 2007). Similarly organizations are not merely the passive vehicle for government action. They may inflect or interpret policy directions to fit with organizational, managerial or local predispositions.

Turning to the *occupational-organizational* relationship, professionals have always occupied an ambiguous space in public organizations, balancing peer loyalties and identities with their membership of a particular organization. Managerialism has certainly sought to shift this balance. One strategy here has been to make managers out of professionals, asking senior professionals to take on managerial roles or inventing new kinds of 'hybrid' posts (such as the clinical director in the UK). This strategy has been extended as managerialism has pervaded occupational groups working in new business units or cost centres, being 'responsibilized' for the budget and performance of that unit. This means that for occupations, autonomy has remained one critical focus of concern, whether this is the space of 'clinical judgment' for doctors or the discretion built into 'front-line work' in local offices. Most studies of managerialization in public services have pointed to the attempts to control, constrain and diminish the sites and forms of professional autonomy, although evaluations of the success of managerialism's impact on public service professionalism vary (e.g. Exworthy & Halford 1999; Kirkpatrick et al. 2004). Some occupations have been hard hit by managerialism and other reforms, while others – notably medicine – seem to be remarkably resilient.

However some professionals have become adept at creating new spaces of agency within the expanding market of public services. The professional 'social entrepreneur' – the group of nurses setting up an agency, the social care and housing workers setting up cooperatives or companies to supply new kinds of supported living, the social workers setting up personal advocacy and support services selling their work to the holders of individual budgets – are all features of the changing landscape of professional work in the UK. This gives them greater control over the organization they work for and an escape from increasing performance pressures within public sector organizations. And the supposed exhaustion of the NPM is opening up spaces in which both professionals and managers are talking the language of democratization, involvement, co-production, empowerment and choice (Duyvendak et al. 2006). I am not necessarily convinced that we are now looking to something 'beyond' the NPM, but nevertheless I think attention needs to be paid to the different ways in which such concepts are emerging and being deployed. Professionals are developing new skill bases – patient and public involvement in health, risk assessment in social work, community safety in policing, and capacity building in all of those professions that deal with the shift of responsibilities from states to citizens and communities.

Such shifts tend to be made in the name of the public and/or in the interests of clients and users, taking us to the *professional/public* relationship. Professionals have tended to privilege their relationships with individuals (as clients, service users) but they also have much wider public roles, attempting to secure better health, improved educational achievements, and indeed to address problems of inequality and injustice. A whole range of governmental initiatives has played a part in reconfiguring these professional-public relationships – disrupting the claims of professional expertise and authority. Here governments lay claim to be the 'public's friend', serving the user interest by challenging the knots of professional power. However professionals, in turn, stress their place close the user that allows them to both serve and defend the user interest (against a distant and intrusive government). New pressures are arising in this relationship with the public, including those of managing unpredictable and excess demand; dealing with varieties of acquiescence and assertiveness; and managing modes of access and interaction.

But key is the issue of legitimacy. Despite the decline in deference and the rise of mistrust, public service professionals tend to command a relatively high degree of public trust and confidence in surveys (especially by contrast with other occupations that sometimes claim the 'public interest' defence – politicians and journalists, for example). However, legitimacy now appears more fragile and more contextually contingent, rather than being available 'en bloc' to a public service organization or occupation. The challenge to legitimacy coupled with the orientation to responding to new social and professional goals has led to considerable shifts in the relationship between professionals and the public. Some groups of professionals have developed a discourse of 'coproduction' that sets out to overcome some of the disparities of knowledge and power between professionals and users. This is not only in the name of 'democratizing' the professions (Kremer & Tonkens 2006) but also in the name of securing better outcomes from interventions and better resource use.

Each of the relationships captured in the model in Figure 1 is thus the site of contestation. This is not just a case of professional resistance to governmental and organization constraints, but of contestation within the professions themselves – for example between those wedded to 'coproduction' or democratization and those who wish to retain their traditional knowledge and power, or between those who view public legitimacy as a priority and those who view greater scrutiny and accountability as impeding their discretionary space. Finally of course there may be profound tensions between those who combine managerial and professional logics in their individual work and those who wish to retain a 'pure' professional status.

JANET NEWMAN

Remaking professional work: Governance and governmentality

Throughout this chapter I have tried to suggest a dynamic rather than linear view of change: a view in which multiple forces and pressures, and the practices that flow from them, are assembled in specific contexts. Contexts make a difference, both in terms of the different professional groupings and the different places (and trajectories of reform). I have tried to illuminate the ways in which new pressures and new spaces of agency are articulated. That is, I have argued that professionals are not just the passive victims of reform but have an active role in shaping not only large-scale reform programmes but also specific spaces of agency. This does not, however, mean that I want to offer a rosy picture of the resilience of professional power. Rather, I want to offer two different theoretical framings that might help illuminate the complex articulations of new pressures and new spaces of agency.

The first framing returns us to the well worn metaphor of governance, and the idea that we are witnessing some kind of shift from hierarchical authority to more network-based modes of steering and coordination (Rhodes 1997; and see critiques in Newman 2001, 2005). This is certainly a helpful metaphor for capturing some of the dynamics I have described. The demise of respect and deference, coupled with the challenge to professional power bases, seems to represent a move away from hierarchical authority. So too does the shift towards coproduction, public participation and user involvement. Here the public, in its various forms, become drawn into more collaborative and partnership-based relationships with professionals: knowledge is shared (to some extent) and patients take on some responsibility for the success or otherwise of the treatments or interventions they participate in.

Ideas of network governance also apparently dissolve the rigidity of the boundaries between professionalism and managerialism. Different kinds of actor are brought together in partnership bodies, or work across organizational boundaries in order to achieve common purposes. New organizational forms challenge 'old' distinctions between public, private and 'third' sectors and between different roles and labour market categories. As I noted earlier, many professionals are becoming market actors, heading up new kinds of community-based agency, becoming 'social entrepreneurs' or setting up new kinds of trust or cooperative ventures with colleagues, often from different occupational groups. Such developments lead to them having to combine professional, managerial and business logics. The generative potential of combining different skill sets, knowledge and forms of influence power is crucial to such endeavours.

Governance theory, then, offers a view of professionals as part of newly significant networks and relationships, both with the public itself (new forms of coproduction, involvement) and with other agencies (in interorganization and multidisciplinary partnerships). They are also important players in policy networks, exerting influence and shaping new policy directions. At the same time, such directions tend to bring to the fore forms of knowledge and power that have operated only on the margins of the mainstream professions (though sometimes have evolved from them). I am talking here about the contemporary significance of behaviour change strategies, public engagement policies, community capacity building, place shaping, community safety policies, advocacy work for the holders of Individual Budgets in social care, good parenting or 'well being' policies and so on. These blur the boundaries of professionalism and managerialism in complex ways. On the one hand they 'belong' to neither, requiring new skill sets – and sometimes new categories of quasi professionals. On the other, these strategies are often translated into governmental goals and targets and thus subject to managerial forms of priority setting, measurement and performance management.

Network governance thus has a paradoxical effect. It opens up the space for new occupational groups aspiring for professional status to demonstrate the importance of their skill base and to take their place in the policy landscape, often leading new policy developments. Again in the UK the community safety officer has been a prime example (Hughes & Gilling 2004). At the same time, however, the emphasis on organizational collaboration or 'joined up government' and the focus on achieving policy outcomes has led to some softening of the boundaries between established professions. Again the UK, partnership relationships between health and social care have blurred some boundaries and opened up new forms of contestation over 'who owns' particular kinds of knowledge or expertise. This blurring of boundaries challenges the integrity of some professional disciplines. Partnership working certainly demands new skills and personal resources; but it also produces new orderings of power (Glendinning, Powell & Rummery 2002), while offering the possibility of new forms of agency and influence.

The significance of partnership work in challenging professional boundaries can of course be overstated. As I have argued (Newman 2001) network governance is uneasily aligned with other governance regimes, including those of managerial governance, hierarchical governance and self-governance. I am not sure this original categorization continues to hold up, but the point that the dissolution of boundaries between different knowledges and skill sets is cross cut by new orderings of power and lines of tension remains valid. The governance thesis would tend to suggest that we need to transcend old-style thinking about professionalism and managerialism as distinctive forms of knowledge and power. But this may not pay sufficient attention to how 'network' regimes interact with other forms and practices of governance: the continued role of hierarchy, the capacity of managerialism to adapt into new forms, and the changing relationship between public and private authority in the evolving market place of public services.

It seems to me that academic engagement with the interaction of professionalism and managerialism has given way to a concern with, on the one hand, performance, accountability and 'good governance'; and on the other to 'big' explanatory concepts such as governmentality and neo-liberalism, or some combination thereof. The latter draws attention to governmentalities that constitute both professionals and managers as self-governing, self-regulating actors. Rather than turning to governance theory for the answer, then, we might look to notions of governmentality. Whether the governmentalities are those of professionalism or managerialism might matter less, this argument would go, that the ways in which public service work is increasingly concerned with constituting managers, professionals and front-line workers, as well as citizens, service users and communities, as self-governing subjects.

Governmentality theory helps us reframe the idea of 'professionals under pressure'. The focus shifts to discursive regimes and to the technologies of power that draw on the agency of 'free' actors to regulate themselves. Dent & Whitehead explore the relationship between discourse and identity in the following terms: 'It is through immersion in (these) discursive regimes that the individual is enabled into existence and by which the individual comes to (re)present certain truths about the world. The extent to which this is subjecting the individual to an embodied regulatory effect, or whether the individual is drawing, more agentically, on these knowledges to constitute themselves as 'works of art' is one of the contested interpretations of Foucauldian theory' (2002: 9). I want to emphasize this contestation in order to avoid oversimplistic notions of the constitutive power of discourse. But the conceptualization of power as productive, mobilizing the empowered subject, rather than constraining him or her, is, I think, helpful to the analysis of professionals under pressure, transforming the notion of multiple pressures coming from outside into a concern with the remaking of professional agency and identity in individual life projects. It also directs attention to how professionals and other workers occupy the spaces of change; and offers a conceptual vocabulary of work that, I think, can operate across the boundaries between different professional disciplines and between professional and other workers.

But the difficulty is that governmentality, like governance, tells too big a story. It recounts how professionals are being empowered through programmes of devolution and decentralization, and how their capacities as self-regulating actors are being summoned and mobilized to address the necessities of change. Perhaps, rather than being satisfied with such big stories (and the theories they draw on) we need to look at how different – and multiple – forms of power (discursive, institutional, knowledge based, coercive etc.) are brought together and how they are ordered and aligned in specific sites. This does not of course present a wholly satisfactory answer, but it does open up questions about the specificities of what is going on in particular places, how this is experienced by different

groups of actors, and what processes of translation, mediation and negotiation are opened up to the analytical gaze. Finally, it directs attention to
the work of assembling – the alignment of disparate programmes and
practices, and the search for coherence in the face of an increasing multiplicity of governmental objects and actors. Perhaps this struggle for
coherence – and the work of translation, mediation, negotiation, and the
containment of personal and social trauma – is now at the core of professional work.

Notes

1. In 'The Managerial State' John Clarke and I analyzed the rise of managerial-
    ism through analysis of three different settlements: the political/economic;
    the social; and the organizational. I have drawn on a simplified version of
    this here.
2. In Newman, J. and Tonkens, E., (Eds.) (2011) we analyze the ways in which
    notions of choice, participation and responsibility in discourses of active ci-
    tizenship flow from, but rearticulate, the demands of earlier movements
    and citizen claims.

References

Clarke, J. (2005). Performing for the Public: Doubt, Desire and the Evaluation of
   Public Services. In P. du Gay (Ed.), *The Values of Bureaucracy*. Oxford: Oxford
   University Press.
Clarke, J., & Newman, J. (1997). *The Managerial State: Power, Politics and Ideology
   in the Remaking of Social Welfare*. London: Sage.
Clarke, J., & Newman, J. (2009). Elusive Publics: knowledge, power and public
   service reform. In S. Gewirtz, P. Mahony, I. Hextall & A. Cribb (Eds.), *Chang-
   ing Teacher Professionalism: international challenges, trends and ways forward*.
   London: Routledge.
Clarke, J., Newman, J., Smith, N., Vidler, E., & Westmarland, L. (2007). *Creating
   Citizen-Consumers: Changing Publics and Changing Public Services*. London:
   Sage.
Dent, M., & Whitehead, S. (2002). Introduction. In M. Dent & S. Whitehead
   (Eds.), *Managing Professional Identities: knowledge, performativity and the 'new'
   professional*. London: Routledge.
Duyvendak, J., Knijn, T., & Kremer, M. (2006). *Policy, People and the New Profes-
   sional: De-professionalisation and Re-professionalisation in Care and Welfare*. Am-
   sterdam: Amsterdam University Press.
Exworthy, M., & Halford, S. (Eds.) (1999). *Professionals and the New Managerial-
   ism in the Public Sector*. Buckingham: Open University Press.
Glendinning, C., Powell, M., & Rummery, K. (Eds.) (2002). *Partnerships, New
   Labour and the Governance of Welfare*. Bristol: Policy Press.

Hansen, H.K., & Salskov-Iversen, D. (Eds.) (2008). *Critical Perspectives on Private Authority in Global Governance*. Basingstoke: Palgrave-Macmillan.

Hughes, G., & Gilling, D. (2004). Mission impossible? The habitus of the community safety manager and the new expertise in the local partnership governance of crime and safety, *Criminal Justice, 4*(2), 129-49.

Kirkpatrick, I., Ackroyd, S., & Walker, R. (2004). *The New Managerialism and Public Service Professionals*. Basingstoke: Palgrave Macmillan.

Kremer, M., & Tonkens, E. (2006). Authority, trust, knowledge and the public good in disarray. In T. Knijn & M. Kremer, *Professionals between people and policy* (p. 122-136). Amsterdam: Amsterdam University Press.

Kuhlmann, E., & Newman, J. (2007). Consumers enter the political stage: the modernisation of health care in Britain and Germany, *Journal of European Social Policy, 17*(2), 99-111.

Newman, J. (2001). *Modernising Governance: New Labour, Policy and Society*. London: Sage.

Newman, J. (2005). *Remaking Governance: Peoples, Politics and the Public Sphere*. Bristol: Policy Press.

Newman, J., & Clarke, J. (2009). *Publics, Politics and Power: remaking the public in public services*. London: Sage.

Newman, J., & Nutley, S. (2003). Transforming the Probation Service: what works, organisational change and professional identity, *Policy and Politics, 31* (4), 547-63.

Newman, J., & Tonkens, E. (2011). *Responsibility, Participation and Choice: Summoning the active citizen in western Europe welfare states*. Amsterdam: Amsterdam University Press.

Newman, J., & Vidler, E. (2006). Discriminating customers, responsible patients, empowered users: consumerism and the modernisation of health care, *Journal of Social Policy, 35*(2), 193-209.

Pollitt, C., & Bouckaert, G. (2004). *Public Management Reform: a comparative analysis*. Oxford: Oxford University Press.

Rhodes, R.A.W. (1997). *Understanding Governance*. Buckingham/Philadelphia: Open University Press.

Schram, S., & Soss, J. (2002). Success stories: welfare reform, policy discourse and the politics of research. In S. Schram, *Praxis for the Poor*. New York: New York University Press.

4 Professionals dealing with pressures[1]

Peter Hupe & Theo van der Krogt

Introduction

Full and semi-professionals appear to have more in common than their distinction suggests. They experience pressures on the way they do their work, and they feel these pressures have increased. In the preceding chapter Janet Newman showed that increasing pressures on professionals can be explained in two ways. First, existing pressures have exacerbated, and, second, new kinds of pressures have arisen. Her focus on pressures within knowledge-power knots illustrates that these pressures are relative, depending on the perspective that is taken. Whereas some professionals might be troubled by pressures and seek ways to cope, others might be consciously causing pressures or might profit from pressurized professional spaces. Moreover, pressures might be an unavoidable part of professional work – although professionals might still complain if they dislike certain work aspects.

This shows that it is necessary to specify and differentiate when we study what professionals do and how pressures affect outcomes of professional work: what are we talking about? Pressures, for instance, that are emphasized in order to resist policy changes might also be seen as 'normal' pressures, inherent to professional work. In addition, pressures might add up and make things unworkable, but they might offer professionals more space to be selective as well. In this chapter we analyze how professionals deal with 'old' and 'new' pressures on their work, while explaining variation in professional work. Specifying what we know and what we do not know and taking Newman's change narratives one step further, is what we aim at in this chapter. We do so by addressing the following question: Given the variety of tasks full and semi-professionals fulfil, the different degrees of institutionalization of their professions, and their varying personal characteristics, what kinds of pressures on their work, including contemporary pressures, can be observed? And which patterns can be identified in the ways professionals deal with such pressures? In the next section we explore how professionals and their work might vary: which dimensions are relevant for classifying types of professional work? In the third section we distinguish between types of pressures. We will focus on regular constraints on professional work, i.e. constraints on the autonomy of individual professionals, as well as on contemporary or 'new' pressures. Next, we explore the ways in which professionals deal with these pressures; which patterns can be identified? In the final section we draw some conclusions.

Professionals in public service

Institutionalization

Many sociologists have addressed the question 'what constitutes a profession?' Two dimensions turned out to be of crucial importance: the specific nature of the work involved and the position of that work in society, often addressed in terms of power (Johnson 1972; Freidson 1986). Greenwood (1957: 45), for instance, suggests that 'all professions seem to possess: (1) systematic theory, (2) authority, (3) community sanction, (4) ethical codes, and (5) a culture'. This collection of attributes of a profession seems to combine characteristics of an occupation (systematic theory, ethical codes and culture) with the way in which society treats that occupation (authority and community sanction).

Likewise, many sociologists have asked the question, 'what is a professional?' The terms professions and professionals refer to different levels of aggregation. Professions are situated at the institutional level: professional groups have defined professional work and established occupational spaces or jurisdictions (e.g. Abbott 1988). Professionals are situated at the individual level: they are members of a profession which results from but also regulates professional practices. The distinction between these levels can be specified one step further: professionals work in varying organizational settings. Differences in organizational circumstances and specific work conditions will influence how both professional regulation and practices will work out. In other words, the nature of a specific profession and the degree of societal acceptance of its relative autonomy (*institutionalization*) have consequences for the way the individual members of that profession do their work (*professional practice*) in a particular setting (*organization* and *work circumstances*); see Table 1.

Against this background the classical theme of the relationship between institutions and individual action is relevant. More specifically, the degree of institutionalization of a profession and the autonomy available to its members seem to be mutually reinforcing. DiMaggio & Powell (1983: 152) describe a profession as an occupation whose members have had success in defining 'the conditions and methods of their work' and in establishing 'a cognitive base and legitimacy for their occupational autonomy'. Occupational closure is aimed at (Abbott 1988), as well as professional control (Freidson 2001). Internal professional control makes the delegation of responsibility towards a profession, like the medical one, feasible. At the same time such delegation makes the mentioned control more necessary in order to protect the autonomy of the profession as an institution, as well as of its individual members.

PETER HUPE & THEO VAN DER KROGT

Table 1 Dimensions of professional variety

Level of aggregation	Category	Dimensions
Profession	Institutionalization	Nature of vocation
		Contents of vocation
		Social status
		Self-regulation
Organization	Organization and work circumstances	Public-administrative layer
		Policy formation/implementation
		Organizational structure
		Function of IT in primary process
		Superior/subordinate
		Nature and frequency of client contacts
Professional	Individual characteristics	Formal education
		Nature and length of vocational training
		Habitus
		Work experience
		Experience in present job
		Personal experiences
		Gender
		Age
		Personal traits

The nature of the norms inherently related to his or her profession – e.g. the doctor dealing with matters of life and death – might enhance the institutionalization of the profession involved. The result may be that the needs of the patient or client are always in the forefront; in any case, they are used in a legitimizing way. This may even be the case when professionals merely protect particular interests. More than a matter of becoming better experts, the degree and pace of institutionalization of a profession seem to involve power relations and legitimation. In a comparative perspective this means that occupations are accorded the status of a traditional 'profession' by virtue of the combination of the inherent characteristics of such occupations and the esteem they have in society.

It is obvious that the term 'professional' – certainly when opposed to 'bureaucrat' – refers to a rhetorical construct, implying a positive or negative connotation, dependent on the one who uses the word. The usage of these terms in public discourse is part of political language, employed in order to convince others, while implying a normative claim (Edelman 1975). A substantial freedom to act, addressed as 'autonomy', is argued to be one of the defining characteristics of professional work (Day & Klein 1981). Full professionals like the medical specialist, the lawyer, the architect – functionaries seeing themselves as representing the 'real' professions – traditionally have been accorded a high degree of autonomy, both institutionally and in their day-to-day practices (see, for instance, Witman 2008). While such autonomy may arise from the nature of the task, the according of power is involved. The latter is justified on two grounds. First, professionals possess specialized expert knowledge (e.g. Brint 1994). Such knowledge is the product of controlled entry, a lengthy training and accreditation by the professional body itself. Second, professionals make a corresponding (and constraining) claim to serve the public good, rather than their own interests. This may be expressed in a professional code, enforced by internal regulations (Kultgen 1988). The members of a profession that legitimately can claim that their relationships with citizens, in their various roles, are governed by ethical codes and altruistic values, may claim autonomy more effectively than members of another profession. The extent to which these two justifications of professional autonomy are expressed in the degree of institutionalization of the profession involved, is an empirical question. However, despite developments towards further professionalization, the distinction between the so-called full and semi-professions remains relevant (Etzioni 1969).

Professional practice

As indicated, the notion of autonomy is inherent to the term profession. As an idealtypical construct, professional autonomy would mean that the professional always possesses the unlimited possibility to act exclusively according to the internalized standards of his or her profession. In contrast, the term discretion is used to label the constrained freedom of bureaucrats to act. The freedom of the latter is by definition limited, it is argued, not only by the nature of the rules bureaucrats are supposed to apply, but also by the fact that they have to do so.

Rather than being fixed as an inherent characteristic of a profession, the freedom to act of individual professionals, both granted and taken, will vary empirically. This goes particularly for how the freedom is used. In their work actors will always have a certain degree of freedom to act. What is usually called discretion refers to the limits of such freedom as granted by a rule-maker. As such, discretion is a characteristic of a formal rule or range of rules formulated by a specific rule-maker. The latter expects the presumed rule-applier to act accordingly, in a relationship thought of as one of compliance that has a one-to-one and hierarchical nature.

Autonomy can then be described as the freedom to act as taken by an actor. It is a characteristic of an individual, often working inside an organization. While professional norms and other action prescriptions, coming from different sources, are valid, it is the individual actor who in a given situation decides both on the applicability of these action prescriptions and on how to apply them. It is obvious that the usage of the freedom to act will empirically vary along a range of dimensions. We already mentioned the nature of the profession, the degree of its institutionalization and the contents of the values embodied in the profession; these are dimensions of the occupational system. As far as individual members of a profession are concerned, there are characteristics like years of experience, moral stances and the personalities involved.

This means that no professional is ever completely free. The freedom to act, even in the case of full professionals, is always constrained, both theoretically and empirically.

Organizational context

This bounded freedom is constrained even further when we take organizational surroundings into account. Work circumstances of professionals vary along a range of dimensions. A person with a degree in law, for instance, can work as a policy adviser at a ministry, but can also head a judicial unit of a Social Services Department in a large city. Among the variety of dimensions on which agencies or 'street-level bureaucracies' may differ, the frequency of contacts with citizens in various roles, is a particular one. In fact, there is a relational dimension involved as well. Teachers at a primary school, for instance, see the pupils in their classroom daily, GPs see their patients only a few times per year, but a surgeon may operate on his patient perhaps once in a lifetime. It can be expected that in the latter case, professional autonomy is less constrained than in the former ones. Pupils in the classroom, and indirectly the expectations of their parents, will influence the way the teacher teaches.

Both Lipsky's (1980) street-level bureaucrats and Wilson's (1989) operators see themselves as doing their job in a professional way (Hupe & Hill 2007). They have this in common with Freidson's full professionals, irrespective of the degree of institutionalization of their professional fields. On the other hand, a doctor employed by the National Health Service, or working as a medical inspector, actually is a public servant. This enables us to define professionals in public service (Hupe 2010). These are employees that:
- practise a particular profession for which they have been formally trained,
- organize their accountability related to practising that profession, and
- practise that profession while working in a public organization.

When summarizing the dimensions of variety identified in this section, three clusters can be distinguished, each concerning a specific level of aggregation. The degree of institutionalization of a profession refers to the occupational system. The distinction between full and semi-professions is still relevant, but within each of these categories there are major differences. Differences at the institutional level may influence the position and work of individual members of the profession, the second cluster of dimensions. Education, ethics and trust are relevant here, along with experience, moral stance and other person-bound characteristics.

The frequency of client contact, the visibility of activities (tasks of individuals) and results belong to the third cluster of dimensions of variety. These characteristics refer to work circumstances in specific organizational settings.

All in all, the term professional is a broad concept with multiple meanings, and the notion of (full) professional autonomy is a generic claim that has to be related to many empirical 'givens' before statements can be made about the degree of and pressures on autonomy. In fact, the image of free professionals with full autonomy is a fiction, which might be useful in public discourse but says little about actual organizational processes and occupational practices. Like bureaucrats working at the street level, doctors, lawyers and other full professionals face certain kinds of *rules* (cf. the action prescriptions implied by the standards of their profession), *discretion* (norm-bound constraints on their freedom to act), and *accountability* (organizing their own feedback, but also being held accountable). The next step is to investigate the nature and impact of the factors functioning as pressures on professionals in public service while doing their work.

Specifying pressures

Pressures and accountability regimes

In the previous section we concluded that the freedom to act for individual professionals is always constrained. We also observed that some of the constraining influences – pressures – on their work are sought by themselves. Occupational rules set by their profession, inter-professional relations regulating their work, and even peer consultation can be observed as all limiting their individual freedom. This implies that the opposition between 'professional autonomy' and 'bureaucratic discretion' is a relative one, and primarily concerns a claim. The members of a profession do not have unlimited freedom to act according to the standards of the profession they belong to. They are accountable to their profession and their professional peers.

Public accountability appears in several forms (see for instance Meijer & Bovens 2005). Hupe & Hill (2007) speak of 'accountability regimes' as systems of social control in which mutual adjustment of action takes place. They distinguish, respectively, *professional* accountability oriented towards peers, *participatory* accountability oriented towards clients, and *public-administrative* accountability oriented towards the law, political authorities and public managers (ibid.: 289-291). While the latter category takes the form of hierarchical relations, the former two regimes have a horizontal character. As Hupe & Hill state, in the practice of any individual professional there is always a mix of actual accountability regimes – although the composition of that mix will vary empirically. Besides, the different forms of holding to account are practised at the level of individuals (for instance between a street-level bureaucrat and his or her first-line supervisor), organizations (for example a National Audit Office and a ministry), as well as systems (between a ministry and implementation organizations (ibid.: 290)).

Table 2 Constitutive elements of work pressure in public service (objective component)

Sorts of action prescriptions	Source of action prescriptions	Sorts of accountability regimes	Sorts of pressures experienced on the work floor
Formal rules	Public administration – Laws – Public policies – Managerial targets	Political-administrative	Rule pressure
Professional norms	Profession	Professional	Vocational pressure
Expectations	Society	Participatory	Societal pressure

Elaboration of: Hupe & Hill (2007: 289)

Table 2 summarizes the basis for assessing empirical variation in pressures on professional work. Beneath, we sketch three types of pressures. First, we assume that increased demand plus scarcer resources lead to more *rule pressure*. Second, the rising expectations of clients enhance *societal pressure*. Third, changed ideas about 'good practice' as well as ongoing specialization mean higher *vocational pressure*. Thus, we can analyze the pressures on the work of professionals in public service and investigate them in a comparative perspective.

Rule pressure: Increased demand, scarcer resources

Several authors highlight the combination of increased demand for public services on the one hand, and scarcer financial resources on the other (e.g. ABIM 2002). After decades of rising public expenditures, welfare states and especially sectors like public health and education are experiencing major financial cuts. At the same time most Western countries are also confronted with rising demands for these very same services. Several factors contribute to this asymmetrical situation. When citizens know more about available resources – professionals may have helped them here, aided by media coverage – this knowledge can raise demand and expectations. The constant introduction of technological innovations, especially in the health sector, has raised productivity, but also possibilities and hence demands. The gap between demand and resources urges professionals to work both more efficiently and more transparently.

What has been labelled as New Public Management (NPM; see Hood 1991) expresses both the possibility and the need to approach government like a corporation. This approach, if not ideology, is characterized by a focus on cost-efficiency and value-for-money, customers, and transparency and accountability, as well as a reliance on businesslike instruments like performance measurement and audits. Such instruments have been introduced in many countries (see Pollitt & Bouckaert 2004; Bouckaert & Halligan 2007). Public organizations, ranging from tax offices to general hospitals, are addressed as 'normal' organizations. They should be managed in efficient and effective ways, especially by using businesslike mechanisms like planning and control, measurement and analysis of inputs, processes and outputs.

Although there is a lack of empirical findings from cross-sectoral and cross-national comparative research, NPM seems to play an important role in what professionals perceive as increased pressure on their work (compare the arguments presented by Ackroyd in chapter 2). Managers of public organizations are supposed to realize higher efficiency and to provide evidence for it, which in many cases invites more control and supervision of professionals by those managers. Some authors indicate that this extended 'bureaucracy' may lead, in an opposite way, to less efficiency. Professionals need more time to justify themselves, which may enhance a spiral of performance measures and account giving (Tonkens 2008a).

Thus within the government-organizational relationship (compare the chapter of Newman), we can observe that a range of managerial targets is added to professional environments, in addition to the laws that have to be enforced and the public policies that have to be implemented. The term 'rule pressure' seems appropriate here.

Societal pressure: Rising expectations

In modern society citizens in general have become better educated. The result is more demand for value-for-money as well as for proven quality, with respect to both the quality of services and the ways in which clients are treated. Not as objects, but as semi-expert 'coproducers', contemporary citizens want to have a say on where and when the professional is available and how he or she treats them in their role of client, patient, pupil or parent. Dubious acts and idiosyncrasies of professionals are no longer blindly accepted. Furthermore, the acceptance of misfortune is reduced considerably. Pain should be cured; parents think their kids are all brilliant and easy-to-handle; unhappiness is unacceptable. Risk should be zero; mistakes – always made by others only – are unforgivable. Professionals should have answers and solutions for everything; that is what they have studied for and are paid for.

At the same time the expertise-based authority of professionals has diminished considerably. This may be seen as a side-effect of the cultural

PETER HUPE & THEO VAN DER KROGT

individualism and democratization movement that originated in the 1960s and 1970s. Under this influence the reluctance of professionals to interfere may have grown, or in any case was legitimized. New moral cadres for interference turned up missing (Tonkens 2008b). In the *post-liberal* era that we are said to have entered, however, the legitimacy of more interventionist measures may have become larger.[2]

As far as various professions are concerned, the pressure referred to here comes from outside, but may be adopted within their institutions. Most quality aspects are integrated in what peers expect from their colleagues and in what organizations demand from the professionals employed by them. Here the media play an important role. Under the influence of the growing competition between media organizations, the hunt for scoops is permanent. Politicians are important (and sometimes easy) victims, but also professionals are closely watched and scrutinized.

Vocational pressure: 'Good practice' and enhanced specialization

The ideas about 'good practice' in many professions seem to have changed. Those ideas may stem from the professionals themselves, from the ministry involved or from other 'outsiders' to the profession, such as the media. An example is the changed set of ideas about education in the Netherlands. Teachers at secondary schools are no longer primarily supposed to transfer knowledge, but to 'coach' their students to develop their talents. That was the prevalent idea underlying the most recent, extensive system reform in the Netherlands (see also chapter 8). In general, major changes in educational philosophy imply changed expectations from the didactic community about the way professional educators should fulfil their role (see the Dijsselbloem Committee, 2008, for this Dutch example). Such changes at the system level have consequences for judgments on the actual role performance of professionals, not only by peers, but also by managers, clients and the public in general.

Although quality is supposed to be at the heart of professionalism, professionals are sometimes seen as needing encouragement, in order to give quality the priority it deserves. In the Netherlands, one can observe a growing importance of 'demonstrated' professional quality, to be proved in evaluations of all sorts. This attention results in additional tasks, sometimes for new functionaries, both at the system level and in the separate organizations. Quality needs to be assured through policies, procedures, reporting and control processes, and this is obviously accompanied by corresponding paper work. While independent control is preferred, the role of peers in such procedures is limited. Quality assessment is seen as too important to leave it to the professionals concerned. Hence a whole new 'profession' of evaluators seems to have been created (Daemen & Van der Krogt 2008).

At the same time and maybe partly as a result of the growing importance of quality assessment, one can observe a tendency towards harmonizing practices, often culminating in the establishment of protocols. In most cases members of the profession concerned develop such protocols in order to improve the quality of their work. In this context, the term 'evidence-based treatment' has become popular. Problems arise when managers try to force professionals to follow the protocol in all cases, or when following protocols is used to avoid responsibility. An exemplary expression of the enhanced importance of protocols can be found in Dutch medical practice (see chapter 7).

Another factor leading to enhanced vocational pressure is the phenomenon of ongoing specialization and the related appearance of domain conflicts. Scientific developments not only give professionals more possibilities to diagnose and treat clients, but also to enhance specialization. Ever more super-specialists can be found, while at the same time tasks that are less cutting-edge are left to others – peers or subordinates. Fields for expert knowledge become smaller, while the risk of domain conflicts between professional specialists grows. In any case, it becomes more difficult to find effective and efficient ways of collaboration. This can be seen in fields like law (Moorehead 2008) and psychiatry (Brown & Bhugra 2007). It seems also the case in youth welfare work, where different problems like ADHD, dyslexia, problematic behaviour, etc, are diagnosed and treated by different categories of professionals (Tonkens 2008b). In most of the cited publications, the connection between specialization and de-professionalization is made. Professionals become 'technicians (...) with reduced skills, reduced power and control by financial decision-makers' (Brown & Bhugra 2007: 282).

In the next section we will explore what these various pressures mean for the work of professionals in public service and look at how they deal with the pressures differentiated here.

Dealing with work pressure

In the previous sections we distinguished between formal rules and societal expectations, as action prescriptions 'adding up' to professional norms. These three categories of constraints, affecting professional work and autonomy, have developed into accountability regimes. Rule pressure originates in public administration, with its laws, public policies and managerial targets. Societal pressure is exerted through the demands from citizens, groups and associations. Vocational pressure comes from professional norms that originate in distinctive professions.

We assume that these pressures can be identified and measured in real-life practices, and we expect that these constraints interact on workfloors in public service. Not the formal rules and/or other categories of action prescriptions *as such* matter most, but the ways individual professionals deal with them. Next, we assume that there is variation in how people deal with these constraints and that, *ceteris paribus*, person-bound

characteristics will be relevant. These assumptions will be elaborated below.

The three sorts of constraints distinguished above can be seen as exerting 'pressures' on work, and when they are combined a well-rounded
picture of 'work pressure' can be established. We propose to use this
term as an operational concept, so that pressures can be measured.
Work pressure (singular) characterizes particular workfloors, where actors experience the three sorts of pressures (the *objective* component) in
individually varying ways (the *subjective* component). Hence, work pressure is a measure for the combined action prescriptions as experienced,
in a given setting, by individual professionals working in public service.
These action prescriptions vary in source, nature, number and mutual
relationship.

Individual or collective rule-makers, like the policy advisers at the
ministry writing a white paper on behalf of their minister, formulate formal rules in the form of policy measures. They will expect the application of these rules to happen in a one-to-one, hierarchical relationship of
compliance. On the other end, however, at the 'street level' the professional in public service sees him- or herself confronted with more than
the rules laid down in a single white paper. Next to the managerial targets to be met in his or her organization, there are several other action
prescriptions to be reckoned with, like demands from clients. The need
to act continuously – i.e. what Hupe & Hill (2007) call the 'action im-
perative' – means that professionals decide how to apply a specific rule.
It also implies that they decide which formal rules and other action prescriptions are applicable in a given situation. Multiple prescriptions may
induce a certain decision, but they may also conflict, or even oppose one
another.

Given a measured degree of work pressure in a given setting (objective component), the way this pressure is experienced individually will
vary, strongly influenced by personal characteristics (subjective component). A medical specialist working in a public hospital, for instance,
may complain about bureaucracy and 'red tape' in Whitehall (UK central
government) causing him to spend too much time on paper work. His
colleague, however, working in the same hospital, acknowledges the ra-
tionale of cost control and considers desk work as a perhaps less pleasant
but necessary element of his professional work.

Professionals can experience the increased number of managerial targets or other action prescriptions to be followed as putting strains on
their work. It may also be the case, however, that the mixed character of
the sources these action prescriptions stem from is experienced as causing the straining effect. Given the various pressures sketched in the
third section, one can assume that changes in the mix of accountability
regimes professionals have to deal with daily, will have an important impact on the experienced work pressure. Traditionally, both the full professional on the one hand and the public servant or street-level bureau-

crat on the other, are seen to have primarily worked within a single re-gime of accountability. As far as this has been historically true, currently, however, this is no longer the case. Professionals face a multiplicity of regimes, adding up to hybrid accountability regimes characterized by mixed control from different formal and other 'authorities'. This implies that shifts can be identified in how constraints and ('new' as well as old) pressures are perceived.

Adopting a term from psychology, we propose to call the latter phe-nomenon *shifts in locus of control*. The combination of types of account-ability by way of which the work of professionals is judged, continually changes, and at the individual level this in itself is experienced and dealt with in different ways. Individual professional A who is confronted with work pressure entailing a perceived shift in locus of control, will deal with it in a different way than colleague B working in the same profes-sion and even in the same organization. This will be more the case when ways of dealing with work pressure are compared across various profes-sions and (sub)sectors.

Modes of dealing

The assumptions identified above imply that person-bound characteris-tics will substantially affect how professionals deal with similar pres-sures. On the basis of these very same assumptions we can distinguish three general modes of dealing with given work pressure: coping, net-working and activism; see Table 3. Below we briefly explore each of these modes.

Table 3 Modes of dealing with work pressure

Mode of dealing	Elaboration	Response to work pressure
Coping	Accepting the work pressure as given and trying to make the best of it	The individualist reaction
Networking	Compensating the work pressure by seeking feedback and creating shared goals	The professional reaction
Activism	Attempting to reduce the work pressure by tackling its sources	The political reaction

Coping

By coping we mean that professionals accept their work pressure as giv-en, perceive circumstances as hard to change, and try to make the best of it. In this way, coping seems to be an obvious and prevalent strategy of 'occupational survival' (Lipsky 1980; Satyamurti 1981). It does not imply

PETER HUPE & THEO VAN DER KROGT

a fatalist or cynical world view, but rather a pragmatic one. The term is connected to how Lipsky (ibid.) conceptualizes the work of street-level bureaucrats. He explores 'patterns of practice' of what we have called professionals in public service. Lipsky (ibid.: Part III) distinguishes various coping mechanisms: queuing, creaming, triage and other ways of rationing services and limiting access and demand. Social workers, police officers and similar public servants working at the street level, 'process' citizens as clients or in other roles, whilst they try to control both the latter and their own work situation. Apart from anything else, coping can be seen as the *individualist* way of dealing with work pressure.

Networking

A certain freedom to act is inherent to professional work. Most specifically, the nature and length of the received professional training and the developed professional *habitus* offer a counterweight to limitations set by hierarchical rules. This is especially relevant in situations not foreseen in legislation. Furthermore, professionals organize their own feedback. By definition, they do so in a case-related way, asking advice in processes of decision-making on specific cases. Their networking tactics may go further, however, reaching beyond their specific tasks and aiming to enhance organizational or personal goals. Then networking is practised as a strategy, which may function as a compensation for some of the effects of work pressure that are experienced as negative. The example of Newman in the preceding chapter about the professional 'social entrepreneur' fits this strategy.

Sometimes professionals are active in a broader context, for instance within their occupational association. When professionals belong to a profession with an established institutionalized position, they will have potential influence, also acknowledged by Newman's emphasis on the organization-occupational knowledge-power knot. They may better succeed in protecting and maintaining their discretionary room to move. The urge towards effectiveness and efficiency as far as individual practice is concerned, vis-à-vis organizations and institutional settings, may be countervailed by the power of the practised profession. This type of dealing with work pressures can be called the *professional* type.

Activism

Professionals may enter into power struggles within the organization they work in. They may seek relations that resemble working coalitions, while engaging themselves not only with clients, but also with managers. Accepting the realities of scarce resources, emancipated clients and a sometimes pertinent public opinion can be a wise option for both professionals and managers (Noordegraaf 2006: 191-193).

In addition to these possibilities, a new phenomenon can be observed. Irrespective of the professions and professional fields they belong to, professionals are increasingly organizing themselves. They become visible actors in the public domain, initiating movements with a semi-political character. In the Netherlands, for instance, the discontent of many professionals working in the (semi-)public sector and coming from various kinds of professions and professional fields, has been bundled by a highly visible movement that has called itself 'BeroepsEer' ('professional honour'). Their discontent is called the reverse: 'BeroepsZeer' ('professional pain'), while the association now focuses on enhancing 'Beroeps-Trots' ('professional pride') (see Jansen et al. 2010). The explicit use of such normatively loaded labels seems to indicate a growing resistance against what is perceived as a 'bureaucratization' of professionalism, or perhaps as an excessive 'public managerialism'. Similar complaints can now be heard in many professional groups, as well as more generally, also in political circles. It looks as if coalitions are formed to counter developments perceived as undesired. At the same time, the public is sought as an ally as well, which fits Newman's observation that professionals still seem to have a relatively high degree of public trust. This way of dealing with work pressure – illustrating professionals acting within the government-public knowledge-power knot – can be called the *political* type.

It is obvious that these three modes of dealing with work pressure in empirical reality will not exclude each other; after all, actors may show behaviour at multiple levels of action. Nevertheless, we might also empirically observe that some professionals may primarily practise the individualist response of coping, whilst others seem to focus deliberately on networking. How influential the response of activism is remains to be seen.

Conclusion

Given the variety of tasks that full and semi-professionals perform, the different degrees of institutionalization of their professions, and their varying personal characteristics, what kinds of pressures on their work, including contemporary pressures, can be observed? And which patterns can be identified in the ways professionals deal with such pressures? This was the twofold question central in this chapter.

Beyond reduced professionalism

Nowadays full professionals feel themselves sometimes reduced to 'technicians' or 'bureaucrats'. At the same time, other workers like public servants consider themselves as professionals. This does not protect them from being occasionally (and seemingly randomly) perceived as mere subordinates in formal, Weberian hierarchies. Both categories are confronted with demands from a third side. Citizens organized as clients or active in similar roles hold professionals accountable for the way they perform their tasks. Therefore, the idea of a professional practising accountability only to his peers – which might have been a functional fiction anyway – has become all the more obsolete. Not one, but several forums of public accountability may and do demand justifications for how a professional, whether publicly employed or freelance, fulfils his or her task. Of course, this development fits the broader narrative of governance as outlined by Newman in the preceding chapter.

Despite a range of dimensions on which they empirically vary, as shown in the second section, professionals of all sorts have much in common. First and foremost, they have left behind their supposed natural state of a singular accountability within their respective professional fields. In addition, professionals see themselves confronted with what is perceived as new pressures. We have identified increased demands but also increasingly scarcer resources (rule pressure); rising expectations from society (societal pressure); and changes in the ideas about 'good practice', accompanied by an ongoing specialization that seems to complicate rather than facilitate collaboration (vocational pressure).

To a large extent, these pressures are attributed to managerialism as an ideology and to New Public Management as a mode of organizing, and indeed, these are embraced by governments in almost any contemporary welfare state. Although the impact of these managerial ideology and techniques cannot be underestimated, it is too simple just to blame 'managerialism' or 'the managers'. Rules are piled upon rules, while action prescriptions come in many forms, as explained in this chapter. Many of these action prescriptions, however, do *not* entail managerial targets, but stem from substantive policy objectives as agreed upon between government and the institutions of representative democracy. The logic of politics implies that all policy objectives are equally important. So the weighing of priorities, what to give more attention to and what less, is left to individual 'implementers' in their day-to-day action. As professionals in public service, they have been central in this chapter. The managers are not to blame, but neither are 'the politicians'. It is us, the citizens, who want to avoid risks and desire guarantees, security and safety as much as possible, and who expect our governments to take care of this (Beck 1992). Although rules and other action prescriptions might be piled upon each other on work floors, to a substantial extent this is caused by an accumulation of policy objectives, stemming from ever-rising expectations from society itself.

Towards a refined understanding of pressures

We have observed that being held accountable by alternative accountability regimes may enhance the feeling of work pressure beyond acceptable limits. These experienced shifts in locus of control may be more relevant than the quantitative accumulation of formal rules and other action prescriptions as such. At the same time we have emphasized the subjective component involved. Given a certain objectively generated work pressure as the result of pressures stemming from one's own profession, from public administration, and directly from society, individual responses to the hence 'added up' work pressure may vary a lot.

Professionals might complain about too much managerial control, certainly in public, but in the meantime just deal with the pressures as experienced. We formulated patterns in the reactions of professionals to what we, in an aggregated way, described as work pressure. In what was called an *individualist* reaction, professionals pragmatically deal with the 'given' circumstances at hand. In a *professional* reaction, practising networking is regarded as more than just fulfilling functions in case treatment. In a *political* reaction, professionals engage in power struggles in the organization in which they work. They do so by negotiating and coalition building, whether or not backed by the institutional strength of the profession they belong to. They also may seek coalition partners in the broader public domain.

In this way we have elaborated Newman's change narrative and localized the knowledge-power knots with respect to the varying work pressure felt by professionals. The three sorts of distinguished pressures from which work pressure originates, are embedded in broader knowledge/power relations, between government, professions and other societal spheres. Simultaneously they are also part of local service practices, in which human beings see themselves confronted with them. In the following chapters this perspective will be taken one step further. On the basis of empirical investigations other authors will refine our understanding of professionals under pressure. Looking at a range of professional fields they will analyze whether and how pressures pervade the practice of professionals in public service in its various forms.

Notes

1. The argument presented here was developed as an original contribution to this edited volume. However, the authors introduced some elements in earlier papers. At the 2007 EGPA Conference (In EGPA Study Group 3 Public Personnel Policies, Madrid, Spain, 19-21 September 2007), Theo van der Krogt presented the paper 'Towards a New Professional Autonomy in the Public Sector'. In a special session of the NIG Colloquium 'Professionals under Pressure' (2007 Annual work conference of The Netherlands Institute of Government (NIG), 8 November 2007, at Tilburg University) Peter Hupe presented the paper 'The State or the Client: Street-Level Bureaucrats as Professionals in Public Service', co-authored by Michael Hill. The audiences of both presentations are thanked for their reactions, and the editors of this volume for their suggestions.

PETER HUPE & THEO VAN DER KROGT

2. NRC Handelsblad (2007). *Postliberaal.* Chief editorial, 15 February.

References

Abbott, A. (1988). *The System of Professions: An Essay on the Division of Expert Labor.* Chicago: University of Chicago Press.

ABIM (2002). *Medical Professionalism in the New Millenium: A Physician Charter.* Philadelphia, PA: American Board of Internal Medicine Foundation.

Beck, U. (1992.) *Risk Society: Towards a New Modernity.* London: Sage.

Bouckaert, G., & Halligan, J. (2007). *Managing Performance: International Comparisons.* London: Routledge.

Brint, S. (1994). *In an Age of Experts: The Changing Role of Professionals in Politics and Public Life.* Princeton, NJ: Princeton University Press.

Brown, N., & Bhugra, D. (2007). 'New' Professionalism or Professionalism Derailed? *Psychiatry Bulletin, 31,* 281-283.

Daemen, H.H.F.M., & van der Krogt, T.P.W.M. (2008). Four Functions of International Accreditation. In G. Jenei & K. Mike (Eds.), *Public Administration and Public Policy Degree Programs in Europe: The Road from Bologna* (pp. 23-25). Bratislava: NISPAcee Press.

Day, P., & Klein, R. (1981). *Accountabilities: Five Public Services.* London: Tavistock.

Dijsselbloem, J.R.V.A. (2008). *Eindrapport Parlementair onderzoek onderwijsvernieuwingen: Tijd voor onderwijs. [End Report Parliamentary Investigation Educational Innovations: Time for Education]* Tweede Kamer. 2007-2008. 31 007 006. http://www.tweedekamer.nl/images/kst113842.8s_tcm118-149847.PDF

DiMaggio, P.J., & Powell, J. (1983). The Iron Cage Revisited: Institutional isomorphism and collective rationality in organizational fields. *American Sociological Review, 48,* 147-160.

Edelman, M. (1975). *Political Language: Words that Succeed and Policies that Fail.* New York: Academic Press.

Etzioni, A. (1969). *The Semi-Professions and Their Organizations.* New York: Free Press. Freidson, E. (1970). *Profession of Medicine: A Study of the Sociology of Applied Knowledge.* New York: Harper and Row.

Freidson, E. (1986). *Professional Powers: A Study of the Institutionalization of Formal Knowledge.* Chicago: University of Chicago Press.

Freidson, E. (2001). *Professionalism, the Third Logic: On the Practice of Knowledge.* Chicago: University of Chicago Press.

Greenwood, E. (1957). Attributes of a Profession. *Social Work, 2,* 45-55.

Hood, Ch. (1991). A Public Management for all Seasons? *Public Administration, 69,* 3-19. Hupe, P. L., & Hill, M.J. (2007). Street-level Bureaucracy and Public Accountability. *Public Administration, 82,* 279-299.

Hupe, P.L. (2010). The Autonomy of Professionals in Public Service, In Th. Jansen, G. van den Brink & J. Kole (Eds.) 2010. *Professional Pride: A Powerful Force* (pp. 118-137). Amsterdam: Boom.

Jansen, Th., G. van den Brink & J. Kole (Eds.) 2010. *Professional Pride: A Powerful Force.* Amsterdam: Boom.

Johnson, T. (1972). *Professions and Power.* London: MacMillan.

Kultgen, J. (1988). *Ethics and Professionalism.* Pittsburgh: University of Pennsylvania Press.

Lipsky, M. (1980). *Street-Level Bureaucracy: Dilemmas of the Individual in Public Services.* New York: Russell Sage Foundation.

Meijer, A.J., & Bovens, M.A.P. (2005). Public Accountability in the Information Age. In V.J.J.M. Bekkers & V.F.M. Homburg (Eds.), *The Information Ecology of E-Government* (pp. 171-182). Amsterdam: IOS Press.

Moorehead, R. (2008). Lawyer Specialisation: Managing the Professional Paradox. *Cardiff Law School Research Papers.* Cardiff: Cardiff Law School.

Noordegraaf, M. (2006). Professional Management of Professionals. Hybrid Organizations and Professional Management in Care and Welfare. In J.W. Duyvendak, T. Knijn & M. Kremer (Eds.), *Policy, People, and the New Professional: De-Professionalization and Re-Professionalization in Care and Welfare* (pp. 181-193). Amsterdam: Amsterdam University Press.

Pollitt, C., & Bouckaert, G. (2004). *Public Management Reform: A Comparative Analysis.* Oxford: Oxford University Press.

Satyamurti, C. (1981). *Occupational Survival.* Oxford: Blackwell.

Tonkens, E. (2008a). Bevrijd Vaklui uit de Bureaucratie [*Free Craftsmen from Bureaucracy*]. *de Volkskrant,* 13 september 2008.

Tonkens, E. (2008b). *Herwaardering voor Professionals, maar Hoe? [Recognition for Professionals, but How?]* ROB-lezing 2008. Den Haag: Raad voor het Openbaar Bestuur (ROB).

Wilson, J.Q. (1989). *Bureaucracy: What Government Agencies Do and Why They Do It.* New York: Basic Books.

Witman, Y. (2008). *De Medicus Maatgevend: Over Leiderschap en Habitus. [Doctor in Charge: On Leadership and Habitus]* Thesis. Rotterdam: Erasmus University.

PETER HUPE & THEO VAN DER KROGT

5 A managerial assault on professionalism?

Professionals in changing welfare states

Romke van der Veen

Introduction

Long ago, professionals were seen as neutral experts who used their skills and knowledge for the betterment of society. This functionalist perspective on professionalism, embodied in e.g. the works of Emile Durkheim (1957), treats professionals as the bearers of important social values. Professionals are defined by the idealtypical traits of their profession, as described in the previous chapter, including a body of abstract and specialized knowledge and professional values. The idealtypical image of the impartial professional who uses his expert knowledge to the best interest of his clients is under attack since Ivan Illich's (1976) famous criticism of the medical profession. Illich argued that medicine is harmful to the individual. He spoke of 'iatrogenesis': harm caused by medical intervention. Illich did not only observe clinical iatrogenesis – harm caused by direct medical intervention – but also social and cultural iatrogenesis. This concerns the medicalization of everyday life and thinking. The medical profession extended its reach and medical intervention became more and more perceived as a solution for many individual and social problems.

In Illich's thesis that professional intervention creates the needs it responds to, is coupled with the idea of counterproductivity of professional intervention. This approach is applied to professionalism in general by, for example, the Dutch philosopher Achterhuis, who wrote a very influential critical review of social work in 1979, 'The Market for Welfare and Happiness'. At that moment, social workers had experienced a long period of expansion, mainly because of the rapid growth of the welfare state in-between World War II and the 1970s. Achterhuis portrayed social workers as semi-professionals engaged in a process of professionalization. His conclusion was that these (semi-)professionals created their own expansive markets of well-being and happiness, which make people dependent on professionals and in the end fail to solve problems. This failure, however, is answered with more professional intervention, not less (Achterhuis 1980).

The critical analyses of professionalism by Illich, Achterhuis and many others undermined the high status and autonomy of professionals. This loss of status almost automatically contributed to the pressures experienced by professionals, especially the rule and societal pressures identified in the preceding chapter. Institutional shelters crumbled and professional fields lost some of their power to other fields. Client associations appeared, opposing medical professionals. Managerial control on professional work, moreover, also intensified, facilitating the rise of new roles through different work contexts. Both in classic professional domains as well as in semi-professional domains, professional action was constrained. Professionals working in public services were particularly affected. The 'managerial assault' on the welfare state directly affected public services and street-level workers had few means to counter the assault. This chapter analyses the evolution of managerial control of professionals in order to contextualize the pressures exerted on them. Whereas the previous chapter stressed the differentiated nature of professional fields and work, this chapter stresses shifting relations between (welfare) states and professional fields.

The organizational professional and the professional organization

Reed (1996) offers a critical reading of the distinctions between types of professionalism as already presented in the previous chapter. Reed identifies liberal, entrepreneurial and organizational professions. Liberal professions are those such as law and medicine, which are traditionally independent and work for fees. The entrepreneurial professions exploit the market and are represented by accountants, management consultants and the like. Organizational professions owe their status to the organization in which they work. As already mentioned by both Newman and Hupe & Van der Krogt, public professions are also a distinctive category in this respect. They became more important within the growing bureaucracies of the welfare state. Many organizational professionals are employees of the welfare state. The idealtype of professionalism – stressed in the preceding chapter – that is often used to understand public professionals, however, appears to be mainly based on the image of the liberal professional. In reality however, most public professionals are organizational professionals, and often semi-professionals and even liberal professionals have to some extent become organizational professionals. Liberal professionals, especially medical doctors, have also become part of (publicly) regulated work settings. Classic professional autonomies are all the more constrained.

As expressed by Newman in her chapter, administrative and bureaucratic logics are at work. But how all of this affects 'real' professional work is an empirical question. Administrative and bureaucratic logics were always operative and classic studies show that professionals in organizational contexts can be constrained and autonomous at the same time. Perrow (1970), for instance, characterizes professional organizations by the technology used to produce goods or services. The production process is little routinized and is characterized by variability and many exceptions. The organizational structure is consequently non-routine: the organization members have high discretionary power, interdependency is high and coordination takes place backward. In terms of Burns & Stalker (1961) this non-routine organization represents a classic organic regime: organization members enjoy a high autonomy but organizational integration is also high. This is the result of a strong professional ethos and membership of a professional community (Lammers 1997). Hence, Perrow's characterization of the professional organization does not necessarily conflict with the idealtype of the liberal professional. The same can be said of Mintzberg's characterization of what he calls the professional bureaucracy. Characteristic is the autonomy of the operating core: professionals 'work relatively freely not only of the administrative hierarchy but also of their own colleagues' (Mintzberg 1980: 334). Professional organizations are decentralized, have a small technostructure and a relatively large support staff who work at the machine bureaucratic margins.

A well-known research topic concerning professional organizations is their reaction to pressures towards bureaucratization. Scott (1965) introduced the concepts of autonomous and heteronomous professional organizations. Autonomous professional organizations are those in which the professionals play the central role in achieving the organizational objectives. Scott illustrates this type of professional organization by pointing to hospitals and universities. In a heteronomous professional organization, professional employees are subordinated to an administrative framework and the autonomy granted is limited. Rules and systems of supervision control the tasks performed by the professional employees. Many public agencies correspond to this heteronomous type of professional organization: social welfare agencies, schools, libraries, etc.

Scott investigated the acceptance of supervision by professionals in a public welfare agency and concluded that professional workers accepted the system of supervision, although the degree of acceptance varied with the professional orientation of workers and supervisors. More professionalized workers were more critical of the system of supervision, and more professionally oriented supervisors were better accepted. Most workers looked chiefly to their supervisors for their professional norms and standards (Scott 1965: 81). Scott's findings suggest that professionalization and bureaucratization do not necessarily conflict. This finding is supported in later research (see Van Bockel 2009).

In this chapter, we will investigate the functioning of (organizational) professionals in professional organizations. We try to grasp what is happening with them, especially within the occupational-organizational relationship as characterized by Newman in the third chapter. We will focus on attempts to control the practices of professionals. In this chapter we will analyze developments in the organization and delivery of public services and the consequences of these developments for the professionals and professional organizations that produce these services. Often, these consequences are discussed in terms of deprofessionalization (e.g. Broadbent et al. 2005). Increasing control of professional practices is linked to the rise of managerial practices – of businesslike ideas and practices that fit the NPM movement, as discussed in the preceding chapters.

I follow Ackroyd's and Hupe & van der Krogt's observation that the rise of NPM plays a role in the increased pressures perceived by professionals. More explicitly, I assume that the NPM logic conflicts with professionalism. The role and position of professionals within an organization are characterized by discretion and autonomy (Hasenfeld 1983), as also expressed by Hupe & Van der Krogt. *Discretion* is necessary because it gives professionals the freedom to apply their knowledge, following their own interpretation, to individual cases. Managerial control in whatever form can conflict with this professional discretion. In the same way, organizational *autonomy* makes professionals to some extent independent from the organization in which they work. This is necessary in order to organize the trust that is the foundation of the relation between professionals and their clients. Autonomy is also conditional to the incorporation of the individual professional in the wider (extra-organizational) network of the profession. Again, such autonomy conflicts with managerial control. The assumption to be tested in this chapter is that NPM will lead to a *deprofessionalization* of professional work in public services, e.g. a *decline in the discretion and autonomy* professionals enjoy. Based on this, the central question is *how and to what extent the organizational practices of New Public Management lead to deprofessionalization in service delivery.*

Towards a managerial state: Consequences for professionals

The changing logic of public service delivery results from transformations in public policies. Four trends characterize policy change in most western welfare states: privatization, activation, selective targeting and conditional solidarity (Gilbert 2002: 44). The first trend is a shift from the public provision of services towards private provision, thus introducing price mechanisms and competition in public services. Secondly, the protection of labour is traded for the promotion of work. Universal entitlements are, thirdly, replaced by more selective targeting. Entitlements are becoming gradually more and more limited to the needy and the deserving. Finally, the solidarity of citizenship is exchanged for the soli-

ROMKE VAN DER VEEN

darity of membership: unconditional social rights are transformed in the conditional solidarity of shared membership (e.g. of insurance).

These transformations towards what Giddens calls 'a social investment state' (1994) imply a shift from 'unconditional' entitlements and social protection towards provisional services, and from 'aftercare' (i.e. protection once adversity has struck) towards precautionary measures, i.e. the prevention of adversity. This leads to profound changes in the character as well as the provision of public services: a focus on results and on the effectiveness of public services. Consequently, the bureaucratic '*rechtsstaat*' or legal state is gradually replaced by a 'managerial state' (Clarke & Newman 1997; De Vries 2001). Management philosophies from the private sector are introduced in the public sector, they are lumped together under the banner of New Public Management. In a managerial state rules and hierarchy are replaced by financial incentives and market relations. Normconformity is exchanged for efficiency. Public officials become 'managers' who focus on their mission. The goal-rationality of market efficiency becomes dominant over the value-rationality of the traditional bureaucratic *rechtsstaat* (De Vries 2001: 8).

New Public Management is paradoxical and combines contradictory developments. Increasing freedom is combined with increasing control; freedom is increased by giving 'choice' to 'consumers' of public services. Freedom is also increased by using the market in the delivery of public services: the introduction of so-called 'quasi-markets'. Control is increased by reducing discretion and by increasing duties and obligations. This is enacted by increasing legal constraints (bureaucratization) or by decreasing professional freedom through the introduction of protocols. Control is also increased by enhancing the role of managers in public service delivery.

New Public Management gives ample freedom to the manager of public services. The manager will consequently be evaluated according to the outcome and not to the legitimacy of his or her efforts. Pollitt (1990) has illustrated that this paradoxically implies a form of neo-Taylorization on workfloors: managerial freedom implies intensive control of work and work forces. The development towards New Public Management not only results in paradoxical developments in public services but also in public policies. Again, control is tightened while at the same time freedom is increased. The following legal, organizational and policy changes are generated in welfare arrangements (Van der Veen & Trommel 1999):

- *reduction of discretion* in the administration and provision of public services by creating more precise legal rules and by stressing the duties and obligations of consumers of public services;
- *introduction of financial incentives* in the delivery of public services by a (partial) privatization of services, by the introduction of quasi-markets and by increasing the freedom of choice for consumers;
- *institutional redesign* of the organization of policy sectors by (partial) dismantling of complex, interdependent (corporatist) structures and

by the introduction of principal-agent relations (i.e. contractualism) in the organization of public service delivery.

In the next paragraph I will analyze several cases of changing public service delivery. The leading question is how and to what extent deprofessionalization (defined as a loss of discretion and/or autonomy) can be observed in these cases. The cases are organized along the distinction of increasing freedom and increasing control and each time, I will analyze how professionals are affected. I will first focus on cases in which freedom of choice is increased. The first case concerns the introduction of a personal budget in health care which clients are free to spend. Freedom of choice can also be increased indirectly, for example by the introduction of quasi-markets in public service delivery. Quasi-markets do increase the freedom of the principal on the market. This is my second case. My next three cases focus on increasing control. I investigate three different forms of increasing control: bureaucratic and managerial control and finally the introduction of protocols, which can be seen as a form of professional control.

Deprofessionalization?

Personal budgets in health care

A well-known Dutch example of the introduction of freedom of choice as a deliberate policy instrument is the so called Personal Budget (PGB) that has been introduced in the domain of care for the handicapped and elderly. The PGB is a method to organize what is called 'demand-driven care'. The supplier of care (the professional) does not decide what care is to be given; the one who receives the care decides. Demand-driven care is seen as a threat to professionalism by, for example, Tonkens (2003: 38-39) because it undermines the indispensable dialogue between professional and client. In this dialogue it might be necessary that the professional contradicts the client.

   The PGB was first introduced in the care sector (AWBZ, in Dutch).[1] Clients can get a PGB after assessment of their needs by an assessing agency.[2] In many other policy areas, like reintegration services, health care and social welfare, the idea of individual or group budgets was introduced as well (Tonkens 2003: 37, 69-94) (in 2011 preparations were made to abolish them). A PGB consists of a lump sum that clients can spend at their own discretion. Most recipients of a PGB are chronically ill patients who use their PGB for the daily care and support they need. This was accompanied by innovations in care provision. New services and service providers have been established, such as so-called 'Thomashouses'. These were set up by parents of handicapped young people in order to organize care in family-like environments. Small groups of

ROMKE VAN DER VEEN

(mentally) handicapped young people are taken care of by a family (husband and wife). The houses and the families are paid with the PGBs of the participants. PGBs are also used to pay (formerly) volunteer aid (50% of the budget was used for formerly volunteer aid; CVZ 2005). The financing of volunteer aid with PGBs is controversial, mainly because it is supposed to undermine the willingness to give volunteer aid (CVZ 2005).

A PGB gives people the opportunity to organize the care they need in the way they prefer, at the time and place they like and by the people they have chosen. It makes chronically ill patients independent of the limited service options provided by institutionalized care. The PGBs are mainly used to pay for domestic help and for (what is called) 'accompanying support'. Although there were many implementation problems with the PGB and although the users complain about unnecessary administration, most PGB-owners were very satisfied with the service (CVZ 2004).

The patient movement is a vehement advocate of the PGB, as it gives patients freedom of choice. The consequences of the PGB for professional service delivery are mainly 1) a reduction of the budgets of institutionalized care and 2) the displacement of care from formal, institutionalized care to informal care. These effects are harmful for the market of professional care, but the freedom of choice patients get with a PGB hardly conflicts with professional autonomy as such.

Quasi-markets

Another method to increase freedom of choice is through the introduction of quasi-markets (Bartlett & LeGrand 1993). In 2006, a quasi-market for health care insurances was introduced in the Netherlands. Patients are free to choose their own health insurer and health insurers are free in the choice of the doctors and hospitals they contract. This quasi-market, also known as managed competition, is to produce managed care, that is, controlled service delivery (Van der Veen 2006).

It is the contractual relation between professional and principal – in this case the principals are the health insurance companies – that is seen as a threat to professional autonomy and discretion. Under contractual relations parties have to make agreements on targets, processes and procedures in order to be able to draft a contract, and it is here that professionalism is at stake. 'This [...] standardisation of processes and procedures has a disciplining effect on the work of professionals' (Knijn & Selten 2006: 28). Contracts will also promote transparency and an orientation on results. Following Smith & Lipsky (1994) the risk of transparency and an orientation on results might however increase perverse effects: depending on the sanctions, the contracted party will do everything to meet contractual targets. High targets and sanctions and 'excessively strict performance indicators will damage professional discretion' (Knijn & Selten 2006: 28, 32) and lead to deprofessionalization, it is argued.

The question of whether managed competition limits professional freedom is fervently discussed in countries like the USA. Doctors as well as patients have protested against the introduction of managed care through Health Maintenance Organizations (HMOs). Detailed empirical research, however, showed few negative consequences for the practice of physicians, measured for example in time physicians have per patient, visits per week, direct patient care (Luft 1999) or quality of the services delivered (Cutler et al. 2000; Glied 2000). The negative reactions to managed care were therefore interpreted not as a failure of managed care, but as a reaction to the limitation of choice that the HMO system generated and to resource constraints as such (Enthoven & Singer 1999).

Nevertheless, a limitation of professional autonomy by managed competition might be expected theoretically. A strong dominance of economic interests can undermine professional autonomy when limited resources block the preferred treatment. However, there are also counter forces at work, protecting professional autonomy. The first is the strong position of the medical profession (Starr 1982: 4). Medical professional power is less contested than that of other professions. The second force is the complexity of the field of health care. When horizontal integration of the field is limited, control of professional autonomy is difficult because it is dispersed over several professionals and organizations.

Managed competition in the Netherlands appears to lead mainly to price competition on the insurance market and – in the first few years – hardly to selective contracting (RVZ 2008) and thus professional autonomy is hardly affected.

The idea of contractualism is not limited to quasi-markets. Contractualism has also become increasingly important in organizing care in networks of partners in service-provision. The growing importance of networks and partnerships of service providers is the result of decentralization on quasi-markets, but also the result of the increasing complexity of professional care. This is for example the case in medical care because of increasing technical complexity, but it is also to be observed in juvenile care because of the increasing complexity of the problems of young people. Cooperation between specialized professionals and between different service providers is the inevitable consequence of such increasing complexity. These networks have to be organized and controlled and contractualism is an important instrument to do this. In these cases contractualism is an instrument of control rather than an instrument of increasing freedom. This brings us to our second issue: the increase of control.

Bureaucratization

Bureaucratization is an increase of control through rules and standards in a hierarchical organization. The restructuring of the modern welfare state, as sketched in the third section, has undeniably led to bureaucratization of social policies. Restructuring has led to institutional redesign, to new responsibilities and new interdependencies between administrative organizations. These new relations and responsibilities are conditional to a quasi-market or other forms of decentralization. In the new Dutch Health Insurance Act, which laid the ground for the quasi-market in health insurances, new actors with new responsibilities and new relations and interdependencies were established by law. The same took place in other processes of decentralization. Institutional redesign as has taken place in the Dutch welfare state thus leads to a – on first sight – paradoxical increase in regulation. This type of regulation is necessary to create new institutions, to establish markets and in itself does not limit professional autonomy.

Institutional redesign of the welfare state directed at prevention and precautionary measures also creates new tasks and new organizations. In social security the promotion of work and social inclusion are relatively new tasks. A new field of service providers has appeared on the scene: reintegration agencies. In other domains too the shift from a welfare state to a social investment state has led to the rise of new agencies with new tasks. These new fields have to be organized and new rules had to be established. This too led to bureaucratization as defined above. Again this does not necessarily conflict with professional autonomy. In fact, we can also witness that new opportunities are given to new professional groups, a possibility mentioned earlier in this book by Newman.

Bureaucratization as a result of welfare state restructuring that *does* conflict with professional autonomy can be observed where legal entitlements are curtailed. When these entitlements are established by professionals, these legal changes limit professional autonomy. This has for example taken place in the administration of occupational disability. More than once the government has tried to narrow the right to disability insurance by sharpening the rules for the medical assessment of disability. In this way the government has tried to reduce the professional discretion of the medical doctors involved. Research has shown that the discretion of the medical doctors involved in the assessment has decreased, but only slightly (Berendsen 2007; IWI 2004b). The rules are of a general nature and it is still the doctor who deliberates and decides. What has really changed is the managerial control of these medical assessment procedures (ibid.).

Managerial control

In his chapter Ackroyd noted the fact that professionals are nowadays more under managerial surveillance, and indeed the rise of managers in professional organizations is a widely accepted phenomenon. Reliable figures on this are rare, however, not in the least because of definitional problems. One of the few domains in the Netherlands that has been mapped in some detail is education. Contrary to the expectations, how-ever, the percentage of managerial personnel has declined in the last two decades in favour of the percentage of personnel employed in actual in-struction (Onderwijsraad 2004: 40, 60, 76). This unexpected develop-ment can be explained by processes of up-scaling, e.g. in vocational training: the number of schools has declined and remaining schools have grown bigger. In other educational sectors – where complaints about the increasing burden of management are commonplace – it illus-trates that the experience of increasing managerialism is not necessarily related to an actual shift in the number of managerial personnel. Man-agerial control can also increase without an actual increase in the num-ber of managers.

The results of research in the educational sector are confirmed in a research on 'overhead' (defined as managerial personnel and supporting staff) in the public sector. This research demonstrated that overhead in the public sector is relatively stable (in a period of four years) and lowest in the organizations that actually provide services and highest in admin-istrative agencies (Huijben & Geurtsen 2006). This, too, is contrary to general expectations.

An agency where a new managerial layer has been introduced next to a professional layer is the Dutch public agency for the administration of social insurance (UWV), most particularly in the administration of occu-pational disability. Next to physicians who assess the extent of occupa-tional disability, a managerial layer and supporting staff have been intro-duced. The physicians in the UWV used to enjoy a high level of autonomy and discretion (Van der Veen 1990) and the introduction of managerial control in the process of occupational disability assessment was aimed at a reduction of professional autonomy. In the recent past this autonomy was seen as the main cause of an uncontrolled rise of disability figures.

In 2004, however, researchers concluded that professional autonomy was still very high. The regular re-assessment of the level of occupational disability of clients – which is legally required in order to bring back the level of disability take-up – is often not implemented and in fact only takes place when the clients take the initiative (IWI 2004a: 9). Concern-ing managerial control of these physicians, research has revealed that in this respect changes in working conditions were limited too. With the new occupational disability rules managers focus their attention on the collection of figures and on the quantity and timeliness of the assess-ment procedure. The physicians make it difficult for the managers to inspect their work and the managers avoid conflicts with the physicians (IWI 2004b; Berendsen 2007).

In a study into policy changes in health care in England, Davies (2006) draws similar conclusions. She concludes that the effect of policy changes in the direction of strengthening the control on professional practice is limited. The idea of 'the decline of professionalism' is 'overly simplistic' (Davies 2006: 151). The physicians are still the boss in health care.

All of this illustrates that the reality of managerial control is not as straightforward as suggested by the opponents of managerialism. Even under a managerial regime, professionals keep the power to resist managerial control and to uphold their autonomy. This might be dependent on the type of professional knowledge under managerial control. Physicians will be better able to resist managerial control than semi-professionals like social workers (see chapter 2).

Professional control: Protocols

Hupe & Van der Krogt already noted in their chapter that control of professional practice can also be self-control. Indeed, regulation of professional practice is one of the traditional tasks of professional associations. Nowadays, professional practice is becoming more and more protocolized by the profession itself. Complaints about increasing limitations on professional freedom are therefore also directed at the protocolization of professional practice.

Protocols do not give rules but provide professionals with a manual about how to think and act in specific situations. Protocols structure assessment procedures without determining the outcome. For the assessment of occupational disability, protocols have for example been developed for how to interpret certain situations and how to translate the concepts used in the law – what can be seen as the 'cause' of occupational disability, what is 'fully' occupational disabled – into a medical assessment.

The protocolization of professional work results – among other things – from the movement towards evidence-based practice. The development of evidence-based practice often originates within the professions themselves. It is aimed at founding professional practice on evidence and at creating a professional exchange of opinions, reflection and eventually intersubjectivity. A positivistic translation of knowledge into intervention practices is not the goal of evidence-based practice however and will undermine the professional reflexivity that is necessary for evidence-based practice (Hutschemaekers & Tiemens 2006).

Thus, evidence based medicine (EBM), for example, does not necessarily limit the power of the professional and also does not necessarily result in limitation of autonomy in medical practice. Still, professionals themselves and their professional associations develop the protocols. In the Netherlands professional associations are subsidised by the Ministry of Health Care in order to fulfil this task, in England a highly professionalized organization –NICE – was assigned this task. As the protocols in the assessment of occupational disability do not give rules how to judge clients, neither do protocols in regular medical practice provide rules to physicians. The doctor always has to *translate* the general protocol to the individual case and to decide what is to be done in this particular case. The act of translation is highly dependent on professional knowledge and gives the professional ample discretion. In the UK, Davies studied the workings of medical protocols. She concludes that 'a straightforward loss-of-power argument is hard to sustain', because of '[...] the strong input of doctors [...] to formulate the guideline' and 'the careful formula that emphasises guidelines as advice' (2006: 143).

Conclusion

We started this chapter with the question as to how and to what extent the organizational practices of New Public Management lead to deprofessionalization in service delivery. This question was related to the observation that New Public Management appears to combine contradictory developments with both increasing freedom as well as increasing control for different actors in public service delivery. Using the cases discussed in the previous paragraphs I will provide an answer to the research question.

Autonomy or discretion?

The first conclusion is that increasing the freedom of other actors does not automatically limit professional discretion and autonomy. It does however undeniably affect professional practice. The example of the PGB illustrated that this instrument had budgetary effects and affected the professional domain, but also that it did not make professionals dependent on their clients, as is often suggested. The main effect of the introduction of quasi-market arrangements, the second example, is again not so much that professionals are made directly dependent on their principals; it is mainly to be found in an increasing transparency of professional practice. This can generate perverse effects when performance indicators are becoming too dominant in professional practice. So, in this case, increasing the freedom of other actors hardly affects professional discretion but certainly limits professional autonomy through increasing transparency.

Concerning the increase of control we must conclude that managerial, bureaucratic and professional control are undeniably increasing, but again, this does not necessarily undermine professional discretion and autonomy. Bureaucratic and managerial control is often directed at the control of complex processes and fields of actors. This affects the working conditions of professionals as actors in these processes and these fields, leading to more accounting, consultation and cooperation. Professional self-control through protocols is aimed at the same goals by increasing professional reflexivity and exchange. So, again my conclusion is that professional autonomy becomes restricted but professional discretion is little affected in this process.

Concerning the managers of public services, we must conclude that their control activities are primarily directed at controlling complex policy processes and policy fields which demand that all actors are transparent, cooperative and open for consultation. When managers try to influence professional discretion directly, the lasting power of professionals becomes visible: they are often still able to withstand managerial control of the core of their professional being. They have discretion as far as the application of professional knowledge is concerned.

Managing professionals and autonomy (instead of discretion)

Next, our exploration of the relations between professionals and managers in different public services leads to the conclusion that the oppositional nature of the relationship between professionals and managers that is often assumed, creates a biased image. Reality is more varied and more complicated. Exworthy & Halford (2002) draw the same conclusion: the relationship between professionals and managers can vary from conflict, to compromise to cooperation. This variation can be observed because the relationship between managers and professionals and the specific role of professionals are becoming more and more dependent on the environment in which they operate (cf. Brint 1994: 205).[3] It is the way professions are embedded in markets and organizations that defines the role of professionals. We can see a movement in the direction of an entrepreneurial spirit and a proliferation of services with professions embedded in markets. 'In professions [...] embedded in the public sector, we see, by contrast, a movement toward standardised cultures and highly coordinated organisational fields' (Brint 1994: 206). We focused on these professionals embedded in the public sector. The role and status of these organizational professionals is – in the Netherlands – highly dependent on the organization of the public services in which they operate. Above I have noted a development towards an increase in accounting, consultation and cooperation in professional practices. This development is related to a more comprehensive change of the modern welfare state towards a social investment state. This implies a change in welfare services in the direction of prevention and provisional services. When the integrative results of welfare services become more important than the mere protection they provide to citizens, the focus shifts from entitlements towards the outcome of services. It is this shift towards outcome that has severe consequences for the role of professionals that operate within welfare services.

When outcome becomes leading, this affects the autonomy of professionals that work in public services. In the assessment of occupational disability for example it made professionals think about occupational disability in terms of labour market participation instead of medical limitations. This resulted in a number of protocols for the assessment of occupational disability. It also resulted in more consultation between physicians who assess occupational disability. In a primarily medical context, consultation was organized within the traditional professional association, which is outside the assessment agency. In a result-oriented context the consultation between professionals becomes organized within the agency itself and is seen as a method to improve the quality of the assessment of occupational disability (defined in terms of the possibility to participate on the labour market).

A focus on results affects the autonomy of professionals too because it makes professionals dependent on others. For example when the technology that professionals use becomes more complex we can observe a fragmentation of professional expertise, as has happened in hospitals. Complex technology leads to specialization that asks for cooperation between professionals. Many programmes that aim at standardizing health care practices, in fact organize – among other things – the cooperation between different professionals in and outside the hospital (Zuiderent-Jerak 2007). Next to complex technology, these complex problems make cooperation necessary. An illustrative example of this mechanism is to be found in youth care. When for example the family circumstances threaten children's well-being and children run into problems, several professional groups can be involved: general practitioners, physicians of the child health centre, police officers, social workers of the school, social workers of the child protection agency, psychologists of the mental health office, etc. Effective intervention in family problems thus asks for coordination between the professionals involved.

The orientation on outcome that goes together with a shift in welfare state services towards prevention and social investment, implies a necessity for accounting, in order to create transparency, for consultation, in order to learn, and for cooperation, in order to adjust the intervention of one professional with the interventions of other professionals. It is here that the manager enters the stage. The rise of managers in professional public services does therefore *not* result in a managerial assault on professionalism. Instead, managers often attempt to organize collective professional effort in a context that gives individual professionals limited autonomy but that still needs professional expertise to provide public services and to solve public problems. This limits professional autonomy, but it does not necessarily limit professional discretion.[4]

Notes

1. The AWBZ – the general law on exceptional medical expenses – is a universal care insurance that finances mental care, care for the elderly, home care and care for the handicapped.

ROMKE VAN DER VEEN

2. The assessing agency is staffed with professionals that follow centrally established protocols to establish the need of clients.
3. Brint suggests a changing role of professionals. What remains common to professions is a body of formal knowledge, what is changing is the homogenizing role of the collective morality of professions.
4. Professional discretion is probably limited most when changes in public service delivery are primarily intended to reduce costs.

References

Achterhuis, H. (1980). *De markt van welzijn en geluk [The Market for Welfare and Happiness]*. Baarn: Ambo.

Ackroyd, S., Kirkpatrick, I., & Walker, R. (2007). Public Management Reform and its Consequences for Professional Organization. *Public Administration, 85*(1): 9-26.

Bartlett, W., & LeGrand, J. (1993). *Quasi-Markets and Social Policy*. London: Macmillan.

Berendsen, L. (2007). *Bureaucratische drama's. Publieke managers in verhouding tot verzekeringsartsen [Bureaucratic Dramas. Public Managers and their Relations with Insurance Doctors]*. Utrecht University (Ph.D. thesis).

Bosselaar, H. (2005). *De vraag als antwoord. Vraagsturing en sociaal beleid: voorwaarden en risico's [Demand Based Social Policy: conditions and risks]*. Rotterdam University (Ph.D. thesis).

Brandsen, T., Van de Donk, W., & Kenis, P. (Eds.) (2006). *Meervoudig bestuur: publieke dienstverlening door hybride organisaties [Multiple Governance: Public Service Delivery by Hybrid Organizations]*. Utrecht: Lemma.

Brint, S. (1994). *In an Age of Experts. The changing role of professionals in politics and public life*. Princeton: Princeton University Press.

Broadbent, J., Dietrich, M., & Roberts, J. (Eds.) (2005). *The End of the Professions? The Restructuring of Professional Work*. Routledge : London.

Burns, T., & Stalker, G.M. (1961). *The Management of Innovation*. London: Tavistock.

College voor zorgverzekeringen (cvz) (2004). *Monitor budgethouders pgb nieuwe stijl [Monitor Personal Budgets]*. Nijmegen: its.

College voor zorgverzekeringen (cvz) (2005). *Persoonsgebonden budget en mantelzorg [Personal Budgets and Care]*. Nijmegen: its.

Clarke, J., & Newman, J. (1997). *The Managerial State*. London: Sage.

Cutler, D., McClellan, M., & Newhouse, J.P. (2000). How does Managed Care do it? *Rand Journal of Economics, 31*(3): 526-548.

Davies, C. (2006). Heroes of Health Care? Replacing the Medical Profession in the Policy Process in the uk. In J.W. Duyvendak, T. Knijn & M. Kremer (Eds.), *Policy, People and the New Professional: De-professionalisation and Re-professionalisation in Care and Welfare* (pp. 137-151). Amsterdam: Amsterdam University Press.

De Vries, J. (2001). *Lege staat of lege bestuurskunde? [Hollow State or Hollow Administrative Sciences?]* Leiden: Leiden University.

Durkheim, É. (1957). *Professional Ethics and Civic Morals*. New York: Free Press.

Enthoven, A.C., & Singer, S.J. (1999). Unrealistic Expectations Born of defective Institutions. *Journal of Health Politics, Policy and Law*, 24(5): 931-939.

Exworthy, M. & Halford, S. (2002). *Professionals and the New Managerialism in the Public Sector*. Buckingham: Open University Press.

Giddens, A. (1994) *Beyond Left and Right. The Future of Radical Politics*. Cambridge: Polity.

Gilbert, N. (2002). *Transformation of the Welfare State: The Silent Surrender of Public Responsibility*. Oxford: Oxford University Press.

Glied, S.A. (2000). Managed Care. In A. Culyer & J. Newhouse (Eds.), *Handbook of Health Economics*. Amsterdam: Elsevier.

Hasenfeld, Y. (1983). *Human Service Organisations*. Englewood Cliffs, NJ: Prentice Hall.

Huijben, M., & Geurtsen, A. (2006). Overhead bij publieke organisaties: op zoek naar een norm *[Overhead in Public Organizations]. Tijdschrift Controlling, 2006* (10): 1-11.

Hutschemakers, G. & Tiemens, B. (2006). Evidence-Based Policy. In J.W. Duyvendak, T. Knijn & M. Kremer (Eds.), *Policy, People and the New Professional: De-professionalisation and Re-professionalisation in Care and Welfare* (pp. 34-47). Amsterdam: Amsterdam University Press.

Illich, I. (1976). *Medical Nemesis: The expropriation of health*. New York: The Free Press.

Inspectie Werk en Inkomen (IWI) (2004a). *Herbeoordeeld? Uitvoering van de wettelijke WAO-herbeoordelingen [Implementation of Occupational Disability Assessment]*. Den Haag: IWI.

Inspectie Werk en Inkomen (IWI) (2004b). *De manager de baas? Een onderzoek naar WAO-managers en hun integrale verantwoordelijkheid voor het werk van verzekeringsartsen [Managers as Bosses? Managers and their Responsibilities for the Work of Insurance Doctors]*. Den Haag: IWI.

Knijn, T., & Selten, P. (2006). The Rise of Contractualisation in Public Services. In J.W. Duyvendak, T. Knijn & M. Kremer (Eds.), *Policy, People and the New Professional: De-professionalisation and Re-professionalisation in Care and Welfare* (pp. 19-33). Amsterdam: Amsterdam University Press.

Lammers, C.J. et al. (1997). *Organisaties vergelijkenderwijs: Ontwikkeling en relevantie van het sociologisch denken over organisaties [Sociological Reflections on Organisation]*. Utrecht: Het Spectrum.

Luft, H.S. (1999). Why are physicians so upset about managed care? *Journal of Health Politics, Policy and Law*, 24(5): 957-966.

Mintzberg, H. (1980). Structure in fives: A synthesis of the research on organisation design. *Management Science, 26*(3): 322-341.

Noordegraaf, M. (2004). *Management in het publieke domein [Management in the Public Domain]*. Bussum: Coutinho.

Onderwijsraad (2004). *Bureaucratisering en schaalfactoren in het onderwijs [Bureaucratisation and Scale Advantages in Education]*. Den Haag: Onderwijsraad.

Perrow, C. (1970). *Organisational Analysis: A sociological view*. London: Tavistock.

Pollitt, C. (1990). *Managerialism and the Public Services*. Oxford: Blackwell Publishers.

Raad voor de Volksgezondheid en Zorg (RVZ) (2008). *Zorginkoop [Buying Care]*. The Hague: RVZ.

Reed, M. (1996). Expert *Power and Control in Late Modernity. Organization Studies, 17*(4): 573-598.

Scott, W.R. (1965). Reactions to supervision in a heteronomous professional organisation. *Administrative Science Quarterly, 10*(1): 65-81.

Smith, S.R. & Lipsky, M. (1994). *Non-profits for Hire: The Welfare State in an Age of Contracting*. Cambridge: Harvard University Press.

Starr, P. (1982). *The Social Transformation of American Medicine: The rise of a souvereign profession and the making of a vast industry*. New York: Basic Books.

Tonkens, E. (2003). *Mondige burgers, getemde professionals. Marktwerking, vraagsturing en professionaliteit in de publieke sector [Markets, Demand Based Governance and Professionalism in the Public Sector]*. Utrecht: NIZW.

Van Bockel, J. (2009). *Gevormde kaders. Bureaucratische en professionele regulering van het werk van ambtenaren [Shaped Frameworks. Bureaucratic and professional regulation of the work of civil servants]*. Utrecht: Utrecht University (Ph.D. thesis).

Van der Veen, R. (1990). *De sociale grenzen van beleid [Social Limits of Policy]*. Leiden/Antwerpen: Stenfert Kroese.

Van der Veen, R. (2006). *Interventie en organisatie: Een sociologische analyse van de veranderingen in het gezondheidszorgbeleid [Sociological analysis of changes in health care policy]*. *Sociologie, 2*(2): 188-207.

Van der Veen, R. & Trommel, W. (1999). *Managed Liberalisation of the Dutch Welfare State. Governance, 12*(3): 289-310.

Zuiderent-Jerak, T. (2007). *Standardizing healthcare practices. Experimental interventions in medicine and science and technology studies*. Rotterdam: Erasmus University Rotterdam (Ph.D. thesis).

6 Legal professionals under pressure

Legal professional ideology and New Public Management

Arie-Jan Kwak

Introduction

Elements of New Public Management have also made their entrance in the legal professional world. The Dutch judicial organization has been reorganized in order to improve its transparency and efficiency, backed by the budgetary incentives employed by a supervisory board of adjudication (the so-called *Raad voor de rechtspraak*) and the Ministry of Justice (e.g. Mak 2008a, 2008b). This fits with a changed legal culture: the judiciary is confronted with a critical general public that no longer takes its authority and traditional institutions for granted. Those who seek justice claim a right to transparent and efficient adjudication and so does the Dutch taxpayer who demands value for money. Sometimes Dutch taxpayers behave like angry customers at an airline service counter. After ordering the criminal prosecution of the popular politician Geert Wilders for insulting Islamic minorities, the enlisted judges of the Amsterdam court of appeals were (anonymously) threatened to such a serious degree that the president of the court decided to publicly sound the alarm over our legal order.

Although adjudication is a public service, legal officials are not directly at the service of the personal interests and political preferences of citizens. Many feel however that if judges are not at *their* service, they must be on the side of their political enemies. It goes without saying that in such a climate judges face the considerable challenge of explaining their role and responsibility as independent servants of the law in concrete and accessible terms. In such a climate the struggle for transparency and efficiency of adjudication is essential.

The role and standing of public prosecutors has also changed in recent years. Several commentators in the Netherlands have noted a trend towards a more adversarial (American) type of criminal procedure, partly due to a changing mentality in the public attorney's office. Social order and public safety have been high on the priority list of almost all democratic parties. From a wise public-spirited 'magistrate', committed to social harmony and justice, prosecutors are said to have transformed into assertive 'crime fighters' who see their role mainly as instrumental to the protection of social order and public safety by the reduction of the incidence of crime. At the same time, and connected to this, the Dutch legal order witnessed an institutional reorganization that empowered the Minister of Justice with regard to the office's prosecution policies and decisions. If the minister is democratically responsible to the constituency for the effective fight against crime, the Minister should be able to effectively govern the professionals of the public prosecution office. Subsequently, in order to be more efficient and effective, the prosecution office has gone through several reorganizations in order to modernize its organization.

Attorneys and notaries have also been forced to modernize or 'professionalize' their organizations. Social-economic changes and institutional rearrangements have intensified the (international) competition between these legal professionals. Lawyers who traditionally regarded each other as 'confreres' or 'learned friends' loosely organized in 'partnerships' and 'brotherhoods' are now experiencing stiff competition from their vocational brothers, giving them strong incentives to look at the price and market value of the services they offer. To optimize their response to consumer demand lawyers have become more conscious of costs, benefits and the efficiency of their organizations, gradually transforming them from 'organizations of professionals' into hierarchical 'professional organizations', or what in the British literature is referred to as 'managed professional businesses' (for a critical view: Muzio & Ackroyd 2005; Ackroyd & Muzio 2007). The resulting efficiency is generally thought to be the major selling point of market competition. This trend may, however, have unwanted side effects. Some time ago, the chairman of the Dutch public prosecution office publicly reproached a group of criminal attorneys who personally attacked, even insulted, a public prosecutor in the media. Under the present conditions it is, however, not wholly clear whether the criminal attorneys eagerly searching for media attention do so to serve justice, or whether media exposure is merely part of their marketing strategy in the competition for (wealthy) clients. Although this may sound cynical, reference to economic self-interest should not come as a surprise as it surely is an essential aspect of the whole ideology of efficiency through market competition.

Another incident also illustrates the changing legal culture as a result of institutional rearrangements. A group of notaries in the north of the Netherlands was reproached by the market-competition authority (*Mededingingsautoriteit*) for forming a price cartel, which the notaries claimed was necessary to ensure the quality of their public services. The general public and the *Mededingingsautoriteit*, however, do not take the commitment of notaries to the public good for granted and note that, although it may improve the quality of their public services (which is seriously doubted from an NPM point of view), a cartel obviously also serves private commercial interests. Notaries who claim that price cartels are necessary will not easily convince the general public anymore. Indeed, NPM thanks its ideological appeal to the fact that it suggests that the larger public generally regards such 'disciplining' of legal professionals by market forces as valuable. The market enables consumers to make their own assessments of quality and price of legal services and subsequently 'choose with their feet'. The market is therefore supposed to *empower* the consumers, forcing service providers to become responsive to consumer demands. Who will think of this as a bad thing?

There is, of course, a counterargument to be made. This will be done by addressing in this contribution the following question: Why did legal professionals not succeed in convincing the general public that justice demands professional autonomy and exemption from market forces? The answer I will present is largely inspired by Steven Brint's *In an Age of Experts* (1994). In modern society legal professionals have gradually complemented an 'ideology of subjectivity' with an 'ideology of objectivity,' which leaves them relatively defenseless against NPM ideology. We have therefore not witnessed a true 'revolt of the professionals' in the Dutch legal world, and it is also not to be expected, partly because professionals know that they will not be able to win the hearts and minds of the general public. Our argument gives ample occasion to explore the institutions, values and ideology of legal professionalism that in part resemble other professional worlds. However, particularly the *political* context in which lawyers work accounts for some distinguishing and salient qualities of their working environment. I will argue that the values that motivate legal work do not easily translate into an activist ideology with regard to maximizing professional autonomy. This may sound counterintuitive at first, but its plausibility depends largely on the definition and analysis of the terms used. In particular, it depends on the idea that at the heart of legal professional values and commitments there is a paradox, or even contradiction, that makes it hard to gain public support in the political struggle for the resources to resist democratic demands for efficiency and transparency. Especially transparency, in the sense of objectivity and predictability, is a fundamental legal and professional value and a demand for efficiency easily aligns with this aspiration. From this perspective, professional demands for maximal autonomy will always be ideologically suspect.

Autonomy

Legal professionals claim autonomy with regard to both the content and the organization of their daily work. In the words of Hupe & Van der Krogt in their contribution (see also Van der Veen), legal professionals, like professionals generally, claim 'the freedom to act as taken by the actor', which is to be distinguished from the discretion they experience in their work. Discretion refers to a relative freedom to act in the application of the rules to concrete circumstances as rules always leave room for maneuver, explaining why, according to Van der Veen, bureaucratization of professional work affects the autonomy but not the discretion of the workers. However, Elliot Freidson (2001: 32) states that the monopolistic control over their own work is 'the essential characteristic of ideal-typical professionalism'. Hupe & Van der Krogt note that the claim to autonomy is justified by the idea of disinterested public service which requires that professionals have maximum freedom to follow the imperatives of their public responsibility. The privilege of collegial self-government or 'collea-gue-control' follows from this pivotal premise. This privilege protects the professionals against excessive influence of lay people, whether the public in general, or client/consumers or managers in particular. Another consequence is that professional malpractice is to be judged by a committee of peers and not by outsiders. Moreover, not only because they are not technically equipped, but also because they will not be able to transcend their particular private interests and preferences, outsiders are not to be trusted to manage and judge legal professionals (Brint 1994: 7).

The legal professions' right to self-government has a political aspect, of course. A general characteristic of totalitarian social orders is that the legal professions are hierarchically under the command of the political rulers because an independent 'status group' within society (wielding state powers) allegedly leads to disorder and renders government ineffective. In a liberal democracy, however, an independent judiciary, and legal profession generally, is thought to be a major achievement as it makes *Rule of Law and not of Men* possible. Judges serve the ruling law, and the particular public values and goods that the law is thought to consist of, and under the present division of labor they explicitly do *not* serve the other branches of the state.[1] As servants of the law, from this political theoretical point of view, judges serve the public only indirectly. In as far as the citizenry in a liberal democracy regard, or reasonably should regard, the rule of law as a public good, they cannot and will not expect the judiciary to be under the direct command of public opinion or the people's wishes and demands.

The ideal of the *Rule of Law* – the law is autonomous with regard to the executive and legislative branches of the modern state – requires autonomy of the legal professionals in their daily work practice. Without independence from people who represent other interests than those of the law, the *Rechtsstaat* surely remains a chimera.

But to serve the law, one needs to know the law. Of course, nobody in his right mind, especially not a knowledgeable and competent legal professional, will claim to be omniscient with regard to the law.[2] There is simply too much of it. And to make things worse: with new enactments, new treaties, new decisions the law changes every day. However, judges are selected on the grounds of a general knowledge and competence with regard to the most important sources of law. In this respect judges are typical professionals: they are knowledge-workers who possess a kind of knowledge that is of a rather formal, abstract and complex nature. This kind of knowledge is not very precise and narrowly restricted; judges are supposed to be generalists in the law and not narrow specialists. On the other hand, it is circumscribed and precise enough to be identifiable as typical *legal* knowledge. Indeed, in modern societies such as ours, legal professionals even claim a *scientific* base for the knowledge they bring to the social problems they are committed to solve, just like medical professionals do[3] (e.g. Freidson 2001: 84; Brint 1994: 35). In any case, judges and legal professionals generally claim to possess knowledge that is esoteric and complex enough, but at the same time not too broad and vague, to justify licensing and exclusive jurisdiction (Wilensky 1964: 148-149).

But idealtypical professionals claim more than merely formal knowledge, whether with scientific pedigree or not. Indeed, competent legal professionals generally pride themselves on not merely knowing the given system of legal rules and standards in a particular jurisdiction. They claim to know what to *do* with these rules and standards, translating the 'law of the books' into 'law in action'. Legal professionals are generally action-oriented; they typically *apply* knowledge to resolve concrete human conflicts. But to effectively apply the rules and standards in conflict resolution, professionals need to know more than just the rules; they need to have a 'feeling' for the situation in which they act, for the concrete human needs and interests involved and for the public values or goods that are associated with the law. Such values are only partly made explicit in the formal system of legal rules and standards that is taught to law school students. A large part of the knowledge needed to be a successful practitioner – as opposed to being a successful university student or legal scientist – is embedded in a complex whole of 'tacit knowledge', a phrase coined by Michael Polanyi (1967) and influentially analyzed by Donald Schön (1983). This idea is succinctly summarized in Polanyi's often quoted statement that the practitioner 'knows more than he can tell'.

The tacit knowledge needed to apply general abstract rules and standards to particular concrete problems – and, most significantly, to real human beings – is acquired by means of 'learning by doing'. Legal professionals are therefore, after a formal education in the university, required to complete their education by means of 'on the job learning'. Usually, the formal education is followed by an internship in which they are introduced to the norms and usages of the practice. Moreover, to be successful, 'learning by doing' in legal practices is generally thought to require a sincere personal *engagement* with the legal institutions and practices. It requires a commitment to the law and the public goods it serves, and an identification with exemplary practitioners who personify the law and what is means to society. Thus, the legal practice is more than merely a 'job to pay the rent'; it is a job that pays in a much broader sense of the word. If this is indeed the case, the law is experienced as a *vocation*: 'Professional work can thus be a secular calling, a modern source of meaning and identity [...] such a calling includes concern that it be performed as well as possible. [...] interest in elaborating, refining, and extending a body of knowledge and skill underlying it, and belief in its value both in and of itself and for serving the needs of others' (Freidson 2001: 108; e.g. Martin 2000).

'It is easy (even for a judge) to be a cynical observer of judges, but it is difficult to be a cynical judge' the American federal judge and legal scholar Richard Posner (1999: 206) writes. Posner's admittance that most judges are not solely motivated by money and power is especially noteworthy because he generally demystifies his profession by analyzing legal practices and institutions in rather hard-nosed economic terms. Judges in the US earn significantly less than equally talented people in the big law firms or in the private sector generally, and this is true in the Netherlands as well. From the standpoint of the *homo economicus* becoming a judge is thus irrational. Therefore, in addition to compensation in terms of money and power – often called extrinsic goods – judges are motivated by *intrinsic* goods such as the desire to be a 'good judge' (Posner 2008: 11, 60; e.g. Larson 1977: 220). And this is exactly what justifies their autonomy: the expectation that the professional puts his (tacit) knowledge and skills to good use, that he or she is truly committed to the public good. The right to control their own work, Freidson (2001: 32, 34) writes, 'implies being trusted, being committed, even being morally involved in one's work'. The professional is trusted to do the right thing at least in part because the professional is not only motivated by money and power but derives a sense of personal professional honor, dignity and satisfaction from the quality of his work (as it is recognized by his peers and the wider community).

Ideology

Richard Sennett (1998: 4) writes that the inequality of knowledge and skill between professionals and their constituencies easily leads to 'a feeling of humiliation and resentment' in those who depend on their services. Randall Collins (1979: 136) adds: 'An occupation that monopolizes an important skill and reserves the right to judge its success or failure can provoke considerable antipathy among those who depend on it.' Legal professionals are indeed privileged: they are relatively well off in terms of income, power and prestige. Moreover, they enjoy a degree of autonomy and immunity in their work that is not given to many others. Such privileges tend to evoke envy and scandals involving professional malpractice fortify the ever-present suspicion that professionals are easily tempted to, in Donald Schöns (1983: 11, 12) words, 'put their special status to private use' and are not able to effectively police themselves. This fuels 'a widespread belief that professional overcharge for their services, discriminate against the poor and powerless in favor of the rich and powerful, and refuse to make themselves accountable to the public'. Indeed, from the economic point of view, monopolies generally raise suspicion as they are deemed inefficient and inhibit consumer choice. From a sociological point of view, there is a general fear that the social exclusion effectuated by professional 'status groups' leads to structural social inequality (e.g. Freidson 2001: 199).

Ever more important is also the political context in which legal professionals do their work. In our present political culture, deeply suffused with the principles of modern liberal democracy, all privileges are *prima facie* illegitimate. Privileges are incompatible with the principle of equal rights and entitlements. Modern legal cultures are in fact bent on eliminating most, if not all, traditional (aristocratic) entitlements, whether hereditary or not. In such a society the privilege of judges, and legal professionals more generally, of being beyond managerial or bureaucratic control in how to do their work stands in need of justification to the general public. People will have to be persuaded that this autonomy is indeed a functional necessity for successful conflict resolution by the judicial branch. Only if the general public is genuinely convinced that the professionals need the freedom to act as they think wise, and that they will not betray the trust that is invested in them, will this privilege be a safe possession.

The professional is therefore irredeemably political (Abel 2003, 2004; Muzio 2004). The claims, values and ideas that are employed in the struggle for legitimacy can take the form of a professional ideology which, according to Freidson, is 'the primary tool available to disciplines for gaining the political and economic resources need to establish and maintain their status' (2001: 105-106; e.g. Posner 1995: 54). Against this background we have to consider the argument that loss of professional autonomy will threaten the quality of the public goods that professionals provide. Does this argument mainly serve political purposes? And does it blind us to the empirical reality of professional practices, which will not be able to resist the qualification of such rhetoric as *ideological*?

Building on this, we can ask the following question: What shape might the professional ideology of legal professionals, and that of judges in particular, take? In an effort to answer this question, I propose we map the structural challenges these professionals face to their privileged position. But before I give a (rough) sketch on the basis of two structural challenges that threaten to de-legitimize legal institutions and division of labor as they stand, I want to give a more precise meaning to the concept of a professional ideology by singling out four basic tenets.

First of all, a professional ideology is an ordered and systematic representation of the professional role and position in society that provides a guide or map for professionals in their daily practice (e.g. Geertz 1993). Importantly, ideologies are not merely descriptive representations, but because they are meant to guide human (political) behavior, they generally contain evaluative or normative concepts and ideals as well. In fact, facts and values are intimately intertwined as ideologies intend not only to give a picture of how the (social) world is, and how it came about, but also what it should be or should become. This relates to a second general characteristic of professional ideologies. Ideologies help to *decontest* the particular role, responsibilities and concomitant privileges of the professional group and provide clarity and certainty in a chaotic and uncertain world. This is no mean feat. Clarity and certainty are necessary prerequisites for confident and effective professional action (Freeden 1996: 41, 45, 77).

Third, the decontestation of the privileges is partly achieved by the coherence and consistency of the professional world view, and the cogency of the ideology is bolstered by the fact that the iron logic of the ideology gives it 'a seal of universality' (e.g. Bourdieu 1987). Thus, the interests of the professional group are presented as *universally* shared interests and the privilege of market monopoly and work autonomy is recognized as legitimate. Fourth, the ideology strengthens the coherence and the identity of the group and makes collective action and self-government possible. Michael Freeden, who provided the above analysis of ideology, notes in addition the overt group orientation of ideologies and the collective action they make possible as they formulate communal identities and goals (Freeden 1996: 105; Eagleton 1991: 45). As such, ideologies are the 'glue' that binds, and the inspiration that motivates groups of people. The ideology forges a true community out of a group of otherwise disparate professionals who consequently personally and emotionally identify with the whole. Such identification might become a source of inspiration and passion, indeed. However, the political stakes and the responsibility to the community bound by the ideology accounts not only for the fact that ideological actors sometimes become very passionate, it also, at least partly, explains why ideologies can become rather closed and dogmatic systems of thought and action (Freeden 1996: 81, 134).

The analysis of professional autonomy in the second paragraph suggests two legal professional ideologies. The first I coined an *ideology of subjectivity* which emphasizes and rationalizes the fact that much professional knowledge is of a tacit nature and depends on personal qualities and virtues. The opposing *ideology of objectivity*, by contrast, downplays the role of subjective qualities and emphasizes both the normality of professionals and the objectivity of professional knowledge and practice. My thesis, inspired by Steven Brint (1994), is that in modern society legal professionals have gradually complemented the ideology of subjectivity with the ideology of objectivity, which has left them relatively defenseless against the ideology of New Public Management.

ARIE-JAN KWAK

Legal professional ideology

An ideology of subjectivity is the product of a political struggle for legitimacy of the monopoly of legal services. This right to monopoly implies the right to keep outsiders (laypeople or competing service providers) out and this can be achieved by means of a licensing system policed by the state. Collins (1979: 132-135) argues that the professions branched off from the collegial organization and training institutions of the Church (the medieval universities). From this background they inherited a tendency to mystify their knowledge and skills such that outsiders cannot judge the professional work by its results and thereby cannot control the practitioners. The skills and techniques that are employed are of an *esoteric* kind; the professional here asserts 'knowledge that is not merely the narrow depth of a technician, or the shallow breadth of a generalist, but rather a wedding of the two in a unique marriage' (Freidson 2001: 121). The result, however, is that the quality of the work can only be truly judged and appreciated by peers. But how can outsiders trust the legal professionals with their monopolized powers? The ideological answer is: because we legal professionals, by virtue of our specific background, training and experience, are self-disciplined, honorable and morally committed guardians of justice. Thus, the ideology of subjectivity tends to both overemphasize and idealize the tacit knowledge and the moral concern – the vocation or calling – of the professional. An ideology of subjectivity (over)emphasizes the *personal* qualities and professional commitment.

The appeal of such a professional ideology is largely explained by the fact that it represents the legal professional as a safe haven, an isle of altruism and morality in a sea of social and political conflict and strife. People who seek justice often feel vulnerable and helpless in the face of the powers they confront. The legal professional claims, or at least aspires, to be motivated by a personally disinterested concern for those who seek justice. The fact that he serves only justice is a promise of independence and of character. The ideology represents the professional as the kind of person you would want to have on your side when you feel disempowered and vulnerable: self-reliant, independent, civic-minded and displaying broad general knowledge and cultivated powers of judgment. This is the kind of person whose judgments are experienced as authoritative such that he is truly a 'binding actor' who replaces chaos with order. Consider, for instance, Kronman's (1993: 101, 139) presentation of the good lawyer as someone who does not just 'know', but who is a 'connoisseur' of the law, expressing the idea that the good lawyer is someone who cares for the good of the activity he is engaged in. The good lawyer also masters the art of rhetoric – 'the art of building communities from resistant human material' – such that he can be a source of order in a conflict-ridden and chaotic world.

The ideology of subjectivity represents the ideal lawyer as a gentleman: a man of honor and a man of his word. Such a worldly person is independent or autonomous enough to be a credible and trustworthy representative of the law as a public good, and not the representative of some particular private interest – least of all his own. An 'ideology of objectivity', by contrast, represents the legal professional as an ordinary person, a jobholder like the lot of us. This professional only distinguishes him – or herself by means of the expert knowledge acquired in a formal training and subsequent experience. The professional is merely a proficient and efficient expert trained to get a particular complex job done. The emphasis is on the *impersonality* of the service by pointing to the objectivity – in the sense of the observer's independence and resistance to critical public scrutiny – of the results of professional action. Such an ideology of objectivity is the product of the political struggle for the autonomy of the legal institutions and practices vis-à-vis the political branches of the modern state. The question: Why should we trust you with the legal powers and competences? The answer: You do not need to trust *me* but only positive law. My professional actions will be informed strictly by the law and this will make my decisions both predictable and verifiable.

The confirmation hearings preceding the installation of Justice Sonia Sotomayor in the American Supreme Court (2009) provide us with a perfect illustration of the ideology of objectivity. The nominated Justice has to present herself before the American Senate, part of the legislative branch. Although the President nominated her, during the hearings Sotomayor distanced herself from President Obama's wish that judges be influenced by that 'what is in a judge's heart' in Constitutional and statutory interpretation. She attested to the idea that the American Constitution is immutable, not changeable unless by democratic amendment, repudiating the liberal idea that the Constitution is a 'living' document whose meaning should evolve with a changing society.[4] By ignoring the room for discretion in constitutional interpretation and by downplaying the role of personal engagement or powers of judgment, Sotomayor confesses to 'textualism' as guiding her interpretations of the law. In *A Matter of Interpretation* her new colleague Justice Antonin Scalia succinctly explains why strict textualism should indeed be the official ideology of the Supreme Court: 'The text is the law, and it is the text that must be observed' (1997: 22).

Of course, Scalia recognizes the fact that the Constitution and statutes are grounded in social values and serve social policies. He also knows very well that new times require new laws. The fundamental point, however, is that in a liberal democracy the judicial branch neither has the authority to evaluate legal texts against underlying values and policies, nor the authority to rewrite the law when the law does not live up to its promise. In his book, Scalia underwrites a particular kind of legal formalism which orders the judge to look for the original meaning of the

ARIE-JAN KWAK

legal text at the time of its enactment. Thus the judge knows exactly what he is looking for and Scalia argues that the original meaning will usually be easy to discern and to apply. Moreover, the decision will be predictable and testable as anyone can unearth how the rule was understood at the time it became law. 'The legislative power is the power to make laws, not the power to make legislators. It is nondelegationable.' According to Scalia (1997: 22-45) this political principle leads inevitably to legal formalism which is 'what makes a government a government of laws and not of men'.

The personal characteristics and virtues of the legal professional should be irrelevant, the formal knowledge and expertise explain actions and decisions. Sotomayor and Scalia present themselves as impersonal 'expert professionals' (Brint 1994) not 'preachers of the law'. Preaching is anathema partly because judges do not present themselves as extraordinary legal aristocrats but merely as ordinary 'functionaries' or 'administrators' of the law, employing formal knowledge and analytical skills, while respecting the authority and autonomy of the people ruling themselves democratically by means of elected representatives. Such experts are humble and down-to-earth public servants whose authority does not depend on their personal qualities, virtues and powers of judgment but derives completely from positive law and its democratic pedigree. As unelected officials, they pledge to be as amoral and apolitical as possible against the elected political branch of the state. Indeed, 'the further the courts steer clear of political controversy, the more likely judicial inquiry is to resemble scientific truth-seeking' (Posner 1995: 63). Like the scientist they are committed to a strict separation between fact (posited legal rules with determinate original meanings and the given facts of the case) and value, which is thought to be subjective and arbitrary. And like the scientist who seeks truth for truth's sake, the social and political consequences are beyond the specialist's concern[5] (e.g. Larson 1977: 237).

The demise of an ideology of subjectivity

The ideology of subjectivity does not have a strong appeal in the context of a confirmation hearing. Moreover, it does not have a strong appeal in the context of the political culture in late modern societies. Reference to personal qualities, virtues and judgment, distinguishing oneself both from ordinary people and from business entrepreneurship, is problematic indeed. The amoral (or demoralized) formalist expert, by contrast, needs no sharp distinction from business enterprise and does not claim to have access to a morality that ordinary citizens do not have. Steven Brint (1994: 10): 'There is an appealing note of democratic egalitarianism in this [...] but in the background there is, more importantly, the triumph of expertise as a basis of distinction that needed no additional moral vaulting'. Brint argues that the idealtypical ethos of the expert professional is one of 'principled indifference' motivated by liberal modesty with regard to moral questions and conflicts, and by openness for the demands of society respecting the moral autonomy of the citizens. For expert professionals there is no need for personal judgment and high-minded social responsibilities and aspirations, because the norms of their discipline together with the demands of the market provide an objective and sufficient criterion of the public interest (1994: 37, 103).

This neatly falls in line with the present legal culture which can be characterized as a 'horizontal society' (Friedman 1999): a society populated with citizens with a strong rights consciousness mirrored by a legal system that is to a large degree meant to 'take rights seriously' (Dworkin 1977). Modern law explicitly protects individual rights against the intrusion of the rich and the powerful; including, particularly, the state. Civil rights bolstering respect for the autonomy of those subject to the law by means of respecting the civil rights which bolster this autonomy is a major principle in our civil, criminal, administrative and constitutional law. Some argue it is *the* major premise of any modern legal system. Modern constitutions grant civil rights to citizens and the judiciary has the jurisdiction to review whether state agencies have infringed these rights and thus have not treated them with equal respect and concern. Professionals work daily in such a legal system and are bound to take rights seriously and to experience civil freedom and autonomy as a fundamental public good.

The present legal and political culture also falls neatly in line with one of the basic presuppositions of NPM ideology. Financial pressures in public administration forced the state to make public service delivery more effective and efficient by empowering citizens with the help of market or quasi-markets. According to influential theorists of NPM, efficiency is served by *Reinventing Government* (Osborne & Gaebler 1992). The free market should replace the rigid 'iron cage' of modern bureaucracy that in modern welfare states has become a monolithic autonomous power serving its own needs instead of those of the citizen. The release of the 'entrepreneurial spirit in the public sector' would lead to both 'customer satisfaction' and the reduction of public spending. We only need to replace the word bureaucracy with legal institutions to see how this translates into a criticism of self-serving and inefficient professionals, who are able to ignore the call for efficiency and responsiveness by the citizenry because of their monopoly of service. Here we can refer to Judge Posner again. In the past decades Posner has analyzed again and again how the 'guilds' or 'cartels' of legal professionals may indeed use their monopoly to manipulate the market at the economic expense of the citizenry. By simply keeping the services in short supply, the price indiscriminately goes up. The monopoly is legitimated by an ideological mystification of the professional knowledge and skills, by means of which professionals distinguish themselves from ordinary suppliers of

ARIE-JAN KWAK

ordinary services in ordinary markets (Posner 1995). Indeed, in the ideology of subjectivity the meaning of 'ordinary' borders on 'vulgar'.

Objectivity versus experience

At present, many Dutch notaries undoubtedly have a hard time. The economic crisis has seriously reduced the demand for their services as the volume of real estate transactions declined. Coupled with the prohibition of price fixing to give full reign to market forces, this crisis caused major financial problems. It will not come as a surprise that more and more notaries now try to exert political pressure on the government to attenuate the severe competition for clients by allowing for minimum fees and price fixing. This would guarantee them an income which would not just make them more independent from the market conditions but it would also secure a high quality of service, they argue. By contrast, a further onslaught will seriously threaten their professional independence and concomitantly the quality of their services. In turn, this would threaten the public's trust in these professionals. As the functioning of the whole legal system depends on the public trust, the consequences would be very serious indeed.

But if the quality of the services rendered by the notary is something that is objectively testable by ordinary lay people, the cry for the abolition of market competition loses its bite. If we can trust the consumer to assess the value for money that is offered, why should society pay for all those suppliers of services for which there is presently simply no demand? Notaries made good money when the real estate business was booming; why would the community pay for the survival of those notaries who are not efficient enough to be competitive, and not provident enough to prepare for the present bad times during the good times? What the notaries effectively demand from the Dutch public is that they pay for those among them who have not been responsible and professional enough to face the present crisis and therefore now have financial problems.[6]

However, the argument for the softening of the effect of market forces becomes much more persuasive when we proceed from the premise that consumers to a large extent lack the knowledge and experience to judge the value and quality of the services of the notaries. If customers make bad judgments, the wrong notaries will survive. We will be left with the ones that on the whole offer a socially unacceptable low quality; or with the ones that risk the trust that the public has invested in them by avoiding their public responsibilities. Or, worse, some may even be tempted to occasionally break the law, if customers only put enough pressure on them; for instance, by simply threatening to take their business away from them. The idea is that, given the fact that we cannot really test or judge their practice, notaries might be corrupted *by* the market forces *and* get away with it. One might say that the same is true for a detergent wholesaler that struggles to survive in a very competitive environment, but the quality of detergents is generally more easily assessable by customers than the quality of legal work. Notaries serve the public interest of legal certainty which makes the assessment of the quality of their products a bit more complex and this justifies the reinforcement of their independence from their clients by guaranteeing them a minimum fair price.

Conclusion

In this chapter I argued that it is particularly the *practical* aspect of professional work that justifies the institutional arrangements regarding the 'work autonomy' of the professional. Indeed, I presented an idealtypical ideology of subjectivity which explicitly justifies both the monopoly of service and the professional self-government. In order to fight the competition from other experts, and to resist bureaucratization and commodification in the market, it presents legal practice as an 'ineffable art' and it often leads to the cultivation of a charismatic personality. Legal professionals acquire the appearance of people who are 'in control', and with 'deep, perhaps inarticulable, insight and of masterful, unique competence' (Posner 1999: 188-189). This ideology tends to overemphasize the subjective qualities and virtues at the price of mystifying the professional practice and the closing of the professional mind to external influence; explaining why a profession is often defined as 'an occupation which tends to be colleague-oriented, rather than client-oriented' (Larson 1977: 226). Moreover, this ideology tends to stress the aspiration to excellence at the price of distinguishing the professional from 'ordinary' people. The ideology of subjectivity is uplifting, but it is fundamentally elitist, which clashes with the liberal-egalitarian principles of the present political, legal and economic culture.

The ideology of objectivity represents legal practices as objective decision-making in order to resist popular critique of paternalism, moralism, elitism, and professional mysticism. This ideology of objectivity downplays the role of subjective qualities and virtues and emphasizes both the normality of professionals and the objectivity of professional knowledge and practice. Varying on Steven Brint's influential analysis (1994), we can argue that legal professionals have gradually complemented the ideology of subjectivity with the ideology of objectivity – in his terms: a transition from 'social trustee professionalism' to 'expert professionalism' – but this ideology has left professionals rather defenseless against NPM ideology. If the professional service is both impersonal and objective, why would the professional have to be insulated and protected from bureaucratic and market control? Or in the words of Donald Schön (1983: 289-290): 'Those who would demystify professional knowledge

ARIE-JAN KWAK

[...] would deny his claims to mandate for social control, autonomy in practice, and license to keep the gates of the professions'. In an article on medical professionalism and the demands of the doctrine of evidence-based medicine, Berg et al. (2000: 766) explore exactly this inherent tension between the quest for transparency and objectivity and the justification for medical professional autonomy: 'The same activities that may enhance the scientific image of a profession might reduce the individual professional's autonomy; the instruments that make the profession's decision-making processes more transparent also make that process more vulnerable to 'meddling' by outsiders.'

Indeed, I argued that the basic assumptions of NPM are in line with the fundamentals of our present political, legal and economic culture. However, professional autonomy and social responsibility cannot and will not be totally replaced by consumer sovereignty in a free market. Most distinctive of the present situation seems to be the cautious and pragmatic search for a new balance between professionalism, managerialism and consumerism. I follow Van der Veen's argument in his contribution that the discretion that is typical of professional practices is not at stake here. Their autonomy, however, is. As in professional practices generally, legal professionals inescapably have elbowroom to follow their own interpretation of legal guidelines and standards in applying their knowledge to individual cases. Objectivity is a matter of degree, not an all or nothing matter. The same goes for the autonomy of the professional. The autonomy of legal professionals is undoubtedly affected by the empowerment of the customers or clients and by the managerial controls within the organization that are required to meet the demand of efficiency and responsiveness. Although in the struggle for political resources professionals, like all of us, are forced to reason in terms of black or white ideological dichotomies, NPM policies and institutional rearrangements do not de-professionalize lawyers into bureaucrats or merchants. It is an empirical question to what degree the autonomy is compromised by the new arrangements; the present analysis merely suggests an answer to the question of why legal professionals face a Catch 22 when they enter the ideological struggle for freedom from market and bureaucratic controls.

Notes

1. The fact that the Dutch Constitution does not strictly sever the legislative and executive branches (largely for pragmatic reasons), makes judicial independence all the more important.
2. Actually, as legal subjects, we are all supposed to know the law. But this is, of course, merely a legal fiction; a fiction necessary to disqualify the excuse of legal ignorance which would completely disrupt legal practice.

3. Compare the doctrine of 'evidence-based medicine' (EBM) which urges medical practitioners to ground treatment, and medical standards, protocols and procedures, in sound biomedical evidence about their effectiveness. See, for instance, Harrison (1998) for an analysis of the (political) appeal of this doctrine.
4. See, for instance, 'Future Nominations Are at Stake in Hearings' in *New York Times* 15 July 2009 http://www.nytimes.com/2009/07/16/us/politics/16assess.html?_r=1&ref=politics
5. In short: 'a rule is a rule, don't complain to me' (Kelman 1987: 63).
6. The discussion resembles the debate about the financial institutions that granted huge bonuses to their managers but demanded financial help from the state when the financial markets collapsed, partly because of undue risk-taking by the very same institutions. The comparison is a bit unfair, but the fact is that the government did help some major banks because of the huge public interest involved. The notaries' effectively ask for a something similar.

References

Abel, R.L. (2003). *English Lawyers Between the Market and the State: The Politics of Professionalism.* Oxford: Oxford University Press.

Abel, R.L. (2004). The Professional is Political. *International Journal of the Legal Profession, 11*(1-2), 131-156.

Ackroyd, S., & Muzio, D. (2007). The Reconstructed Professional Firm: Explaining Change in English Legal Practices. *Organization Studies, 28*(5), 729-747.

Berg, M., Horstman, K., Plass, S., & Van Heusden, M. (2000). Guidelines, Professionals and the Production of Objectivity: Standardisation and the Professionalism of Insurance Medicine. *Sociology of Health & Illness, 22*(6), 765-791.

Bourdieu, P. (1987). The Force of Law: Toward a Sociology of the Juridical Field. *The Hastings Law Journal, 38*(5). 805-853.

Brint, S. (1994). *In an Age of Experts: The Changing Role of Professionals in Politics and Public Life.* Princeton: Princeton University Press.

Collins, R. (1979). *The Credential Society.* New York: Academic Press.

Dworkin, R. (1977). *Taking Rights Seriously.* Cambridge: Harvard University Press.

Eagleton, T. (1991). *Ideology: An Introduction.* New York: Verso.

Freeden, M. (1996). *Ideologies and Political Theory: A Conceptual Approach.* Oxford: Clarendon Press.

Freidson, E. (2001). *Professionalism: The Third Logic.* Cambridge: Polity Press.

Friedman, L.M. (1999). *The Horizontal Society.* New Haven: Yale University Press.

Geertz, C. (1993). *The Interpretation of Cultures.* London: Fontana.

Harrison, S. (1998). The politics of evidence-based medicine in the United Kingdom. *Politics and Policy, 26*(1), 15- 31.

Kelman, M. (1987). *A Guide to Critical Legal Studies.* Cambridge: Harvard University Press.

Kronman, A.T. (1993). *The Lost Lawyer: Failing Ideals of the Legal Profession.* Cambridge: Harvard University Press.

Larson, M.S. (1977). *The Rise of Professionalism: A Sociological Analysis*. Berkeley: University of California Press.

Mak, E. (2008a). *De Rechtspraak in Balans [Balanced Justice]*. Nijmegen: WLP.

Mak, E. (2008b). Rechtspraak en Rechtspraak: Een precaire balans *[Justice and Justice: a Precarious Balance]*. *Rechtstreeks, 4,* 9-40.

Martin, M.W. (2000). *Meaningful Work: Rethinking Professional Ethics*. Oxford: Oxford University Press.

Muzio, D. (2004). The Professional Project and the Contemporary Re-organisation of the Legal Profession in England and Wales. *International Journal of the Legal Profession, 11*(1-2), 33-50.

Muzio, D. & Ackroyd, S. (2005). On the Consequences of Defensive Professionalism: Recent Changes in the Legal Labour Process. *Journal of Law and Society, 32*(4), 615-642.

Osborne D., & Gaebler, T. (1992). *Reinventing Government: How the Entrepreneurial Spirit is Transforming the Public Sector*. Reading, MA: Addison-Wesley.

Polanyi, M. (1967). *The Tacit Dimension*. New York: Anchor Books.

Posner, R.A. (1995). *Overcoming Law*. Cambridge: Harvard University Press.

Posner, R.A. (1999). *The Problematics of Moral and Legal Theory*. Cambridge: The Belknap Press of Harvard University Press.

Posner, R.A. (2008). *How Judges Think*. Cambridge: Harvard University Press.

Scalia, A. (1997). *A Matter of Interpretation: Federal Courts and the Law*. Princeton: Princeton University Press.

Schön, D.A. (1983). *The Reflective Practitioner: How Professionals Think in Action*. New York: Basic Books.

Sennett, R. (2008). *The Craftsman*. London: Penguin Books.

Wilensky, H.L. (1964). The Professionalization of Everyone. *American Journal of Sociology, 70,* 137-158.

7 Institutionalizing professional conflicts through financial reforms

The case of DBCS in Dutch mental healthcare

Amanda Smullen

Introduction

Earlier in this book Van der Veen already briefly discussed NPM-related changes in the Dutch healthcare system. His overall conclusion was that these changes appear to limit the autonomy of professionals, but not their discretion. In this chapter, a specific far-reaching change in the Dutch care system – most specifically in Dutch mental healthcare – will be discussed. I will examine how the use of financial instruments creates pressures for professional conflict and change. This chapter describes the introduction of Diagnostic Treatment Combinations (in Dutch Diagnose Behandel Combinaties or DBCS) in the mental healthcare field, and analyzes the challenges this financing system presents to the profession of psychiatry. DBCS are a type of case-mixing system which bring together both clinical and financial knowledge to distinguish and price the 'products' of health professionals. They can be associated with transnational trends towards prospective payment systems in healthcare and are a variant of the more commonly known Diagnostic Related Groups (Schmid & Götze 2009; Van Essen 2009b). While widely applied within somatic healthcare, such financial instruments have rarely been implemented in the broader mental healthcare field (Knapp et al. 2007). In both this respect and in the actual design of the system, the Dutch case is somewhat unique.

However, it is not the primary function of this chapter to examine the technical features of the Dutch DBCS. Rather beyond their technical design, these types of systems are conceived here of as social phenomena which not only represent the work of medical specialists, but also construct that work according to standardized categories (see Hines 1988; Covaleski, Dirsmith & Michelman 1993). It is argued that this is particularly problematic for the diverse specialism of psychiatry which is widely perceived to be at the lower ranks of the medical status (see Buchanan & Bhugra 1992). Historically, the profession of psychiatry was, like its stigmatized patients, quite literally marginalized from mainstream medicine, and in large part relegated to practice in the asylum rather than general hospitals (Shorter 1997). Even today psychiatrists work in a range of organizational settings and struggle with attaining a common professional identity that is equivalent to other medical specialists. This is also complicated by continuing epistemological controversies regarding both the causes of mental illnesses and the appropriate treatments (Lakoff 2005; Shorter 1997). The capacity of DBCS to respond to this diversity will be analyzed by examining and comparing the logic of DBC systems with features of the Dutch psychiatric profession.

In order to capture some of the limits and conflict that has followed from the introduction of Dutch DBCS, we analyzed what have been the limits and conflicts of the introduction of the Dutch DBC system in mental healthcare. More specifically, we analyzed three aspects of this development. Firstly, it was asked to what extent DBCS represent the work activities of psychiatry? This is a question about the relationship between the paper world of financial reporting and exchange, and the professional world of diagnosing and treating patients (Bal 2008). Secondly, following from what has become visible and invisible through DBCS, the chapter also considers the consequences of such systems for the profession of psychiatry. The first part of the chapter briefly describes the introduction of DBCS within Dutch mental healthcare and the promises and controversies that have surrounded them. Furthermore, the Dutch trajectory of DBCS is placed within broader transnational trends towards these systems. The second part of the chapter analyzes the logic and assumptions of DBCS and the kind of information they require to be able to satisfy goals of transparency, distinguish product groups, and cost prediction. The third part of the chapter focuses on the profession of psychiatry and the nature of psychiatric work. It will relate the features of the psychiatric profession to the logic of the DBC system, and explore why the DBC system has become a site for professional conflict.

DBCS in Dutch mental healthcare: From promises to conflict

Since 1 January 2008, the Dutch legislation governing the insurance and thus financing for mental healthcare has changed. While in the past mental health services were entirely funded by the Algemene Wet Bijzondere Ziektekosten (AWBZ) – a compulsory insurance for the chronically ill, the bulk of these activities are now to be covered by new legislation which applies to both somatic and mental healthcare provision (SWZ). This extended the Dutch regulated market in healthcare, which has been underway since 2004, to the mental healthcare field (Helderman et al. 2005). On the one hand, the Dutch regulated market has involved spreading the risk of costs for healthcare to private insurers and thereby encouraging them to act as prudent buyers of health services for their enrollees. On the other hand, it has also guaranteed a basic standard of care by requiring all insurers to offer a basic (mandatory) package to enrollees (Helderman 2007: 227). In order to facilitate the creation of this regulated market, Diagnostic Treatment Combinations (DBCS) were developed by and for each medical specialism.

DBCS play a number of different roles within the Dutch system of regulated healthcare. They were also initially associated with a range of different goals which are not necessarily congruent. Firstly, and at least rhetorically foremost, DBCS were associated with creating transparency within the healthcare field. They were argued to provide a way for the government, insurers, and the general public to obtain greater insight into medical activities and the costs of these activities (DBC Onderhoud 2007). Secondly, as an instrument of the Dutch regulated market, DBCS were also created to promote the reduction of waiting lists in Dutch hospitals and act as an incentive for greater efficiency. They were presented as a commitment to pay medical specialists for what they actually do and encourage them to respond to the growing waiting lists (Van Essen 2009b). Thirdly, DBCS were to provide a pricing system for the Dutch regulated market and thereby enable competition between providers (Van Nooten & Van Agthoven 2006).

A fourth goal that came to characterize the DBC system was the integration of the mental healthcare field into the more general healthcare system. This aspect of DBCS was only agreed upon later in the process to implement the regulated market and complemented existing plans to reform the chronic healthcare insurance. While this integration was primarily of a financial nature, entailing mental health services to be funded in the same ways as other health services encouraged opening up the mental healthcare field to public scrutiny (see Maassen 2005). Finally, though cost cutting was not prominent in the initial discussions to reform the Dutch healthcare system, DBCS can be used in this way and there have been attempts to build in incentives to encourage cheaper treatments. Significantly, concern about the costs of healthcare have increased following the implementation of DBCS as a payment system (Baltesen 2009). Indeed, contrary to activity-based budgeting, a 3.5 % cut has recently been imposed on mental healthcare.

The prospect of being integrated into the DBC payment system was initially welcomed by the elite of the Dutch professional organization for psychiatry. Besides interpreting this inclusion as recognition that mental health illnesses were equivalent to other types of illness, and should be insured accordingly, there was also the hope of achieving equivalence for the specialism (Maassen 2005). At the most rudimentary level, psychiatrists have generally not attained the same kinds of wage conditions as their fellow specialists in the Netherlands. Following from the Commission Ginjaar of the Order of Medical Specialists, there were also indications that achieving greater equivalence in earnings across specialisms was to be part of the DBC package (Commissie Ginjaar 2001).

The desire of psychiatry to be (equally) included within the wider healthcare system was also supported by the Dutch Order of Medical

Specialists who represented all medical specialists in the negotiations to reform the healthcare system. Though psychiatry was incorporated later than other specialist organizations into the project to develop DBCS, like the other medical specialists, representatives from the psychiatric profession were allowed to develop their own DBC healthcare products in collaboration with other stakeholders such as hospitals and insurers (see Van Essen 2009a). For psychiatry this process began in 2002 and actually resulted in a different design of DBCS for mental healthcare compared to somatic care. Moreover, there were indications that earnings differentiation between psychiatrists and other specialists were reproduced, and according to some psychiatrists in private practice it worsened.[1]

By 2008, following on the actual implementation of the DBC system within mental healthcare, the opposition within the professional field to DBCS had become immense. A study conducted by the research bureau of a political party found that 89% of caregivers in the field of mental healthcare (including medical specialists) believed the system should be scrapped (Wetenschappelijk Bureau SP 2008: 89-90). While complaints and disgruntlement had also been experienced in somatic care, this was miniscule compared to the public outrage and even continuing legal action that some psychiatrists instigated against the system.[2] It should be added that there is increasing evidence that medical specialists in somatic care have profited financially from the DBC system (Baltesen 2009). Psychiatrists in private practice, by contrast, have experienced a number of financial difficulties with the system. These have included claims about a reduction in financial returns as a consequence of DBCS and delays in payments from insurance companies which present liquidity problems. At the same time salaried psychiatrists have sometimes publically argued that private practitioners misused the DBC system and have always been more entrepreneurial (Tielens 2011).

Perhaps the greatest indication of conflict was when a group of 148 psychiatrists together with some psychotherapists refused to use the declaration system. They argued it is counter to their professional values such as confidentiality of patient information and treating the patient as an individual.[3] To function as a price and payment system, the DBC system requires information about the patients be sent to insurers. Another aspect of this opposition to DBCS included a rejection of the diagnostic system incorporated into their design. Far from an apparently neutral system which would enable the government to obtain insight into the work of psychiatrists, or from the hopes of the psychiatric profession for status equivalence, DBCS have instead become a site for professional conflict. This has included both conflicts within the psychiatric profession itself and conflicts about jurisdictional boundaries with other mental healthcare professions.

AMANDA SMULLEN

The transnational spread of case mix systems and the Dutch variant

Before analyzing further the source of these conflicts and the logic of Dutch DBCs more generally, it is important to locate the Dutch trajectory within the context of broader transnational trends (Kimberly et al. 2008; Schmid & Götze 2009; Van Essen 2009b, see also chapter 2). Colored by New Public Management, these have included healthcare trends towards developing cost prices for 'health products', the introduction of prospective payment systems, and of competition (Schmid & Götze 2009). The specific origins of case-mixing initiatives have been attributed to American experience with Diagnostic Related Groups (DRGS) (see Chillingerian 2008). These were famously developed by a research group at Yale University headed by Professors Bob Fetter and John Thompson. Based upon clinical work processes, Fetter and Thompson sought to distinguish the acute products of hospitals and associate them with patterns in cost. While the initial intention of the designers was to develop instruments for improving management within the context of hospitals, DRGS eventually became the price-setting system for the Medicare program in the United States (Chillingerian 2008: 4).

Since that time, variants of DRG systems have been developed and implemented as payment systems for hospitals in countries as diverse as Australia, Germany, Japan, Sweden, Belgium and the Netherlands (see Kimberly et al. 2008). While these initiatives share their aim to define hospital services as commercial products, they have differed in their emphasis upon broader healthcare objectives and also in their technical design (Schmid & Götze 2009; Frisina & Cacace 2009). For example, Schmid & Götz (2009: 26) distinguish between DRG systems which were explicitly associated with the goal of cost containment (USA), systems created to promote more efficient production and waiting list reductions (UK, Netherlands), and systems to promote competition within a self-regulating healthcare sector (Germany, Netherlands). In a handful of countries including the Netherlands, Austria and Japan, where case-mixing systems have been applied to health services outside of the hospital setting, DRG systems have also been associated with the goal of fostering integration across the healthcare sector.

Among these initiatives the Dutch system of DBCs has been distinguished from the other DRG systems, and has generally stood out as consensual, complex and generous (Oostenbrink & Rutten 2006). For example, while most countries have had to involve clinicians in the process of developing product groups for these systems, the Dutch approach was exceptional and included setting up project groups per specialism. More than twenty professional organizations representing each specialism were responsible for deciding upon whether and which diagnostic categories should be incorporated in the design of the DBC system. In some instances specialists chose diagnostic systems and in other instances other ways to distinguish patient categories were developed. Furthermore, the Dutch DBC system distinguishes clinical process summaries by episode of care including outpatient visits, clinical episodes, daycare and after care. DRG systems by contrast are only based on inpatient episodes and sometimes daycare (Krabbe-Alkemade et al. 2008). These aspects, together with other design differences concerning co-morbidity, initially resulted in a DBC system in somatic care which contained some 29,000 DBCS in the Dutch system compared to just 600-900 possible categories in other DRG systems (Oostenbrink & Rutten 2006). More recently, a project to reduce the number of DBCS in Dutch somatic care has begun. It should be noted that this was a lesser problem in Dutch mental healthcare as there never existed such a great number of DBCS – approximately 3,000.

Another important feature of the Dutch DBC system for somatic healthcare is the inclusion of a honorarium for the medical specialist. This is similar to a fee-for-service system wherein an hourly specialist fee is included within the DBC. It was an important criterion for the commitment of medical specialists to the healthcare reforms (see Dent 1998). While other DRG systems generally include charges for medical specialists, in the Dutch system the honorarium is made separately visible (Krabbe-Alkemade et al. 2008). This can be of importance when different types of specialists or professions treat the patient. For example, to the surprise of psychiatrists in private practice, the DBC system which was later developed for Dutch mental healthcare did not include a separate honorarium for the medical specialist. This has the consequence that the rate of pay to the medical specialist may vary because DBC cost averages are derived from data including cheaper professionals such as salaried specialists or psychologists.

The ABC of DBCS

In examining the way that DBCS have become a site for conflict within psychiatry, it is useful to examine the logic which underlies this system and thereby informs how the work of psychiatrists is represented. This is akin to understanding DBCS as a system of knowledge. DBCS have been developed by financial/accounting specialists and are the outcome of the application of a range of techniques to measure medical activities in financial terms. Their calculation relies upon a pool of information about the characteristics of different patient groups and statistical averages about the treatments provided to them and their length of duration (DBC Onderhoud 2007). It goes almost without saying that reliable information is the most basic requirement of DBCS and their various functions in the Dutch regulated market. As indicated by their title, a central component and distinction that is made within the DBC system is the diagnosis of the specialist (see also Duckett 2008). This provides an initial starting point for distinguishing financially between different groups of patients, and the kinds of trajectories of care that they receive. It assumes that the diagnosis of the specialist is reliable and also based upon clear distinctions. In the technical language of DRG experts, there should be clinical homogeneity (Sanderson 1993: 50).

A second component of the DBC system concerns the treatments associated with particular diagnoses (DBC Onderhoud 2007). In order to distinguish between the costs related to different diagnoses, information is gathered about the patterns in treatment behavior. For example, when a broken leg is diagnosed, information regarding the kinds of medical activities associated with diagnosing and treating the leg are identified and included on an activity list. This list can include making x-rays, resetting the leg, applying plaster, prescribing painkillers, as well as listing time – such as that necessary for the initial consultation or for follow-up checks. Clearly, some kinds of medical activities are easier to distinguish and represent through this system than others. For example, tangible activities such as an x-ray are more easily quantified and distinguished than the expertise used to diagnose the patient, to comfort them, and to advise them about how they can best promote a quick recovery. These latter kinds of activities are represented in minutes of time. Furthermore, to provide a prediction of costs, DRG systems assume that similar kinds of diagnoses will require similar kinds of financial investments (Sanderson 1993: 52).

Another distinction that has been important to the Dutch DBC system concerns the identity of the caregiver. In developing a financial representation of the costs of treatment given to particular patient groups, it is also necessary to identify the different occupations involved in treating the patient. This is clearly of financial significance since the costs of using medical specialists far exceed those of nurses, social workers, psychologists or other (semi-)professionals in the healthcare field. Indeed, the notion of 'recognizable clinical input' (*medische herkenbaarheid*) has been central to the desire to develop an accurate account of the costs of healthcare services in the Dutch case (see DBC Onderhoud 2006). *Medische herkenbaarheid* refers to the capacity to be able to distinguish the role and effect of the medical specialist in treating a patient from a particular diagnostic group. An example where this criterion is satisfied would be that of the role of the surgeon in treating a patient diagnosed with appendicitis. Following from the diagnosis, it is possible to assess the activity and effect of the surgeon. Aside from legitimating the role of the surgeon, *medische herkenbaarheid* is of relevance to representing medical work financially because it also relates to predicting the length of time necessary for treatment.

It is on the basis of all these kinds of attributes: diagnosis, related treatments, and the role of different types of caregivers that the Dutch DBC system was developed. The financial expert collects existing information, for example records of hospitals, and collates this in a statistical way to develop categories of diagnostic groups with similar treatment patterns. It is possible for a number of different treatment trajectories to be related to the same diagnosis and be recognized within different DBCS. For example, the complex Dutch system allows for the same diagnosis of depression to be applicable to different DBCS depending on the length and type of treatment. Furthermore, the actual payment received for the same DBC product group may vary because of a different range of activities included within the treatment episode. The point is that each activity/cost item within the same DBC group is charged according to the average costs that have been calculated across all providers for those activities within that product group. Indeed, the product group prices are revised each year according to the data collected about earlier years. In order to calculate these averages and distinguish product groups in a statistically reliable way it is necessary to first have that information available, and to collect it about a large number of diagnostic cases and their treatment histories. There is to date no demand for quality incorporated within the DBC system.

The profession of psychiatry and field of mental healthcare

Behind the order that is sought and created through the DBC system, lies the complex world of psychiatry. Arguably, the nature of psychiatric work challenges most of the assumptions of the DBC system such as those regarding diagnosis and patterns of treatment. Standardized classifications for diagnosing mental illness across the globe did not appear until the 1980s (DSM III), and the current system DSM IV remains the subject of criticism (Lakoff 2005: 35). Furthermore, the treatment trajectories of psychiatric patients tend to be variable and long-term which creates problems for the prediction of costs, and there are queries about the role of recognizable clinical input (*medische herkenbaarheid*). Finally, the ability of the profession to unify and institutionalize their economic interests within an instrument like DBCS is hampered by the range of organizational settings within which psychiatrists work. While some of these features of the psychiatric profession may also be relevant to other specialists, the degree to which they characterize psychiatry and the difficulties of directly measuring psychiatric performance presents a number of vulnerabilities. How this acts to create conflict within the profession through the instrument of DBCS is discussed further by focusing upon three aspects of psychiatric work: diagnosis, treatment trajectories and organizational settings.

Diagnostic systems and controversies

The diagnosis of a patient provides one of the primary organizing features of the Dutch system of DBCs, yet diagnostic tools are still undeveloped in psychiatry and subject to controversy. As Lakoff notes: 'Two centuries after its invention, psychiatry's illnesses have neither known causes nor definitive treatments' (Lakoff 2005: 5). Following recent revisions to Psychiatry's Diagnostic Statistical Manual of Mental Disorders (DSM IV) this tool was described, even by those favorable to it, as being based upon superficial scientific research (Kahn 2008: 30). It is primarily a description of different disorders which groups together a number of symptoms, which may or may not be present, and are also not always mutually exclusive. The descriptive character of diagnosis within psychiatry is in large part related to the lack of agreement about the causes of mental illness – is it something organic or is it related to the psyche or social conditions and how can these things be distinguished?

In recognition that there are many factors that play a role in mental well-being, psychiatrists have generally subscribed to a *biopsychosocial* model. This has had various advantages including allowing psychiatrists to identify explanations on the basis of a particular case, but also giving them some discretion to practise their own favored approach to mental illness.[4] There is also some evidence to suggest that the nature of the diagnostic system, and different views on mental illness among psychiatrists, has the consequence that psychiatrists diagnose similar cases in different ways (see Buckingham et al. 1998: 8). This challenges the demand of the DBC system for homogenous patient groups. Indeed, in countries such as Australia and the UK, which are still in the process of developing case-mix systems for mental health, it is preferred to group patients according to severity of illness as opposed to diagnosis (Buckingham et al. 1998).

The inclusion of the DSM IV in the Dutch DBC system could also be interpreted as a preference for biological approaches to psychiatry. This is because the biological approach, together with the pharmaceutical industry, informed the first standardized diagnostic tool (DSM III) within the profession, and has predominated over later revisions (Shorter 1997: 297; Lakoff 2005). More generally, the increasing interest in genetic explanations for health problems and the capacity to conform to the demands of scientific evidence have promoted the prestige and acceptance of biological psychiatry within recent years (Shorter 1997). Lakoff (2005) notes that the favored treatments of biological psychiatrists conform to the budgetary interests of states since prescriptions of medication and shorter term talking (cognitive or psychotherapy) treatments tend to be cheaper than psychoanalytical approaches. Historically, biological psychiatry has also been committed to treating patients with severe mental illness as opposed to some of the more elite clientele of psychoanalysts (Shorter 1997). Nevertheless, in the process to develop Dutch DBCs, it would appear that proponents of the biological approach, or at least the DSM IV system, have prevailed over other traditions in psychiatry including the social, the anthropological and the psychoanalytical. This is surprising since the Dutch psychiatric profession has been historically characterized as diverse and open to different traditions (see Gijswijt-Hofstra et al. 2005). Since the introduction of DBCs, it is the psychiatrists who are also psychoanalysts and psychotherapists who have been the most militant in their rejection of the system.[5]

Though it is not the purpose here to evaluate what should be the correct form of psychiatry, it is nevertheless interesting to note some of the characteristics of biological psychiatry which may be advantageous in the face of DRG-like reforms. Firstly, biological psychiatry characterizes mental illness as an organic problem and therefore reinforces a medical relationship with the patient, as opposed to the analytical role of the psychoanalyst. This medical relationship has also changed over the years with the modern-day (biological) psychiatrist being described as a risk manager (Lakoff 2005). Therapies are used along with medications, but this is primarily to assist the patient in self-management rather than analyzing the self (Lakoff 2005: 109). Secondly, since biological approaches take an objective view to illness they are easier to institutionalize through administrative tools. This is because of the ability to standardize biological approaches (something psychoanalytical approaches are opposed to) and the acceptance of standardization in medical practice more generally. That said, biological psychiatry has not been immune to building new empires for psychiatric services including increasing diagnoses of mental illnesses like ADHD or expanding definitions of depression (Shorter 1997: 288-292).

Treatment types and trajectories

Another problem the DBC system encounters in the field of mental healthcare concerns the patterns and visibility of treatment activities. Contrary to the ideal of using the system of DBCs for the purpose of planning, it has since been recognized that the different mental healthcare categories are unlikely to provide a good prediction of treatment or its duration (DBC Onderhoud 2008). This is related to the use of DSM diagnosis within the DBC, which is not a good predictor of costs (Buckingham et al. 1998). Furthermore, the difficulty of recording and distinguishing between the treatment activities and effects of care providers raises queries about professional jurisdiction. Both of these aspects, variation in treatment and in care providers, also have presented definitional struggles within and across the profession.

Firstly, though variation in the treatment of similar diagnoses is not a new feature of mental healthcare, this variation has become more visible with the introduction of DBCs. Different illnesses may be treated in similar ways such as with a similar number of hours of psychotherapy, and

AMANDA SMULLEN

some patients with the same diagnosis may require quite different medications or hours of therapy (see Kahn 2008). These therapies may be adopted for different purposes, e.g. insight about illness or overcoming anxieties, and they require different kinds of specialist skills. It remains to be seen how policy-makers and insurance companies respond to this variety since clearly the DBC systems provide informational resources for comparing and questioning medical decisions about treatments and their trajectories. In the meantime the Dutch professional association for psychiatrists has been very active in developing and emphasizing its role in initiating protocols for the treatment of illnesses (see NVVP 2009). It is unclear to what extent this is experienced as a limit to psychiatric practices.

Secondly, while the variability in psychiatric treatments may become visible in the DBC system, the actual content of that work is difficult to represent. In contrast to other medical specialists, though not all, few psychiatric activities are characterized by tangible actions such as the removal of an appendix. One exception would be the use of electroshock therapy. Different types of psychotherapy (talking), together with the prescription of medication form the centerpieces of psychiatric treatment trajectories. The knowledge involved in both kinds of work is difficult to represent and quantify within a system such as DBCS. To date, such work has only been recorded in minutes of time (DBC Onderhoud 2007). This makes it difficult, one might suggest impossible, for psychiatrists to relate their daily work – such as treating a schizophrenic – with the representation of this work in the DBC system. In addition, there have been concerns that the reliance on recording of time is likely to be manipulated by medical specialists. It should be added that there are few other medical specialties wherein talking is so prominent in the treatment of patients.

Finally, the criterion of recognizable clinical input (*medische herkenbaarheid*) is not satisfied in the activities that psychiatrists undertake. Unlike the removal of an appendix, it is not possible to make definitive assessments of the role of the medical specialist in changing the mental state of a patient. This has been one argument for not granting psychiatrists the same honorarium as other medical specialists in the Netherlands. The difficulty of satisfying clinical input relates to the range of factors that affect the way a patient responds to psychotherapy or medication. Not to mention that the brain itself is continually changing. While there are tools to make assessments of the state of a patient before and after treatment, evaluating the direct role of the medical specialist in the recovery of the patient is more difficult. Minutes of time in treatment are quickly seen as an expense, as opposed to the contribution of expertise, and it becomes easier to consider cheaper professions such as psychologists or psychiatric nurses (Castel 2008). Indeed, the use of cheaper labor is an appealing and easy alternative for the bigger mental institutions though psychiatrists in private practice have no alternatives but their own labor. While shifting jurisdictional boundaries have a long history in psychiatry, they have been stirred up by DBCS (see Abbott 1998). A recent, but unsuccessful, bid by psychologists to obtain the right to prescribe medication is illustrative of future possibilities.

Organizational settings

A final distinctive feature of the profession of psychiatry, as compared to other medical specialists, is the range of organizational settings in which psychiatrists work. This affects the (financial) interests of different psychiatrists and their capacity to negotiate in the process to design Dutch DBCS. The origins and development of the profession of psychiatry are recognized to have close links with the emergence of mental institutions, rather than simply abstract knowledge (Abbott 1988; see also Oosterhuis 2005). There are also distinctions in the working conditions of psychiatrists across institutions and how they are integrated in the management structure. For example, some psychiatrists, particularly those employed by mental institutions, are salaried employees, while others have their own businesses or work fee-for-service. Furthermore, while general hospitals maintain a tradition of separation between hospital management and the medical representatives, there is more integration between the medical professions and management in the broader mental health sector. In contrast to other medical specialists, the process to design the DBCS for mental healthcare included a large representation from mental health institutions (GGZ 2002). It would seem that their interest in maintaining salaried psychiatrists has, at least to date, defeated the desire of independent psychiatrists to obtain a honorarium in the Dutch DBCS (a court appeal is pending).

Conclusion

This chapter has sought to illustrate the way that financial instruments can create conflict within a profession, and more specifically the differentiated profession of psychiatry. Two main conclusions can be drawn from the chapter. Firstly, the basic components of the DBC system such as diagnosis, patterned treatment trajectories and visibility of medical input are problematic within the field of psychiatry. This is because diagnostic systems are not well developed and are controversial, at least among some psychiatrists. Furthermore, treatment trajectories are variable and often cannot be predicted from diagnosis, while verifying the role of the clinician is difficult. The introduction of DBCS forces attention to this professional *diversity* and creates a clear push for greater *uniformity* towards biological psychiatry. In this way, both professional autonomy as well as discretion of medical professionals (i.e. psychiatrists) are affected, not so much because professional work is increasingly super-

AMANDA SMULLEN

vised and managed, but because professional ideologies are affected and adapted. Like in the legal field (see chapter 6), an ideology of objectivity is increasingly adopted, and this is also supported by the professional groups themselves. Unlike the legal field, this generates much conflict, as psychiatric work can be framed in different ways (whereas objectivity is the hallmark of good legal practice).

Secondly, the ability of DBCs to make visible what psychiatrists actually do in treating patients is limited. Much of psychiatric work involves talk and prescribing pills and these tend to be recorded only through minutes of time or listing pharmaceuticals. This representation of psychiatric knowledge makes it difficult for the information to have meaning for the medical specialist since it gives no indication of the expertise involved in conducting psychotherapy or prescribing pills. It also makes the work of the psychiatric profession vulnerable to cheaper professional jurisdictions. Conflicts then become visible not only within the profession but *across* it. This is strengthened by the diversity of organizational settings in which psychiatrists work. They create barriers to pursuing a common professional interest and attaining the equivalent financial rewards of other specialists.

In short, far from merely making the profession of psychiatry transparent, the system of Dutch DBCs would also seem to be institutionalizing conflict and changes within the profession itself. This fits Ackroyd's emphasis (chapter 2) on the importance of existing conditions of distinctive professions. Both the autonomy and discretion of the involved professionals appears to be under fire, especially where objective biological psychiatry gains ground and stricter models for psychiatric work are adopted. At the same time, this offers chances to other (or new) professional groups to enter medical markets, or strengthen positions, something already mentioned by Newman in chapter 3. Presumed functional (policy) approaches to improve healthcare and apparent technical financing systems actually turn out to be political. They generate conflict, affect psychiatric ideologies and alter professional domains. Paradoxically, these far-reaching effects might weaken the effectiveness of reform projects.

Notes

1. See www.devrijepsyche.nl
2. Van Nierop, L. (2008). Angst voor 'depressie' op factuur; Therapeuten weigeren te declareren op manier die de pyschiatrie kapotmaakt. NRC *Handelsblad*, 18 April, p. 3.
3. See www.devrijepsyche.nl
4. Practices in psychiatry are also regulated by evidence-based research and criteria.
5. See www.devrijepsyche.nl

References

Abbott, A. (1998). *The System of Professions: An essay on the expert division of labor.* Chicago: University of Chicago Press.

Andreasen, N. (1997). What is Psychiatry? *American Journal of Psychiatry, 154*(5), 591-593.

Bal, R. (2008). *De nieuwe zichtbaarheid. Sturing in tijden van marktwerking [New Visibility. Governance in Times of Marketization].* Oratie Erasmus MC, 28 February.

Baltesen, F. (2009, 27 April). Een onbedoelde loonexplosie voor de specialist [An Unintended Wage Explosion for Medical Specialists]. *NRC Handelsblad,* p. 3.

Bruinsma, J. (2008, 18 January). Psychiaters voelen zich door minister Klink geschoffeerd [Psychiatrists feel insulted by the Minister for Healthcare]. *NRC Handelsblad,* p. 7.

Buchanan, A., & Bhugra, D. (1992). Attitudes of the Medical Profession to Psychiatry. *Acta Psychiatrica Scandinavica, 85,* 1-5.

Buckingham, B., Burgess, P., Soloman, S., Prikis, J., & Eager, K. (1998). *Developing a Casemix Classification for Mental Health Services- Summary. Mental Health Classification and Service Costs Project.* Department of Health and Family Services, Australia.

Castel, H. (2008). *DBCs in de GGZ.* Presentation at DBC user's day [DBC Onderhoud Gebruikersdag GGZ] presented June 2008.

Chilingerian, J. (2008). Origins of DRGs in the United States: A technical, political and cultural story. In J. Kimberly, G. Pouvourville & T. D'Aunno (Eds.), *The Globalization of Managerial Innovation in Health Care* (pp. 4-33). Cambridge: Cambridge University Press.

Commissie Ginjaar. (2001). *Opbouw normatief uurtarief medische specialisten [Composition of Normative Hourly Rates Medical Specialists].* Utrecht: Orde Medisch Specialisten.

Covaleski, M., Dirsmith, M., & Michelman, J. (1993). An Institutional Theory Perspective on the DRG Framework Case-mix Accounting Systems and Healthcare Organizations. *Accounting, Organizations and Society, 18*(1), 65-88.

DBC Onderhoud (2006). *De Productstructuur DBC GGZ [Product Structure DBC Mental Healthcare].* Utrecht.

DBC Onderhoud (2007). *De productstructuur DBC GGZ 2008 [Product Structure DBC Mental Healthcare 2008].* Utrecht.

DBC Onderhoud (2008). *Met DBC's op weg naar Transparantie in de zorg [Towards Transparency in Healthcare].* Utrecht.

Dent, M. (1998). Hospitals and New Ways of Organizing Work in Europe: Standardisation of Medicine in the Public Sector and the Future of Medical Autonomy. In P. Thompson & C. Warhurst (Eds.), *Workplaces of the Future* (204-224). London: Macmillan.

Duckett, S. (2008). Casemix Development and Implementation in Australia. In J. Kimberly, G. Pouvourville & T. D'Aunno (Eds.), *The Globalization of Managerial Innovation in Health Care* (pp. 231-253). Cambridge: Cambridge University Press.

English, J.T., Sharfstein, S.S., Scherl, D.J., Astrachan, B., & Muszynski, I.L. (1986). Diagnosis Related Groups and General Hospital Psychiatry: The APA study. *American Journal of Psychiatry, 143*(2), 131-139.

　　　　　　　　　　　AMANDA SMULLEN

Frisina, L., & Cacace, M. (2009). DRGs and the Professional Independence of Physicians. In A.N. Dwivedi (Ed.), *Handbook of Research on IT Management and Clinical Data Administration in Healthcare*. Hershey: IGI Global.

GGZ (2002). *Aankondigen start project Diagnoses Behandel Combinaties in de GGZ [Announcing the Start of the DBC project in Mental Healthcare]*. Project Groep GGZ Nederland.

Gijswijt-Hofstra, M., Oosterhuis, J., Vijselaar, J., & Freeman, H. (2005). *Psychiatric Cultures Compared. Psychiatry and mental healthcare in the twentieth century*. Amsterdam: Amsterdam University Press.

Helderman, J.K. (2007). *Bringing the Market Back In?* Doctoral Dissertation, Erasmus University Rotterdam.

Helderman, J.K., Schut, F.T., Van der Grinten. T.E.D., & Van de Ven, W.P.M.M. (2005). Market-orientated Healthcare Reforms and Policy learning in The Netherlands. *Journal of Health Politics, Policy and Law, 30*, February-April, 189-209.

Hines, R.D. (1988). Financial Accounting: In communicating reality we construct reality. *Accounting, Organizations and Society, 13*, 251-261.

Kahn, R. (2008). *In de spreekkamer van de psychiater [In the Psychiatrists Consulting Room]*. Amsterdam: Uitgeverij Balans.

Kandell, E. (1988). A New Intellectual Framework for Psychiatry. *American Journal of Psychiatry, 155*(4), 457-469.

Kimberly, J., Pouvourville, G., & D'Aunno, T. (2008). *The Globalization of Managerial Innovation in Healthcare*. Cambridge: Cambridge University Press.

Knapp, M., McDaid, D., Ammaddeo, F., Constantopoiulos, A., Oliveira, M.D., Salvador-Carulla, L., & Zechmeister, I. (2007). Financing Mental Healthcare in Europe. *Journal of Mental Healthcare, 16*(2), 167-180.

Krabbe-Alkemade, Y., Groot, T., & Zuurbier, J. (2008). *Case-mix Reimbursement Based upon Episodes of Care: How many DBCs are needed?* Research paper, Vrije Universiteit Amsterdam.

Lakoff, A. (2005). *Pharmaceutical Reason. Knowledge and value in global psychiatry*. Cambridge: Cambridge University Press.

Lien, L. (2003). Financial and Organizational Reforms in the Health Sector: Implications for financing and management of mental health services. *Health Policy, 63*, 73-80.

Maassen, H. (2005). Wij zijn gewone medisch specialisten [We are Ordinary Medical Specialists]. *Medisch Contact, 60*, 1068-1070.

Nederlandse Vereniging voor Psychiatrie (NNVP). (September 2007). *Kracht door kwaliteit; invloed door inhoud [Strength through Quality; Influence through Content]*. Utrecht.

NVVP (2009). Najaarscongres *Psychiatrie en kwaliteit [Autumn Conference Psychiatry and Quality]*. Fort Voordorp Groenekan, 20 November.

Oostenbrink, J.B., & Rutten, F.F. (2006). Cost Assessment and Price Setting of Inpatient Care in the Netherlands. The DBC case-mix system. *Health Care Management Science, 9*, 287-294.

Oosterhuis, H. (2005). A century of outpatient psychiatry and mental health care in the Netherlands 1900-2000. In M. Gijswijt-Hofstra, H. Oosterhuis, J. Vijselaar & H. Freeman (Eds.), *Psychiatric Cultures Compared. Psychiatry and mental health care in the twentieth century* (pp. 73-103). Amsterdam: Amsterdam University Press.

Park, D.W. (2004). The Couch and the Clinic. The cultural authority of popular psychiatry and psychoanalysis. *Cultural studies, 18*(1), 109-133.

Sanderson, H. (1993). DRGS: How well do they define hospital products in Europe? In M. Casas & M. Wiley (Eds.), *Diagnosis Related Groups in Europe* (pp. 46-60). Berlin: Springer Verlag.

Schmid, A. & Götze, R. (2009). Cross National Policy Learning in Health System Reform: The case of Diagnosis Related Groups. *International Social Security Review, 62*(4), 21-40.

Shorter, E. (1997). *A History of Psychiatry. From the era of the asylum to the age of Prozac.* John Wiley: New York.

Tielens, J. (2011, 29 July). De zomernachten van Jules Tielens. Hilversum: NCRV Radio 1.

Van Essen, A. (2009a). *Seeking a Balance?! The emergence of New Public Management in new hospital payment systems in Germany, the Netherlands and the United Kingdom.* Doctoral dissertation, Faculty of Social Science. Amsterdam: VU University.

Van Essen, A. (2009b). New Hospital Payment Systems. Comparing strategies in The Netherlands, Germany and England. *Journal of Health Organization and Management, 23*(3), 304-318.

Van Nooten, F., & Van Agthoven, M. (2006). DBC's: visies en verwachtingen van het veld [DBCS: Perspectives and Expectations in the Field]. ZM (1): 10-13.

Wetenschappelijk Bureau SP en actiegroep Zorg Geen Markt (2008). *De GGZ ontwricht: Een praktijkonderzoek naar de gevolgen van het nieuwe zorgstelsel in de geestelijke gezondheidszorg [Dislocated Mental Healthcare: A Study of the Effects of the New Healthcare System in Mental Healthcare].* The Hague.

8 Public professionals and policy alienation

Lars Tummers, Bram Steijn & Victor Bekkers

Introduction

The chapters of Van der Veen and Hupe & Van der Krogt explored professionals and professionalism in general, as well as the nature of the pressures they face. In this chapter, we explore the pressures faced by professionals when implementing public policy programs. This is relevant, as many of the pressures exerted on professionals are related to the policies that are implemented (Duyvendak et al. 2006; Freidson 2001). In terms of Newman's knowledge-power knots (chapter 3), this chapter will specifically focus on the public professional in his relationship with the government. It will also illustrate how this unilateral relationship of government and professional is complicated by influences exerted by the occupation, the organization and the public.

Many public professionals have difficulties identifying with the policies they have to implement. For instance, Bottery (1998: 143), examining the experiences of professionals with new policies in education and healthcare in Great Britain, states that 'many professionals in both of these sectors would argue that they felt the pressures of legislation designed to produce a greater degree of responsiveness to clients, and to increase competition with other institutions'. The introduction of this legislation resulted in identification problems for professionals. As one teacher states: 'The changes have been outrageous, and have produced a culture of meritocracy and high flyers, there's massive paperwork because the politicians don't believe teachers are to be trusted' (cited in Bottery 1998: 40).

Another example is the introduction of a new reimbursement policy (called Diagnosis Treatment Combinations, see also chapter 7) in Dutch mental healthcare. One large-scale survey showed that nine out of ten professionals wanted to abandon this new policy (Palm et al. 2008: 11). They could not align their professional values with the contents of the policy.

When public professionals cannot identify with the policy they have to implement, this can have serious consequences. Indeed, many scholars examining policy implementation processes state that a minimal level of identification by the implementers is a prerequisite for effective implementation (Ewalt & Jennings 2004; May & Winter, 2009; Peters & Pierre 1998; Sabatier 1986). It might also affect the quality of interactions between professionals and citizens, which may eventually influence the output legitimacy of the government (Bekkers et al. 2007).

Why do public professionals have identification problems with the policies they have to implement? Two lines of thought can be distinguished here. First, many scholars highlight the New Public Management (NPM) characteristics of new policies that pressure professionals (compare chapter 2). They note that contemporary policies focus strongly on economic values, such as efficiency and transparency. Public professionals may have difficulty in accepting the changing trade-off in values which become manifest when implementing a policy program (compare Hood 1991). Here, Emery & Giauque (2003: 475) note that 'to focus on only the economic logic of action poses problems for public agents. They have to set aside some other shared values in order to concentrate solely on "measurement management".'

However, other scholars look at other factors, thereby questioning the statement that NPM is the primary reason why public professionals experience identification problems (Exworthy & Halford 1998; Kirkpatrick et al. 2005; Leicht & Fennell 2001; Noordegraaf 2008). They point to larger forces at work. They examine developments such as the emancipation of clients, the introduction of new technologies, the demands posed by politicians and policy-makers and the influence of the media. This fits a more complicated understanding of the dynamics in and around public and professional services, as Newman stressed (chapter 3; see also Clarke & Newman's (1997) emphasis on knowledge-power knots).

In this chapter we follow this argument; we show that although NPM is indeed an important factor influencing the identification problems of public professionals, we need to consider other factors too. More specifically, one especially needs to look at the degree of professionalism of the policy implementers. In this way, this chapter has theoretical and practical value. It is theoretically important as we do not privilege but position NPM. Newman already noted that NPM cannot be held responsible for everything, but this has not yet been examined thoroughly on the level of actual policy implementation (at 'street level'), where professionals interact with citizens. It is of practical value as a lack of identification with policies might demotivate professionals and hinder high-quality case treatment.

We examine identification problems of public professionals in terms of *policy alienation*. We deal extensively with this concept in the next second section. Section 3 empirically examines the degree of policy alienation and the factors that influence it. This analysis is based on a comparative case study of Dutch insurance physicians implementing a new work disability decree (compare also the contribution of Van der Veen), and teachers implementing the so-called 'Second Phase' model in secondary education. These are interesting cases to compare, as the physicians are situated in a strong NPM-driven context, much more than teachers. We conclude the chapter by showing which factors – next to

NPM – are important for explaining the identification problems of public professionals.

Theoretical framework of policy alienation

Alienation broadly refers to a sense of social estrangement, an absence of social support or meaningful social connection. Its use in the scientific literature can be traced directly to Hegel and Marx. Sociologists, psychologists and other social scientists have used the alienation concept in various studies (for example Blauner 1964; Kanungo 1982: 19; Ramaswami et al. 1993). As a result, a number of different meanings are being attributed to the concept (Kanungo 1982: 24). In an attempt to provide clarity, Seeman clustered these meanings into five alienation dimensions (1959): powerlessness, meaninglessness, normlessness, social isolation and self-estrangement.

Many scholars used these dimensions to devise operational measures for alienation in order to examine the concept in diverse settings. Mau (1992), for example, examined four dimensions of student alienation: powerlessness, meaninglessness, normlessness, and social estrangement. Rayce et al. (2008) looked at adolescent alienation, using three of the five dimensions. Also, many scholars examined the concept of work alienation using Seeman's classification. Here, an important study is that of Blauner (1964), who devised operational measures for three dimensions: powerlessness, meaninglessness, and social isolation.

In this chapter we use the policy alienation concept, as we developed elsewhere (Tummers et al. 2009). *Policy alienation* is defined as a general cognitive state of psychological disconnection from the policy program being implemented by a public professional who regularly interacts directly with clients. Although conceptualized differently, the concept of policy alienation can be seen as a measurement of 'deprofessionalization', the concept used by Van der Veen to find out how the introduction of NPM affects professional practices.

We see policy alienation as a multidimensional concept, consisting of two crucial dimensions: powerlessness and meaninglessness (for a more elaborate explanation, see Tummers et al. 2009; Tummers, 2011).[1] Here, we build on the work of Seeman (1959) and Blauner (1964). Briefly, powerlessness is a person's lack of control over events in their life. Meaninglessness is the inability to comprehend the relationship of one's contribution to a larger purpose. Professionals can feel powerless while implementing a policy, for example when they do not have any influence on the sort, quantity and quality of sanctions and rewards they issue (Lipsky 1980). Further, it is also evident that professionals can feel that implementing a policy is meaningless, as it might not achieve any beneficial outcomes for society (Van Thiel & Leeuw 2002). To make the dimensions more specific, we distinguish between strategic, tactical and operational powerlessness, and between societal and client meaninglessness. The definitions of these sub-dimensions are shown in the table below.

Table 1 Operationalization of policy alienation: Five sub-dimensions

Sub-dimension	Definition	Example of high scores
Strategic powerlessness	The perceived influence of the professionals on decisions concerning the content of the policy, as captured in rules and regulations.	A professional feeling that the policy is drafted without the help of implementing professionals or professional associations.
Tactical powerlessness	The professionals' perceived influence on decisions concerning the way policy is implemented within their organization.	A professional stating that the managers in his organization did not consult him or his colleagues for designing the implementation process of the policy.
Operational powerlessness	The perceived degree of freedom in making choices concerning the sort, quantity and quality of sanctions and rewards when implementing the policy.	Answering 'yes' to a survey question asking whether the professional feels that his autonomy during the implementation process was lower than it should be.
Societal meaninglessness	The perception of professionals concerning the added value of the policy to socially relevant goals.	Stating in an interview that 'I agree with the policy goal of enhancing transparency, but I do not see how this policy helps in achieving this goal'.
Client meaninglessness	The professionals' perceptions of the added value of their implementing a policy for their own clients.	A professional noting that a particular policy seriously harms their clients' privacy.

Factors influencing policy alienation

Policy alienation can be influenced by several factors. Based on the literature, the use of NPM practices and the degree of professionalism seem particularly relevant. As earlier chapters already outlined, New Public Management (NPM) has become prevalent in the public sector (Pollitt & Bouckaert 2004). Hood & Peters (2004: 268) commented that NPM is a rather loose term with no two authors listing exactly the same features. Nevertheless, we will use the widely cited overview developed by Hood (1991) to distinguish various components of NPM; see table 2.

In our view, two NPM components are especially important in explaining the degree of policy alienation: the use of explicit standards and measures of performance (Component 2, referred to as 'performance management' from here on) and a greater emphasis on output controls (Component 3).

LARS TUMMERS, BRAM STEIJN & VICTOR BEKKERS

Table 2 Components of NPM *(BASED ON HOOD, 1991: 4-5)*

No.	Component
1	'Hands-on professional management' in the public sector
2	Explicit standards and measures of performance
3	Greater emphasis on output controls
4	Shift to disaggregation of units in the public sector
5	Shift to greater competition in the public sector
6	Stress on private-sector styles of management practice
7	Stress on greater discipline and parsimony in resource use

A focus on output controls often requires public agencies, managers and employees to work according to performance targets (usually quantitative). Pollitt (2003: 46) argues that this kind of performance management can 'lead to over-concentration on what is precisely quantifiable (for example costs, number of licenses issued) and an under-concentration on other aspects which are not so easily measured'. These quantifiable targets tend to focus on efficiency and results, which can take precedence over values such as equity and security. Public professionals may have difficulty accepting this changed trade-off in values, which becomes manifest when implementing a policy program (Hood 1991; Pollitt 2003). Therefore, we expect public professionals to experience greater policy meaninglessness when performance management and output controls are used in implementing policy. Further, these two NPM components can also curtail professional discretion, the reverse of operational powerlessness. Extensive performance management and output controls often could involve strict internal instructions and managers feel increasing pressure to produce results. Although Van der Veen's analysis (chapter 5) suggests otherwise, we would expect that such developments make it harder for professionals to use their discretion. In summary, public professionals will experience more policy alienation when performance management and output controls are used in implementing a policy.

Next to NPM, we expect the degree of professionalism to also influence policy alienation. An important indicator of a higher degree of professionalism is the existence of a strong professional association (Eraut 1994). We expect that this might influence the degree of policy alienation. Indeed, in the literature the relationships that develop between the professional associations and governments are considered crucial to the policy-making process (Ismaili 2006) as these professional associations can legitimate change by hosting a process of discourse through which change is debated and endorsed (Greenwood et al. 2002).

We can relate this to the policy implementation process. Here, the relationship between 'government' and professional associations is based on a principle of reciprocal return. Governments, for example, can ill-afford to develop policies that will be met with criticism from professionals. Close ties with strong professional groups are cultivated to preclude such occurrences (Smullen's example of how professional groups have been included in the development of DBCs is a good example of this). When professional associations are powerful enough, they can significantly influence policies. Following Hupe & Van der Krogt, this influence of professional associations can be seen as the result of a networking strategy to deal with pressures. However, when professional associations are not considered crucial for the implementation process, they might be by-passed by policy developers. As a result, professionals might feel powerless on a strategic level and, if so, will be alienated from the policy. Therefore, we expect that, the stronger the professional associations, the less strategic powerlessness is experienced by the implementing professional.

The status of the professional group can be considered as a second indicator of professionalism. Professions with high status are, for example, law and medicine (Eraut 1994). Other professions, such as nurses and secondary school teachers, appear to have less status (Etzioni 1969). We expect that professions with a lower status have more difficulty in retaining their discretion when implementing a policy (compare Ackroyd et al. 2007). They might not be able to 'guard' their professional discretion when implementing a policy as much as higher status professions can do. Thus, we would expect public professionals to experience less policy alienation when a) professional associations are stronger and/ or b) the status of their profession is higher.

Based on the previous exploration, we can sketch a theoretical framework about factors influencing the degree of policy alienation; see figure 1.

Figure 1 Theoretical framework: factors possibly influencing policy alienation

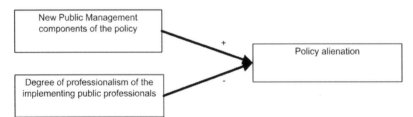

Comparative case study of insurance physicians and teachers

In our empirical research, we examined the degree of and factors affecting the policy alienation of Dutch insurance physicians implementing a new work disability decree and Dutch secondary school teachers implementing the so-called Second Phase system in secondary education. Our

LARS TUMMERS, BRAM STEIJN & VICTOR BEKKERS

goal is to determine how much policy alienation is experienced by the two professional groups and which factors influence this experienced policy alienation. By doing so, we can examine for example a) whether the teachers ('non-NPM group') really experience low policy alienation, and b) whether the factors that induce policy alienation for the physicians (NPM group) are actually related to New Public Management practices, or whether more factors are involved.

In order to get a valid insight we used data triangulation (Yin 2003: 98). Firstly, we conducted extensive document analysis, involving relevant policy documentation, large-scale surveys, professional magazines and newspaper articles. Secondly, twelve semi-structured interviews with individual insurance physicians and teachers were held, which we recorded and transcribed. Thirdly, we checked the validity of our reconstruction by discussing the preliminary results with members of the executive board of the main professional associations – two for the physicians and two for the teachers.

Background of the policies

Work disability decree

In 2004, the Dutch government drafted new, stricter rules regarding welfare benefits for citizens with work disabilities (compare also the chapter of Van der Veen). The so-called adjusted assessment decree (ASB), implemented in October 2004, changed the insurance conditions for people already receiving work disability benefits. One of its aims involved a substantial cost reduction (SWZ 2005). The ASB is implemented through programs run by the Dutch Institute for Employees' Insurance (UWV), a semi-autonomous agency of the Ministry of Social Affairs and Employment. Within the UWV, insurance physicians are involved in implementing the ASB. They 'provide social-medical evaluations with respect to the legislation concerning sick leave and employee disability' (Berendsen 2007: 225).

Second Phase system

In 1998, the Second Phase was implemented in the upper levels of Dutch secondary education. The Second Phase consisted of three elements (Van Veen 2003: 87):
1. The implementation of a 'constructivist' view on teaching and learning, called the Study House.
2. The use of student study profiles, together with new subjects.
3. More autonomy for schools.

The first element needs clarification, as it implies a totally different view on the educational process to that used earlier. Most teachers had a 'behavioristic' training, which emphasizes the process of knowledge transmission and the expert role of the teacher. In contrast, the 'constructivist' view concentrates on the process of learning and the role of the student. Learning is assumed to be an active process of construction, and knowledge is the accumulation of information, as opposed to passive assimilation. Practical implications are for example fewer 'traditional classes': one teacher explaining the material to 30 students at once. Instead, the students learn the material more independently and in small groups, the teacher acting as a facilitator of this process.

Policy powerlessness

Powerlessness refers to the influence (or rather lack of) that public professionals have to shape the policy program at different policy levels. Have insurance physicians and teachers experienced powerlessness and, if so, which factors influenced this?

With respect to powerlessness at the *strategic level*, we have found hardly any evidence that the insurance physicians were able to influence the shaping of the policy. To do so, it would have been necessary to mobilize their professional associations and, although they tried, they did not see any results (uwv 2005: 4). The main professional associations of the physicians, the nvvg and the uwva, did not become involved in the political debate concerning the drafting of the new rules. As a result, many physicians became frustrated with the lack of influence of their professional associations in shaping the asb, and this contributed to feelings of powerlessness.

The strategic powerlessness of teachers also seems to be high. Teachers felt that the implementation was done in a top-down way, without consulting them[2] (Prick 2006). The experiences of the interviewed teachers also showed this. One stated: 'What irritated me enormously was that the Second Phase was presented like: Guys, this is it, this is an important improvement for education. In my view, the knowledge and experience of teachers were not taken into account.' If teachers want to influence the shaping of a policy, they have to do so through their associations and labor unions. The professional associations of the teachers are often subject-based. They did not have a lot of influence, which was mainly due to their lack of collaboration (Parliamentary Commission Education Reforms 2008a: 61, 69, 106). The labor unions of the teachers also did not have a lot of influence on the shaping of the Second Phase (Parliamentary Commission Education Reforms 2008b: 52). This lack of influence of the professional associations and labor unions increased the strategic powerlessness felt by many teachers. Indeed, this problem was acknowledged by a board member of one of the main professional associations. He stated that it was indeed true that the profes-

LARS TUMMERS, BRAM STEIJN & VICTOR BEKKERS

sional associations are less and less able to influence the political debate, also because of declining membership. Further, particularities of the case decreased the power of the teachers to influence the policy. Here, one can consider the development of a steering committee – headed by the State Secretary – without members of the professional associations and the continuous stress on the 'political primacy' of the Minister of Education.

Tactical powerlessness refers to the perceived influence of the professionals on decisions concerning the way the policy is implemented within their organization. For the physicians, the reorganization that created the uwv was a factor that negatively affected their position as professionals since they could no longer effectively influence decisions concerning the way the policy was implemented. The uwv was established in 2002 through a merger of six organizations implementing different social security programs in order to create a 'lean' and more integrated organization. In this merger we can clearly recognize elements of NPM as the relationship between the newly formed uwv and the Ministry is based on a contract form of governance, in which results and costs play an important role. The results orientation is a concretization of the third NPM component – emphasis on output controls. The contract-based form of governance places the uwv 'at arms length' (Component 4). Finally, the focus on cost reduction, through downsizing, resembles the seventh component – stress on greater discipline in resource use.

Following this reorganization, uwv professionals are in a weak position. An interviewed physician stated: 'We could not influence the policy very much. That is clear. The uwv is a top-down administrative organization focused on administrative processes. The professionals re-examining the clients are not the priority of the uwv. We were not consulted about the implementation conditions regarding the ASB.'

Contrary to the physicians, the teachers did not seem to experience a high level of tactical powerlessness. Whereas physicians felt that they operated in a very hierarchic organization, many teachers experienced a more egalitarian structure. As one interviewed teacher put it: 'I believe that the position of the teacher is very strong [in our school]. When you are a school manager you know that it will not work if you oblige teachers to do something they do not believe in.' Many teachers perceived they could influence the way the Second Phase was concretized in their schools. Kips (2003: 48) found, based on a survey of 142 teachers that 45% did (fully) agree with the statement 'I have enough opportunities to influence the way the Study House was implemented in my school', against 28.4% who (fully) disagreed.

But in some schools, managers were dominant in implementing the Second Phase. Prick (2006: 119) states that in these schools 'school management dictates how the Study House has to be modelled', thereby increasing the degree of tactical powerlessness experienced by teachers. Further, not all teachers were taken into account when discussing implementation plans. Many teachers had only an indirect influence, as they did not participate in the working groups that were established at their schools to implement the Second Phase.

At the operational level, many physicians perceived that their level of discretion – after the introduction of the ASB – had decreased: 'physicians had the feeling that they had less influence on their job and could use their own professional standards less' (Kammer 2005). A survey by the De Boer & Steenbeek (2005) drew a similar conclusion: 63% of the respondents answered 'yes' to the question of whether they felt their professional autonomy was lower than it should be. Important reasons given were the strict internal UWV performance criteria plus the managerial focus on results, both associated with the ASB. On the other hand, a number of physicians stated that they still had considerable discretion, but that they have to provide a more thorough argument for their decisions, which takes more time. As one physician put it during an interview, he could still make decisions 'in all freedom'. Van der Veen, in his chapter, concludes that discretion seems not be affected by the ASB. Based on our interviews and also on a survey of De Boer & Steenbeek (2005), we have a slightly different view: in general, physicians experienced a somewhat lower level of discretion.

The introduction of New Public Management is relevant for the discretion physicians experience. The UWV had to implement the ASB and, in a short period of time, more than 325,000 people had to be re-examined. To achieve this, the UWV focused primarily on the number of re-examinations completed, thereby using strict performance criteria and a focus on output controls. Extensive performance management often involves strict internal instructions and managers feel increasingly pressured to produce results. Such developments made it harder for physicians to use their own discretion (De Boer & Steenbeek 2005).

Many teachers also experienced a somewhat lower level of discretion. Kips (2003: 54) notes that 75% of the Second Phase teachers agreed with the statement 'because of the introduction of the Second Phase it became more difficult to deviate from the official program'. An important reason for this decreased discretion was, along with the policy content, the way management introduced the Study House in the schools. Management more or less *obliged* teachers to construct the schedule of the course material before the start of the school year. In this way, the teachers were relatively bound to this schedule, making it more difficult to exercise discretion.

When we compare the two cases, it seems that the discretion of the teachers declined somewhat more than physicians' discretion. The physicians' discretion in their core task – providing social-medical evaluations – did not change substantially (Bannink et al. 2006). For the teachers, their discretion over actual work content did change significantly. This can be explained by the fact that the professional status of physicians is much stronger than the professional status of the teachers. Professional associations of teachers are now trying to tackle this issue by developing a 'professional statute', in which 'professional autonomy' figures prominently.

Policy meaninglessness

Meaninglessness refers to the professionals' perceptions regarding the policy's contribution to a larger purpose. This can be linked to societal and client levels.

Do the physicians see the policy goals of the ASB as meaningless? In the case of the ASB, the official goal is to increase the participation in work of the disabled by focusing on a person's potential rather than his limitations (SWZ 2005). However, in the eyes of many, the economic goal of the ASB seems to be in fact the most important element. As one physician put it, 'I see it more as a cost savings policy than as a method to get people in work.' Here, NPM-based considerations seem to dominate in the trade-off of values in the ASB implementation, leading to a shift in value orientation – a move not welcomed by a number of physicians (De Boer & Steenbeek 2005). This can be seen as the operationalization of the seventh component of NPM: a greater discipline in resource use.

Another factor contributing to societal meaninglessness, as witnessed by our respondents, was the multitude of policy changes regarding work disability. Between 2002 and 2006, major policy changes included the 'Gatekeeper Improvement Act', the ASB and a new Law on work and income. Before physicians were able to work out what one policy meant for their work, there was already another policy to implement. Such a situation contributes to feelings of societal meaninglessness. As one physician put it: 'Lately there have been so many changes. [...] It happens all the time. I do not feel "connected" with politicians. Often they propose things which are not well thought out, and which have to be implemented right away.'

One aspect of the ASB, which many physicians did agree with, was the fact that almost everyone receiving a work disability benefit had to be re-examined. Many claimants who were re-examined had not been examined for years, and so it became possible to assess changes in their condition, as well as to remedy any previous judgmental errors.

Contrary to the physicians, many teachers experienced low societal meaninglessness. The official objectives of the Second Phase are to increase the quality of education in secondary schools and to improve the connection with higher education. Obviously, almost all teachers experienced these goals as laudable. Kips (2003: 49) states that only 10% disagrees with the goals of the policy. Again, another factor influencing societal meaninglessness was the number of policy changes. Like with the physicians, this factor contributed positively to societal meaninglessness (NRC 2007; Parliamentary Commission Education Reforms 2008b: 648;

Prick 2006), although the interviewed teachers experienced this factor less prominently than did the interviewed physicians.

At the *client level*, meaninglessness refers to the perception of the professionals concerning the added value of their own implementation of the policy.

Between physicians, significant differences existed in how they experienced client meaninglessness. Of the 230,000 clients they re-assessed, 90,000 saw their benefits lost or reduced. One and a half years after re-examination, 52% of them still had not found a job (Van der Burg & Deursen 2008: 80). A number of physicians identified strongly with this unfortunate group. They felt that they did not help them, experiencing a high degree of client meaninglessness (De Boer & Steenbeek 2005; LVA 2006). As one commented (cited in Kammer & Jorritsma 2005): 'I cannot put my signature to a medical evaluation which inevitably results in state assistance for the person [...] someone who is unemployed for ten years, and searching for a job again, that is impossible.'

However, not all shared this view. Numerous respondents stressed that, especially for younger claimants, it could be worthwhile to decrease work-disability benefits. In fact, in their view, being labeled as work-disabled for a very long time is detrimental to people's health. In this way, they identified more with the policy program and less with the immediate wishes and concerns of clients.

Examining this, we can see that the professional orientation of the physicians influenced the experienced meaninglessness. Some interviewed physicians differentiated between so-called 'hard' and 'soft' physicians. Hard physicians believe that lowering a benefit can induce people to search for a job. When they ultimately do so, this is beneficial for them. Softer physicians do not believe that lowering a benefit will result in a client becoming more active. It is ultimately harmful for their clients as their benefits are reduced. Seen in this way, the *professional orientation* influences the experienced meaningfulness of the ASB policy. In terms of Hupe & Van der Krogt, one can state that the 'hard' physicians have a better coping strategy to deal with the pressures they experience. Given their personal values, it is more difficult for 'soft' physicians to cope with (policy) pressures.

The professional orientation of the teachers also seemed to influence their experienced client meaninglessness. Van Veen (2003: 103) discerns between two types of teachers. On the one hand you have teachers who are 'student-oriented' and consider personal and moral development to be among the goals of education. On the other hand there are 'content-oriented' teachers, who consider qualification to be more or less the only goal of education. Looking at the two types of teachers, the Second Phase constructivist orientation fits better with the student-oriented teachers. As a result, they can cope better with the Second Phase as they perceive it as more meaningful for their students (Kips 2003: 50-51; Van Veen 2003: 127). This constructivist view resulted in, among other things, the fact that students had to work more independently. In many schools, management framed this by diminishing the number of hours teachers had to teach per class. Many content-oriented teachers experienced this situation as detrimental for the students (Kips 2003: 54; Nierop 2004: 24; Parliamentary Commission Education Reforms 2008b: 139). More student-centered teachers, however, felt that their implementation of the Second Phase was very meaningful (Van Veen 2003: 60). As one teacher put it: 'Because of the Second Phase, I feel that I am better able to help the students. Before, it was only old-fashioned teaching. Then you do not have that many opportunities to really help them. In that way, I think it is better now.'

Comparative analysis

Our empirical goal was to determine how much policy alienation is experienced by the two professional groups and which factors influence this experienced policy alienation. We can now answer these questions. Table 3 presents the degree of policy alienation as experienced by physicians and teachers. Scoring high on a sub-dimension means that, on average, the professionals experienced high pressures on this dimension. To obtain an overall policy alienation score, we allot 2 points for scoring high on a sub-dimension, 1 for scoring medium and 0 for scoring low. We add these to obtain a score for overall policy alienation, ranging from 0 (very low policy alienation) to 10 (very high policy alienation). This gives us a rough estimate of the policy alienation experienced by the different professional groups.

Table 3 Comparing the degree of policy alienation felt by insurance physicians and teachers

	Strategic powerlessness	Tactical powerlessness	Operational powerlessness	Societal meaninglessness	Client meaninglessness	**Degree of policy alienation**
Insurance physicians	High (2)	High (2)	Medium (1)	Medium (1)	Medium (1): Differs between 'hard' and 'soft' physicians	**7**
Teachers	High (2)	Low (0)	High (2)	Low (0)	Medium (1): Differs between 'content-oriented' and 'student-oriented' teachers	**5**

Two main observations can be made. First, we see that both groups experience a certain level of policy alienation. The teachers experience moderate policy alienation (a score of 5), although they do not operate in a NPM context, but they seem to experience less policy alienation than the insurance physicians (who score 7). Now that we have established an estimate of the degree of policy alienation experienced, we can determine which factors induce this. Our comparative case study provided us with a number of factors, which are summarized in figure 2.

Figure 2 Main factors influencing the degree of policy alienation felt by teachers and physicians

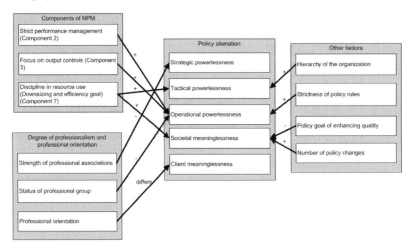

Many factors influence the degree of policy alienation. We clustered these variables into three categories: New Public Management (mainly influential for the physicians), degree of professionalism and professional orientation (influential for both cases) and other factors.

The degree of strategic powerlessness experienced is mainly influenced by the strength of the *professional associations*. In both cases, these professional associations were classified by respondents as not strong enough to substantially influence the political debate. This led to a high feeling of strategic powerlessness for both insurance physicians and teachers. Further, for the physicians, as a result of the constant downsizing and the hierarchical nature of the UWV, it appears that they did not experience sufficient influence on a tactical level. Teachers, in contrast, experienced a more egalitarian structure, thereby experiencing significantly less tactical powerlessness. Operational powerlessness, or the discretion open to professionals, seemed to be influenced by numerous factors. For the physicians, we see that two components of New Public Management influence their perceived discretion: strict performance measurement and a focus on output controls. However, their high status as physicians made it possible for them to still use some discretion in their core task: providing social-medical evaluations. The discretion open to the teachers, however, was reduced somewhat more, as a) the strictness of the policy rules substantially reduced their discretion and b) their professional status was not legitimized enough for them to be able to counter the attack on their discretion.

With respect to societal meaninglessness, we see that the NPM goal of cost reduction of the ASB led to a shift in value orientation, which was not welcomed by many physicians. The re-examination goal seemed to be more appreciated. For the teachers, the Second Phase goal of enhancing educational quality was obviously appreciated. As a result, they experienced low societal meaninglessness. Looking at client meaninglessness, we see that this sub-dimension is particularly dependent on the professional orientation of the implementer. For instance, teachers who are more student-oriented experience less client meaninglessness.

Conclusion

In this chapter, we examined the pressures professionals face while implementing public policies. Based on the policy alienation framework and the empirical results, a number of conclusions can be drawn, which can add to the debate of public professionals in service delivery.

Firstly, we see that the introduction of NPM elements is indeed an important factor for the experiences of professionals with the policy they have to implement. However, other factors are relevant as well. We found that both insurance physicians and teachers experience a certain degree of policy alienation. This is important, as the teachers did not operate in a NPM context. Further, in the case of the physicians, factors not related to NPM influenced their degree of policy alienation. Clearly, New Public Management is not the only factor pressuring professionals, as has been claimed by some authors. Our analysis shows that more forces are active, which necessitates a broader view when examining pressured professionals.

Being more specific, the degree of professionalism is an important factor influencing the pressured experienced by professionals. A first indicator of this is the strength of the professional associations. Professional associations can serve the role of advocate for the profession, and thus reduce the level of policy alienation. This is in accordance with possible effects of 'networking' as a mode of dealing with pressures as outlined by Hupe & Van der Krogt.

Further, the status of the professional group is important in explaining the pressures professionals face. The physicians proved more capable of maintaining discretion in their core task than did the teachers. We are thus able to amend the conclusion of Van der Veen that recent changes seem to affect autonomy, but not the discretion of organizational professionals. According to our analysis, professional status is here an important mediating factor. It could be that 'semi-professionals', such as teachers, nurses, labor experts and home care workers, are experiencing increasing pressures: their professional status does not guard them against demands posed by new policies (see also Hayes 2001). This finding both concurs with as well as contradicts a basic observation in Ackroyd's chapter 2. It concurs with it, as it underlines his point that the existing condition of a profession affects the way its members perceive the introduction of new policies. It contradicts his view that the more professionalized members perceive these policies as a threat.

Lastly, we noted that the professional orientation of the implementers strongly influenced the pressures they experienced. Not all professionals experience the policy in the same way. Something like this is already mentioned in the contributions of Newman and Hupe & Van der Krogt, such as the importance of 'coping' as a way of dealing with pressures. Our analysis provides further empirical illustration for the importance of individual characteristics or values of professionals with respect to their views upon governmental policies. It appears that the degree of 'professional orientation/policy fit' seems to influence the pressures experienced by individual professionals, similar to the well-known person-organization fit (Kristof 1996). This might influence the success of the implementation of a policy (Van Veen et al. 2001: 191).

In summary, our chapter shows that although New Public Management is indeed an important factor influencing the identification problems of public professionals implementing public policies, we need to consider other factors too. The degree of professionalism, both in terms of status and professional association, is an important factor which should be taken into account. Further research could benefit by applying this in a more rigorous way, to add to the knowledge of the experiences of varying groups of professionals in the public sector.

Notes

1. In Tummers et al. (2009) we also considered role conflicts as a dimension of policy alienation. Here, we do not opt for this as in alienation literature; role conflicts are generally not considered a dimension of alienation. Secondly, during empirical research for this article we found that the degree of role conflicts is more an effect of policy alienation, than a dimension of policy alienation.
2. NRC (2007, October 10). Havo 'voor dummies'; de geschiedenis van de tweede fase. NRC Handelsblad, pp. 10.

References

Ackroyd, S., Kirkpatrick, I., & Walker, R.M. (2007). Public Management Reform in the UK and its Consequences for Professional Organization: A comparative analysis. Public Administration, 85(1), 9-26.

Bannink, D., Lettinga, B., & Heyse, L. (2006). NPM, bureaucratisering en de in-vloed op de professie [NPM, Bureaucratization and the Impact on the Profes-sion]. *B en M, 33*(3), 159-174.

Bekkers, V.J.J.M., Edwards, A., Fenger, M., & Dijkstra, G. (2007). *Governance and the Democratic Deficit: Assessing the legitimacy of governance practices.* Alder-shot: Ashgate.

Berendsen, L. (2007). *Bureaucratische drama's: Publieke managers in verhouding tot verzekeringsartsen [Bureaucratic Dramas: Public Managers in Relation to Insur-ance Doctors].* (Ph.D thesis, Tilburg University).

Blauner, R. (1964). *Alienation and Freedom.* Chicago: University of Chicago Press.

Bottery, M. (1998). *Professionals and Policy: Management strategy in a competitive world.* London: Routledge.

Bucher, R., & Stelling, J. (1969). Characteristics of Professional Organizations. *Journal of Health and Social Behavior, 10*(1), 3-15.

Clarke, J., & Newman, J. (1997). *The Managerial State: Power, politics and ideology in the remaking of social welfare.* London: Sage.

De Boer, W., & Steenbeek, R. (2005). *Probleemsituaties en dilemma's in de verzeker-ingsgeneeskunde [Problem Situations and Dilemmas in Insurance Medicine].* NVVG.

Duyvendak, J.W., Knijn, T., & Kremer, M. (Eds.) (2006). *Policy, People, and the New Professional: De-professionalisation and re-professionalisation in care and wel-fare.* Amsterdam: Amsterdam University Press.

Emery, Y., & Giauque, D. (2003). Emergence of Contradictory Injunctions in Swiss NPM Projects. *International Journal of Public Sector Management, 16*(6), 468-481.

Eraut, M. (1994). *Developing Professional Knowledge and Competence.* London: Routledge.

Etzioni, A. (1969). *The Semi-professions and their Organization: Teachers, nurses, social workers.* New York: Free Press.

Ewalt, J.A.G., & Jennings, E.T. (2004). Administration, Governance, and Policy Tools in Welfare Policy Implementation. *Public Administration Review, 64*(4), 449-462.

Exworthy, M., & Halford, S. (Eds.) (1998). *Professionals and the New Managerial-ism in the Public Sector.* Maidenhead, UK: Open University Press.

Freidson, E. (2001). *Professionalism: The third logic.* Cambridge: Cambridge Uni-versity Press.

Greenwood, R., Suddaby, R., & Hinings, C.R. (2002). Theorizing Change: The role of professional associations in the transformation of institutionalized fields. *The Academy of Management Journal, 45*(1), 58-80.

Hayes, D. (2001). Professional Status and an Emerging Culture of Conformity amongst Teachers in England. *Education, 29*(1), 43-49.

Hood, C. (1991). A Public Management for all Seasons. *Public Administration, 19* (1), 3-19.

Hood, C., & Peters, G. (2004). The Middle Aging of New Public Management: Into the age of paradox? *Journal of Public Administration Research and Theory, 14*(3), 267-282.

Ismaili, K. (2006). Contextualizing the Criminal Justice Policy-Making Process. *Criminal Justice Policy Review, 17*(3), 255-269.

Kammer, C. (2005, November 3). *De Geus ziet nog steeds geen crisis bij UWV [Minis-ter of Social Affairs Still Doesn't See Crisis at UWV].* NRC Handelsblad, pp. 3.

Kammer, C., & Jorritsma, E. (2005, November 5). *Gefeliciteerd! U kunt aan het werk; keuringsartsen onder druk bij de herkeuring van WAO-ers [Congratulations! You can go to work; Insurance Doctors under Pressure].* NRC Handelsblad, pp. 3.

Kanungo, R.N. (1982). *Work alienation: An integrative approach.* New York: Praeger Publishers.

Kips, M. (2003). *Van taakoverdracht naar procesbegeleiding [From Task Transfer to Process Guidance].* Rotterdam: Erasmus University Rotterdam.

Kirkpatrick, I., Ackroyd, S., & Walker, R. (2005). *The New Managerialism and Public Service Professions.* New York: Palgrave MacMillan.

Kristof, A.L. (1996). Person-Organization Fit: An integrative review of its conceptualizations, measurement, and implications. *Personnel Psychology, 49*(1), 1-49.

Leicht, K.T., & Fennell, M.L. (2001). *Professional Work: A sociological approach.* Oxford: Blackwell Publishers.

Lipsky, M. (1980). *Street-level Bureaucracy.* New York: Russell Sage Foundation.

LVA (2006). *We zijn gedwongen strenger te keuren [We are forced to Re-examine more Strictly].* Digitale Nieuwsbrief LVA, 44(December 2006), 2-6.

Mau, R.Y. (1992). The Validity and Devolution of a Concept: Student alienation. *Adolescence, 27*(107), 731-741.

May, P.J., & Winter, S.C. (2009). Politicians, Managers, and Street-Level Bureaucrats: Influences on policy implementation. *Journal of Public Administration Research and Theory, 19*(3), 453.

Nierop, D. (2004). *Geen tijd voor het studiehuis [No Time for the Second Phase].* Utrecht/Den Bosch: APS.

Noordegraaf, M. (2008). *Professioneel bestuur.* The Hague: Lemma.

Palm, I., Leffers, F., Emons, T., Van Egmond, V., & Zeegers, S. (2008). *De GGZ ontwricht: Een praktijkonderzoek naar de gevolgen van het nieuwe zorgstelsel in de geestelijke gezondheidszorg [Dislocated Mental Healthcare: A Study of the Effects of the New Healthcare System in Mental Healthcare].* Den Haag: SP.

Parliamentary Commission Education Reforms. (2008a). *Interviews tijd voor onderwijs [Interviews Time for Education].* 31007(10).

Parliamentary Commission Education Reforms. (2008b). *Tijd voor onderwijs [Time for Education].* 31007(6).

Peters, B.G., & Pierre, J. (1998). Governance without Government? Rethinking public administration. *Journal of Public Administration Research and Theory, 8* (2), 223-243.

Pollitt, C. (2003). *The Essential Public Manager.* Maidenhead: Open University Press.

Pollitt, C., & Bouckaert, G. (2004). *Public Management Reform. A comparative analysis.* Oxford: Oxford University Press.

Prick, L. (2006). *Drammen, dreigen, draaien [Resisting, Threatening, Turning].* Alphen aan den Rijn: Haasbeek.

Ramaswami, S.N., Agarwal, S., & Bhargava, M. (1993). Work Alienation of Marketing Employees, Influence of Task, Supervisory, and Organizational Structure Factors. *Journal of the Academy of Marketing Review, 21*(3), 179-193.

Rayce, S.L.B., Holstein, B.E., & Kreiner, S. (2008). Aspects of Alienation and Symptom Load among Adolescents. *The European Journal of Public Health, 19* (1), 79-84.

Rosner, M., & Putterman, L. (1991). Factors behind the Supply and Demand for less Alienating Work, and some International Illustrations. *Journal of Economic Studies, 18*(1), 18-41.

Sabatier, P.A. (1986). What Can We Learn from Implementation Research? In F. X. Kaufmann, G. Majone & V. Ostrom (Eds.), *Guidance, Control and Evaluation in the Public Sector* (pp. 313-325). Berlin: De Gruyter.

Seeman, M. (1959). On the Meaning of Alienation. *American Sociological Review, 24*(6), 783-791.

swz (2005). Nieuwe wet werk en inkomen naar arbeidsvermogen per 1 januari 2006 ingevoerd [New Law Work and Income 2006]. swz.

Tummers, L.G. (2011). Explaining the Willingness of Public Professionals to Implement New Policies: A policy alienation framework. *International Review of Administrative Sciences, 77*(3), 555-581.

Tummers, L.G., Bekkers, V.J.J.M., & Steijn, A.J. (2009). Policy Alienation of Public Professionals: Application in a new public management context. *Public Management Review, 11*(5), 685-706.

uwv (2005). *Het woord is aan de professionals [It is up to Professionals]*. Amsterdam: uwv.

Van der Burg, C.L., & Deursen, C.G.L. (2008). *Eindrapportage herbeoordeeld... en dan? [Re-examined End report ... What next?]*. Leiden: Astri.

Van Thiel, S., & Leeuw, F.L. (2002). The Performance Paradox in the Public Sector. *Public Performance and Management Review, 25*(3), 267-281.

Van Veen, K. (2003). *Teacher's Emotions in a Context of Reforms*. Nijmegen: Radboud University.

Van Veen, K., Sleegers, P., Bergen, T., & Klaassen, C. (2001). Professional Orientations of Secondary School Teachers towards their Work. *Teaching and Teacher Education, 17*(2), 175-194.

Yin, R.K. (2003). *Case Study Research: Design and methods* (3rd ed.). Thousand Oaks, CA: Sage.

9 Loyalties of public sector professionals

Gjalt de Graaf & Zeger van der Wal

Introduction

Hupe & Van der Krogt discerned three different modes of dealing with pressures available to professionals: coping, networking and activism. In the preceding chapter Tummers, Steijn & Bekkers showed that certain types of professionals differed in their coping strategies, backed by their professional orientation.

In this chapter we will elaborate on this. We will describe how public sector professionals – street-level professionals, to be more precise, who possess ample discretionary powers – deal with clashes and tensions between values, interests, and loyalties. They face multiple work influences, which cannot be respected all at once. For public sector professionals, such tensions are part of their daily lives. On a daily basis, they have to relate to various objects of loyalty, often contradictory. Besides the clients they interact with daily, they can be loyal to their own moral conscience, their organization, managers, political masters, society, private life, and so on (e.g. Bovens 1998; 't Hart & Wille 2002, 2006). Somehow tensions between the interests of all these possible objects of loyalties must be tractable (De Graaf 2005). But if the interests conflict, whose are considered more or most important?

Arguably, public professionals experience more difficulties when prioritizing objects of loyalty than a few decades ago. The literature on political-administrative relations and public management shows that the ways in which street-level professionals interact with their political and external environments are subject to ever changing dynamics (see Noordegraaf 2008; 't Hart & Wille 2006). Among these are shifts in citizen expectations towards public services (Noordegraaf 2008), the politicization of civil service positions and appointments (Lee & Raadschelders 2008) and increasing attention to integrity and accountability of the public service (Dobel 2005). These dynamics have been fuelled by governance developments such as increasing policy co-production across organizations and sectors, and the rise of networks (see also Newman's contribution) in addition to a variety of public sector management reforms including NPM. They make it more complex for public administrators to relate to one single stakeholder and may result in increasing tensions between different objects of their loyalties.

The situation used to be clear, at least in terms of functional and structural separation between tasks, roles and values expected from public professionals and their various 'masters', predominantly the politicians they were supposed to serve. The classical 'politics-administration dichotomy' prescribes that the function of politics is to make policy, or more precisely, 'setting the task for administration' (Wilson 1887: 210). The function of public administration, then, is 'neutral policy implementation' (Demir 2009: 877) or as Goodnow (1900: 23) stated more explicitly, 'execution of the state will.' Given some of the developments sketched above, the position that the modern civil servant is still the distant, politically neutral figure he used to be is not widely held anymore (Noordegraaf 2004; Peters & Pierre 2001).

It should be noted that there are differences between various types of public administrators. Senior civil servants or 'public managers' (O'Flynn 2009) are increasingly recognized as active and motivating agents, rather than actors that passively execute the will of their political masters (2009: 2). Street-level bureaucrats in the lower administrative echelons might still be considered mainly implementers and executors of grand plans formulated by politicians. However, the combination of changes implies that their moral obligation of 'obedience to the mandates of law and policy mediated by the elected and appointed officials of democratic regimes' (Dobel 2005: 159) might no longer prevail in every situation. Again, rather than just being actors that execute policies with adherence to classical Weberian values such as lawfulness, neutrality and impartiality, public sector professionals are increasingly seen as 'co-creators of public value'.

Where do the loyalties of public professionals lie?

Even before 'the public manager' emerged as such, the classically neutral, almost amoral notion of the civil servant made various scholars criticize the ethical implications of the dichotomous view (Demir 2009: 877). For instance, Adams & Balfour (1998), taking the seminal work of Arendt (1963) as a starting point, and Denhardt (1989) have argued that the idea of a strict separation of policy formulation and implementation seemed to strip public administrators of their moral responsibilities. Arguably, the strict dichotomy has been a problematic concept from the start and loyalties of civil servants have always been perceived of as being more differentiated than just obedience to politicians (Aberbach et al. 1981; Putnam 1976).

However, we argue here that the recent developments described above – increased pressures not only from political masters but also from new types of managers, clients, media and society in general – result in more difficulties for public street-level professionals in deciding to what and to whom their loyalties should be directed. What do these developments mean for the loyalty conceptions of public administrators, in this case street-level workers? In this chapter we analyze these conceptions empirically by studying different types of street-level public sector professionals in Dutch municipalities, using Q-methodology. After identifying the most commonly recognized tensions and pressures in the literature, drawing upon earlier chapters in this volume (in particular the one of Hupe & van der Krogt), we describe the different ways in which they deal with conflicting loyalties. The main research question of this chapter is: *Where do the loyalties of street-level public professionals lie?* Our results reveal five conceptions of loyalty among street-level bureaucrats. These conceptions matter because they are not merely ideational; the attitudes of public administrators directly influence and guide behavior, mostly by prioritizing signals, issues, and meetings (cf. Fletcher 1993). In other words, public professionals' loyalty conceptualizations are important because they are indicative of their moral and decision-making behavior (De Graaf 2005). Furthermore, having different conceptions means having different loyalty dilemmas and conflicts; the perception of loyalty will determine the type of loyalty conflicts experienced. The chapter ends with a discussion of the results in light of the central theme of this volume; that is, public professionals' pressures from different interests, masters, and organizations, and how they deal with the resulting loyalty conflicts.

Public professionals under pressure from different directions

Although pressured professionals are not a novel phenomenon, those within the public sector – particularly between professionals and managers – have received enormous attention in recent years from both popular and scholarly media (e.g. Jansen et al. 2009; Noordegraaf 2008; Van der Wal et al. 2007; Weggeman 2008). The general sentiment seems to be that nowadays managerial rather than political masters are responsible for restraining professionals' discretionary powers. Whereas scholars differ substantively in their views with regard to whether the management side is to blame for the alleged clashes and increased pressure on professionals (e.g. as expressed in the contrasting views of Verbrugge (2005) and Noordegraaf (2008)), a broad consensus is that public professionals occupy a difficult position in modern public sector environments.

A specific complaint from professionals is that they feel increasingly like bureaucrats and technocrats at arm's length from their managerial masters rather than professionals in the classical sense. Although they may not have lost much formal autonomy and status, the rise of different forms of managerialism and the 'proofs of performance' many professionals are subjected to, have led to new sorts of pressures and loyalty conflicts (see Hupe & van der Krogt). Public professionals today have to prove their performances to managers and politicians, serve their clients and stakeholders to the best of their abilities, respect the values of the public interest, *and* adhere to their own professional values, norms, and standards. Which pressure – that is, which object of loyalty – is addressed first in complex situations?

Public professionals are confronted with various pressures within various venues. Hupe & van der Krogt (chapter 4) distinguish between the following:

- *Accountability-regime pressure.* Professionals have to deal with a) accountability to the profession, b) professional accountability towards peers, c) participatory accountability towards clients, and d) public-administrative accountability towards the law, political authorities, and public managers (Hupe & Hill 2007: 289-291).
- *Rule pressure.* Increased demand and scarce resources urge professionals to work both more efficiently and transparently, resulting in more time spent justifying their work, and possibly leading to spiraling performance measures and account-giving (Tonkens 2008).
- *Societal pressure.* Rising expectations (increased demand for value-for-money and proven quality from citizens acting as semi-experts and co-producers) coincide with the diminished expertise-based authority of professionals.
- *Vocational pressure.* 'Good practice' and enhanced specialization have in many professions placed quality and quality control outside the direct scope of the profession itself, and ongoing specialization leads to complex interrelations between super specialists.

Such pressures, and especially the way public professionals deal with them, strongly influence loyalties and values just as they, in turn, strongly influence pressures and conflicts. The pressures identified above show many similarities to Petter's (2005) responsibilities of administrators' loyalties (table 1).

How public professionals deal with tensions and pressures

Inspired by the work of Lipsky (1980) and others, Hupe & van der Krogt distinguish between three modes of dealing with work pressures: coping, networking, and activism. Within the context of this chapter, the first mode merits special attention. *Coping* means that a professional accepts existing work pressures as given, and tries to make the best of his or her job in circumstances that are considered difficult or even impossible to change. Lipsky (1980) has famously described coping in the work of street-level bureaucrats, who operate in an environment where the demand for services almost by definition exceeds what they are able to supply (resulting in all sorts of pressures, as described above). Whereas Lipsky explores 'patterns of practice' in how individuals use coping strategies, we focus on the specific loyalties professionals are expected to adhere to (it follows that adhering to certain objects of loyalty could also result in networking or even activism). While these are obviously related to strategies to adhere to a specific loyalty or group of loyalties, our interest lies with the final phase in the professional's deliberation: the choice for a specific object of loyalty (e.g. the direct boss, the client) and not another (e.g. the peer group, the public interest).

In the next sections we observe how street-level public professionals cope with different pressures and tensions, and how they choose between the various objects of loyalty before them: colleagues, the public good, their consciences, their organizations, the law, their organizations' clients, and elected officials.

Research methodology: Q

There are various ways to empirically study where the loyalties of public administrators lie. Q-methodology was deemed most suitable here because its results are clusters that are functional rather than logical (see De Graaf 2011). In other words, rather than being logically constructed by the researcher, the clusters result from the empirical data; they are operant. Q-methodology can reveal a characteristic independently of its distribution and relative to other characteristics in a population. Unlike surveys, which provide patterns of variables, Q-methodology provides patterns of persons, in this case, street-level professionals. It is a mixed qualitative-quantitative small-sample method that provides a scientific foundation for the systematic study of subjectivity, such as people's opinions, attitudes, preferences, and so on (Watts & Stenner 2005; Brown 1980, 1993). On the type of research question of this article, Petter (2005: 211) has said:

> For instance, do administrators who evaluate subordinates based on hierarchical responsibility also emphasize other low-autonomy perspectives? Or do they balance it by also stressing an outcome focus, such as public responsibility? A Q-methodology study may reveal patterns.

Q-methodology was applied to this study through four steps (discussed below): selection of relevant statements (Q-set), selection of respondents (P-set), respondents' ranking of statements (Q-sort), and interpretation of the results (Q-analysis).[1]

The Q-set

In a Q-methodological study people are typically presented with a sample of statements about some topic (here, issues concerning the loyalties of public administrators), called the Q-set. We compiled a list of all the quotes on loyalties, responsibilities, and role conceptions found in academic and popular literature. The original list contained more than 600 quotes. A Q-set of 42 statements was chosen by first discarding overlapping statements and second, by applying the following framework to the statements:

Table 1 Logic of the Q-set

Type of Loyalty	Thick	Thin
Hierarchical		
Personal		
Social		
Professional		
Societal		
Legal		
Customer		

Adopted from: Petter (2005) and Bovens (1998)

Table 1 is based on Bovens' (1998) objects and Petter's (2005) responsibilities of administrators. In other words, we ensured that each theoretically relevant category was represented in the 42 statements, both the object and the background of different loyalties.

The P-set

The set of respondents, or P-set, is usually not randomly chosen, but theoretically structured (Brown 1980) and all viewpoints should be included. In this case, the 42 statements were sorted by 29 respondents. For the interviews, only street-level bureaucrats were approached: public professionals with direct daily client relationships. Street-level bureaucrats have certain discretionary powers, which always lead to certain loyalty dilemmas and conflicts (Lipsky 1980). We selected social benefit and permit providers, both of which are local authority group workers. The municipalities that cooperated were Venlo (both permit and social benefit providers), Leiden (social benefit providers), Dordrecht (both permit and social benefit providers), and Stadsdeel Slotervaart in Amsterdam (permit providers). The P-set consisted of thirteen permit providers and sixteen social benefit providers (see Appendix).

GJALT DE GRAAF & ZEGER VAN DER WAL

The Q-sort

By Q-sorting, people give subjective meaning to the set of statements, and so reveal their subjective viewpoint. Stephenson[2] has presented Q-methodology as an inversion of conventional factor analysis in the sense that it correlates persons instead of tests (i.e. by-person factor analysis). If each individual had unique likes and dislikes, their Q-sorts would not correlate. If, however, significant clusters of correlations exist, they can be factorized and described as common viewpoints, and individuals can be mapped to a particular factor.

Using a quasi-normal distribution, respondents were asked to rank-order the 42 statements from their own point of view according to some preference, judgment, or feeling (figure 1).[3] The two statements he or she agreed with most were put on the right (for a score of +3); the two he or she disagreed with most on the left (-3). The statements they felt indifferent about (or did not understand) were put in the middle (the 0 category). The final distribution was the Q-sort. The Q-sorts were factor-analyzed with the objective of revealing a limited number of corresponding viewpoints.

Figure 1 Fixed distribution of the Q-set

Least Agree					Most Agree	
		(Statement Scores)				
-3	-2	-1	0	+1	+2	+3
(2)	(4)	(9)	(12)	(9)	(4)	(2)

After the statement sorting, a second interview was held with each respondent to gain insight into the reasons behind their choices, for example: 'Why did you put these two statements in the +3 category?' 'Do you see an issue concerning loyalty that is missing in the statements?' This helped with the final analysis of the different factors.

Q-analysis

The individual Q-sorts were factor analyzed using PQMethod 2.11[4] (extraction method: centroid; rotation method: varimax) in order to reveal the distinct ways in which the statements were rank-ordered. The analysis led to the five factors (or loyalty types) A, B, C, D, and E. For each factor a composite sort was computed based on the rankings of the respondents' loading on that factor[5] using their correlation coefficient with the factor as weight. This idealized Q-sort represented the way a person loading 100 percent on that factor would have ranked the 42 statements. The appendix shows the factor loadings of the 29 subjects.

Each factor was interpreted and described using the characterizing and distinguishing statements and the explanations of respondents loading on the factor. A statement is *characterizing* by its position in the outer columns of the idealized Q-sort of the factor and is *distinguishing* if the position is statistically significantly different from its position in the idealized Q-sorts of all other factors. Respondents' explanations (which were transcribed literally during the post-Q-sort interviews) are cited below in italics to illustrate administrators' ways of thinking and support the description of that viewpoint. Corresponding statement numbers from the Q-set are noted in parentheses.

Results: Five types of street-level professionals

Factor A: The Objective Judge

Street-level professionals falling into factor A believe that public administrators should not base decisions on personal values (41) so that citizens can trust that policies and rules are followed uniformly. 'Whatever goes to citizens cannot be a personal opinion. For the citizen my opinion is irrelevant.' 'Once you start to base decisions on personal values, the end is near. Who then determines what is right and what is wrong?' Their motto is to follow the rules without interference from personal values (32).

Rules and professionalism are valued very highly by administrators with conception A; that is where their most important loyalty lies, certainly not with their own conscience or identity (34). 'The rules are leading, because they guard us from arbitrariness. Our society then depends on the law.' Professionals in this factor thus feel that it is important to know the rules and regulations and adhere to them (11). Of all street-level professionals, they most strongly reject the notion that administrators should be able to refuse a task if their consciences dictate so (16). The administrator cannot base a decision on a personal opinion or their own conscience and cannot refuse assignments based on personal objection. Their own political values should not play a role in their work (13) and administrators' opinions should not be expressed in public (5). 'If you make an administrative decision based on your own feelings, you're out of your mind.' Forming opinions on the morality of actions at work is strongly rejected (15). An administrator is a 'serving hatch of the law'. 'You can say something internally, but if nothing changes, you simply should do what management wants.' 'You can't make up your own rules.' 'How an administrator feels about something personally should be of no consequence.' When decisions are based on personal opinions, 'democracy is governed by administrators', which, according to these administrators, is undesirable. There is no loyalty dilemma between this professional's conscience and assignments from the top: the latter al-

GJALT DE GRAAF & ZEGER VAN DER WAL

ways prevail. A typical remark is, 'you can never refuse an assignment. Your own conscience is minor.' A few respondents mentioned the current discussion of some administrators' refusing to marry gay couples. This group believes that administrators so tasked cannot refuse such an assignment; that is, they should follow the law and their directives or find another job.

Factor B: The Defender of the Public Interest

Notable about the street-level professionals in factor B is that they consider public administrators who focus on societal effects good and those who focus on bureaucratic output bad (22). 'The public interest is exactly what is so important for us civil servants.' The loyalty of these administrators lies in the first place with the public interest, certainly not their superiors: 'Superiors cannot always be right.' 'It cannot be that the superior is more important than the public interest' (26). Nor does it lie with their organizations (19) or their colleagues, whom they will easily abandon in the case of conflict (33). They are decidedly against colleagues who are more focused on their own careers than the public cause (28). Administrators in factor B are the only ones who do not mind not knowing all the rules and regulations and sticking to them (11). 'You cannot know all the rules. And that is not necessary. You can always look up something or ask someone.'

Just what the public interest constitutes is something public administrators make explicit for themselves based on common sense rather than political party standpoints. 'If an assignment is in conflict with something, I will not do it. You cannot unthinkingly follow orders; you have to use your common sense.' It follows that acting with integrity means acting according to one's own conscience. (27): 'Your own conscience is the most important thing. You should always follow that.' 'I'm an administrator and don't want to be put in a certain pattern. My opinion also counts and I want to express it when I feel I have to.' 'I find it important to help people who have a difficult time.'

Administrators in factor B are the only ones who state that they work for government because they want to serve society (7): 'I do this job because of its service-rendering character' but it is notable that they find their private lives more important that their jobs (1). Interestingly, no permit providers fall into this category, only four social benefit providers.

Factor C: The Neutral Intermediary

The title of this loyalty conception comes from statement number 6: administrators in factor C see it as their main duty to mediate between conflicting interests. 'It is my task to keep a good relationship between the law and the client.' For administrators in this factor the point of departure is to find a common path between different parties, but not based on their own judgment. 'Solving problems is what I do on a daily basis. But I have to stay within the rules, of course.' The administrator should always be as neutral as possible; he or she cannot act on personal values. They have strong loyalties to their own management (18) and organizations (19): 'We are one organization. I took an oath of office. How our organization comes across to citizens is important', and their own conscience (25): 'You have to follow the rules, the elected politicians, and your superior.'

It is good to know all the rules and regulations and follow them strictly. Saying that the rules for dealing with clients lower the street-level administrator's efficiency and effectiveness is therefore nonsense (37): 'You have to deal with clients all the time anyway' and doing that does not lower efficiency. 'Rules are there for a reason. Without them you might treat someone you liked better than someone you didn't like. It is therefore also a matter of quality service delivery. Rules guarantee that you offer a certain level of quality to all clients.'

Factor D: The Conscientious Administrator

Administrators in factor D are typified by the important role their consciences play in their daily work. Their loyalty is clearly drawn from their own conscience. They strongly believe that they should form their own opinion on the morality of their actions at work and cannot leave the matter up to their superiors (15). When they find an assignment irresponsible, loyalty to their conscience and identity is the decisive factor (34): 'If I disapprove of something, I won't do it. I have a responsibility to myself. That for me is most important, not whether the policy will be carried out or not.' This is clearly different from aiming for societal effects (22) like the respondents in factor B. Their own identities matter in that 'you cannot do things that do not adhere to your conscience. Not all rules are clear. Their interpretation depends on your personality.' In the end you have to be able to live with yourself, which is why loyalty to one's own conscience is the most important thing in the professional's work (25): 'When you disapprove of something and you still do it, the question is whether you can live with yourself.' Administrators should be allowed to refuse a task when their conscience so dictates (16).

The quality of the relationship with their superiors is irrelevant to their own commitment to their work (42): 'I have had my differences with a superior for a long period of time. My work cannot suffer for that because citizens become the victims.' Differences of opinion cannot influence functioning at work.

Factor E: The Objective Service Provider

Most striking about respondents in factor E is their devotion to client interests. The client is central: 'Impartiality is much more important than efficiency. It is important that we judge everything objectively. People's lives depend on the money we provide.' 'In our department we take care of the less fortunate citizens – that is important and necessary.' Impartiality and fairness far outweigh the importance of efficiency (4, 41): 'When companies request a permit, they simply have to provide all the necessary data on time. Other people I help with things like applications and forms.' 'I sometimes help people with their applications by making a small drawing. Officially that's not allowed, but it saves them the cost of an architect.' The loyalty lies with the client, not the supervisors, elected officials (2), or their own consciences (27): 'We all have different values and norms.' 'Personal opinions should not play a role. Yet, you do more for some clients than others; that can't be avoided.' To help clients well, impartially, and honestly, rules play an important role (11).

Street-level professionals in factor E worry about the well-being of less privileged citizens (10). Also, they feel a stronger loyalty to their own organizations than to the government in general (35). 'I did not choose to work for "the public sector" in general, but to function at a place where I can express myself.'

More than any other street-level professionals, the 'objective service provider' considers private life much more important than work: 'Private life always goes above my work. Work is a means to provide for myself, nothing more than that.' 'After working hours I really close that door and that's that.' 'When I'm dealing with a tough issue I stay until it's finished; that way I don't take it home with me.'

Conclusion

The results of the Q-study show differences in how today's street-level bureaucrats weigh their loyalty to clients vis-à-vis other loyalty objects and revealed five different loyalty conceptions. The loyalties of *Objective Judges* are for a large part legal and professional. *Defenders of the Public Interest* want to serve society in general and create what they consider to be 'public value' (cf. Bozeman 2007), having a strong loyalty to what they envision as the common good and definitely not to their superiors, their own organizations, or their colleagues. The 'soft' physician in the preceding chapter can be seen as an example of this type. *Neutral Intermediaries* have a strong loyalty to their clients, a type identified in the literature on street-level bureaucrats (e.g. Lipsky 1980) but they are also strongly loyal to their own organization and superiors. *Conscientious Bureaucrats* bring to mind administrators who refuse to marry gay couples, but one can also think of the content-oriented teachers (who see qualification as the ultimate goal of education) in the preceding chapter. They strongly believe that they should form their own opinions on the morality of their actions at work and final decisions cannot simply be left up to superiors or a rule with which they disagree. If they find an assignment irresponsible, loyalty to their own conscience and identity is the decisive factor. They are certainly not amoral Weberian public servants. Finally, *Objective Service Providers* are typified by their loyalty to the interests of their clients. Also, they feel a stronger loyalty to their own organizations than with 'government' in general.

These conceptions matter because they are not merely ideational; the dedication and attitudes of street-level bureaucrats directly influence and guide behavior, mostly by prioritizing signals, issues, and meetings (cf. Fletcher 1993). Administrators' conceptualizations of their loyalties are thus morally important: they indicate how administrators behave and make decisions (De Graaf 2005). Furthermore, as becomes clear from the four loyalty descriptions, *different conceptions mean different loyalty dilemmas and conflicts,* which are in turn indicative of different solutions and modes of coping. Which particular dilemma an administrator perceives and how he or she frames the moral question within it depend on the public servant's loyalty type.

The results have implications for the broader theme of this book, that is, public professionals being under all sorts of different pressures. They provide evidence to refute notions held by the general public and particular groups of professionals that 'managers are the root of all evil'. Earlier, Noordegraaf (2008) and others convincingly demonstrated that a narrow focus on a clash between professionals and managers is not very productive and that professional realities in modern public sector environments are much more nuanced than is often assumed in the common 'professional versus manager' debates. This study corroborates just that by showing how loyalties of public servants can differ. The same applies to the more old-fashioned sentiment that emphasizes the 'primacy of politics' and the civil servant's obedience to elected officials (e.g. Rhodes & Wanna 2007). Daily life of public professionals is simply more diversified as they experience having more 'masters' than just managers and politicians.

The debate is dependent on the priorities of a professional in terms of loyalties and the particular clashes and tensions he or she actually experiences. *Defenders of the Public Interest,* for instance, may experience tensions with their managers when asked to comply with managerial dictums because their loyalty lies with the broader public good and not the manager or organization. But *because* they pay less attention to superiors when making a decision, they might be less bothered by managers' expectations in other situations. These deliberations might be opposite for *Objective Service Providers* whose loyalties towards the organization and manager are much stronger, while their conscience and morality are distanced in decision-making dilemmas.

There is no one best way in which public professionals in this century deal with the variety of pressures that influence their profession and the way they make sense of their professionalism. Depending on where loyalties lie, vocational or societal pressures might for instance be experi-

GJALT DE GRAAF & ZEGER VAN DER WAL

enced more strongly and taken more seriously by one particular type of professional than another. In other words, how professionals interpret reality and how they use their conceptions and discourses directly influence the pressures they actually experience. In a sense, professionals experience different realities, and thus their experienced pressures are shaped by very different external factors, interests, and stakeholders. *The* public sector professional does not exist, nor do public sector professionals *agree* on which pressures are most problematic and which solutions are paramount. General statements by outsiders that clients should be more important than managers and citizens more important than political masters are thus of limited use.

Generalizing the empirical results to other parts of the public sector and related domains – let alone other countries and regimes – surely warrants further research but has a 'however' clause. Street-level public professionals may form a particular group within the public sector, but they are also a highly relevant group for similar study because, like many professionals, they deal with clients on a personal level and possess the discretionary powers to weigh loyalties differently on a daily basis. In that sense, the pressures of the professionals studied here are comparable to those of healthcare professionals, police officers, and so forth.

The results give rise to a number of interesting questions and issues that merit attention in future research. Clearly, more research needs to be conducted in different parts of the public sector on why, when, and how different types of professionals create different types of loyalty conceptions because it will enhance our understanding of actual professional realities. Q-methodology is appropriate for doing so because it is capable of operantly revealing clusters of subjectivity. The result of this and similar studies can be used for further research and as inputs for other methods. For example, a survey in order to find out what the percentage of each of the four types of professionals is in a wider population. A more detailed and nuanced understanding of how professionals actually go about professional decision-making is urgently needed to improve the quality of the debate on 'professionals under pressure'.

Notes

1. The main source for Q-methodology is Stephenson (1953). Within the social sciences, Brown (1980) is the classic reference.
2. William Stephenson, the inventor of Q-methodology, served as the last assistant to Charles Spearman, the inventor of conventional factor analysis (Brown 1997).
3. Even though a forced distribution was used, some deviations were tolerated. If the Q-sorters found the forced distribution too much unlike their positions, they were allowed to slightly vary the number of statements they were 'supposed to' have in a category.

4. Dedicated software and manual can be downloaded from www.rz.unibw-muenchen.de/p41bsmk/qmethod.
5. A respondent loads on a factor if: i) he or she correlates statistically significantly with that factor; i.e. the loading of a respondent on a factor should exceed the multiplier for the statistical significance level (p=.05) divided by the square root of the number of statements (in this case: $1.96/\sqrt{42} = 0.30$) or ii) the factor explains more than half of the common variance; i.e. the square of the loading on that factor should exceed the sum of squares of factor loadings on other factors.

References

Aberbach, J.D., Putnam, R.D., & Rockman, B.A. (1981). *Bureacrats and Politicians in Western Democracies.* Cambridge, MA: Harvard University Press.

Adams, G., & Balfour, D. (1998). *Unmasking Administrative Evil.* London: Sage Publications.

Arendt, H. (1963). *Eichmann in Jerusalem: A Report on the Banality of Evil.* London: Faber and Faber.

Bovens, M. (1998). *The Quest for Responsibility.* Cambridge: Cambridge University Press.

Bozeman, B. (2007). *Public Values and Public Interest. Counterbalancing Economic Individualism.* Washington: Georgetown University Press.

Brown, S. (1980). *Political Subjectivity: Applications of Q-Methodology in Political Science.* New Haven/London: Yale University Press.

Brown, S. (1993). A Primer on Q methodology. *Operant Subjectivity, 16*(3/4), 91-138.

De Graaf, G. (2005). Tractable morality. *Journal of Business Ethics, 60*(1), 1-15.

De Graaf, G. (2011). The Loyalties of Top Public Administrators. *Journal of Public Administration Research and Theory, 21*(2), 285-306.

Demir, T. (2009). The Complementarity View: Exploring a Continuum in Political-Administrative Relationships. *Public Administration Review, 69*(5): 876-888.

Denhardt, K. (1989). The Management of Ideals: A Political Perspective on Ethics. *Public Administration Review, 49*(2): 187-93.

Dobel, J.P. (2005). *Public Integrity.* Baltimore: The John Hopkins University Press.

Fletcher, G.P. (1993). *Loyalty. An Essay on the Morality of Relationships.* Oxford: Oxford University Press.

Goodnow, F. J. (1900). *Politics and Administration.* New York: Macmillan.

Hart, P. 't, & Wille, A.W. (Eds.) (2002). *Politiek-ambtelijke verhoudingen in beweging [Shifting Political-bureucratic Relations].* Amsterdam: Boom.

Hart, P. 't, & Wille, A.W. (2006). Ministers and Top Officials in the Dutch Core Executive: Living Together, Growing Apart? *Public Administration 84* (1):121-146.

Hondeghem, A. (Ed.) (1998). *Ethics and Accountability in a Context of Governance and New Public Management.* Amsterdam: Ios Press.

Hupe, P.L., & Hill, M.J. (2007). Street-level Bureaucracy and Public Accountability. *Public Administration, 82*(2), 279-299.

Jansen, T., Van den Brink, G., & Kole, J. (Eds.) (2009). *Beroepstrots. Een ongekende kracht [Professional Pride. An Unprecedented Power]*. Amsterdam: Boom.

Lee, K., & Raadschelders, J. (2008). Political-Administrative Relations: Impact of and Puzzles in Aberbach, Putnam, and Rockman, 1981. *Governance, 21*(3), 419-438.

Lipsky, M. (1980). *Street-Level Bureaucracy: Dilemmas of the Individual in Public Services*. New York: Russel Sage Foundation.

Nieuwenkamp, R. (2001). *De prijs van het politieke primaat: Wederzijds vertrouwen en loyaliteit in de verhouding tussen bewindspersonen en ambtelijke top [The Price of the Political Primacy: Mutual Trust and Loyality in the Relation between Ministers and Senior Civil Servants]*. Delft: Eburon.

Noordegraaf, M. (2004). *Management in het publieke domein. Issues, instituties en instrumenten [Management in the Public Domain. Issues, Institutions and Tools]*. Bussum: Coutinho.

Noordegraaf, M. (2008). *Professioneel Bestuur. De tegenstelling tussen publieke managers en professionals als 'strijd om professionaliteit.' [Professional Governance. The Contradiction between Public Managers and Professionals as 'Contest for Professionality']*. Den Haag: Lemma.

O'Flynn, J. (2009). The Public Value Debate: Emerging Ethical Issues. Paper presented at the *Third Annual ANU Leadership Workshop*, Canberra, Australia, 26-27 November 2009.

Peters, B.G., & Pierre, J. (Eds.) (2001). *Politicians, Bureaucrats and Administrative Reform*. London: Routledge.

Petter, J. (2005). Responsible Behavior in Bureaucrats: An Expanded Conceptual Framework. *Public Integrity, 8*(3), 197-217.

Putnam, R.D. (1976). *The Comparative Study of Political Elites*. Englewood Cliffs, N.J.: Prentice Hall.

Rhodes, R. & Wanna, J. (2007). The Limits to Public Value, or Rescuing Responsible Government from the Platonic Gardens. *Australian Journal of Public Administration, 66*(4), 406–421.

Tonkens, E. (2008, September 13). *Bevrijd vaklui uit de bureaucratie [Free Craftsmen from Bureaucracy]*. De Volkskrant.

Van der Wal, Z., Van Hout, E.J.Th., Kwak, A.J. & Oude-Vrielink, M. (Eds.) (2007). Managers en Professionals. Waarden in een hybride praktijk [Managers and Professionals. Values in a Hybrid Practice]. *Bestuurskunde, 16*(4), 2-52.

Verbrugge, A. (2005, June 18). *Het procesdenken van managers berooft de wereld van zijn bezieling [The Process Focus of Managers Deprives the World from its Animation]*. De Volkskrant.

Watts, S., & Stenner, P. (2005). Doing Q Methodology: Theory, Method and Interpretation. *Qualitative Research in Psychology, 2*, 67-91.

Weggeman, M. (2008). *Leiding geven aan professionals? Niet doen! [Managing Professionals? Don't!]*. Schiedam: Scriptum.

Wilson, W. (1887). The study of public administration. *Political Science Quarterly, 2*(2): 197-222.

Appendix

Factor matrix of the 29 respondents and their loadings (X indicates a 'defining sort')

Q-SORT	1	2	3	4	5	M/F	Fx*	Mun**
1	0.7644 X	0.0845	0.1857	-0.0827	0.1021	F	Uit	L
2	-0.1248	0.1812	0.3702 X	-0.0067	0.2662	M	Uit	L
3	0.5096	0.3746	0.3681	0.0583	0.1970	F	Uit	L
4	-0.0409	0.0583	0.1476	-0.4581 X	0.0957	M	Ver	V
5	0.2089	0.3880	0.2768	0.1344	0.3736	F	Ver	V
6	0.7038 X	-0.0927	-0.0389	0.0503	0.0890	M	Uit	V
7	0.0076	0.3649	0.5067 X	0.0564	0.2998	M	Uit	V
8	0.3311	0.4488	0.2205	0.2059	0.1575	F	Uit	V
9	0.3401	-0.0100	0.2422	0.2811	0.5157 X	F	Uit	D
10	0.0004	0.1318	0.4723	-0.0744	0.4828	F	Uit	D
11	-0.0093	0.0884	0.0745	0.5515 X	0.0601	M	Ver	S
12	0.1270	0.0791	0.5061 X	0.2297	0.0530	F	Ver	S
13	0.4577 X	0.1560	0.1727	0.1545	0.1454	M	Ver	D
14	0.2159	0.0931	0.0691	0.0517	0.4784 X	M	Ver	D
15	0.1613	0.0250	0.6371 X	-0.0777	0.0380	M	Ver	D
16	0.0791	0.3459	0.0842	0.4827	0.4056	F	Uit	L
17	-0.1963	0.4074 X	-0.0872	0.0011	0.0205	F	Uit	L
18	0.1499	0.7463 X	0.0994	0.1012	0.0921	M	Uit	L
19	0.4091 X	0.1890	0.1128	0.1374	0.2572	M	Ver	V
20	0.0556	0.4722 X	0.0472	0.0449	-0.0307	M	Uit	V
21	0.6799 X	-0.0068	0.0676	0.0503	0.0854	M	Uit	V
22	0.2330	0.1106	0.1037	-0.2549	0.6467 X	F	Uit	V
23	0.4582	0.0130	0.0542	0.1280	0.4623	F	Ver	V
24	0.4614	0.0895	0.4708	0.1267	0.0935	F	Uit	D
25	0.0316	0.3857 X	0.1402	-0.0268	0.1633	M	Uit	D
26	0.4388	-0.1001	0.5512 X	0.1036	0.2053	F	Ver	S
27	0.1493	0.1500	0.3580	0.6314 X	0.0218	M	Ver	S
28	0.7645 X	-0.0204	-0.0311	-0.0012	0.1664	M	Ver	D
29	0.5861 X	0.1900	0.4467	-0.0615	0.0064	F	Ver	D

* Fx = function (Uit = social benefits providers, Ver = permit providers)

** Mun = municipality (D = Dordrecht, L = Leiden, V = Venlo, S = Amsterdam Slotervaart)

GJALT DE GRAAF & ZEGER VAN DER WAL

10 Democratizing social work

From New Public Management to democratic professionalism

Evelien Tonkens, Marc Hoijtink & Huub Gulikers

Introduction

The concept of NPM and its consequences for professional work have already been discussed in previous chapters of this book. Newman stressed that NPM is not a singular entity, but a wide range of reforms that have been enacted and experienced very differently in various countries. Nevertheless, the overview of Hood (cited in the contribution of Tummers, Steijn & Bekkers) can be seen as giving the essence of what is generally meant by the introduction of NPM reforms. In this chapter we will especially focus on the second component mentioned in Hood's overview, e.g. the introduction of explicit standards and measurements of performance, or more specifically, performance-based accountability.

We will focus our attention on its consequences, in the light of relations between professionals and people who need social care or social support. Interestingly, NPM became attractive because it promised to democratize professional practices, including social work. It promised to take citizens seriously: they should be listened to and have influence on what social workers offer. Although this democratic promise certainly covers not all of what NPM promised, it is a crucial element in the embrace of NPM in the field of social work. The promise of performance accountability is that 'performance information is not merely managerial useful, but also contributes to the quality of democratic debate and to the ability of citizens to make choices' (Pollitt 2006: 52).

The critique on social work as an undemocratic practice preceded the rise of NPM. It was uttered fervently from the mid-1970s onwards and can be summarized by highlighting four components: social work was a) disempowering, b) paternalistic, c) self-centred, and d) unaccountable. NPM was put forward as a more democratic practice, by empowering citizens, by giving them voice and choice, and by serving their demands and providing accountability. The core question of this chapter is to what extent NPM manages to fulfil this democratic promise in social work. Our empirical data are derived from interviews with Dutch social workers and their managers.

We will first have a closer look at the major criticisms and argue why they can be understood as attacks on the undemocratic features of social work. Then we will discuss how and why NPM was offered as a more democratic alternative. Our own empirical research work will be used to analyse how this promise works out in practice in local social work in the Netherlands. Our study is therefore linked to the first of the 'candidate contradictions of public management reform' that Pollitt & Bouckaert (2004: 165-167) have stressed: how is it possible that NPM simultaneously empowers consumers, frees managers and strengthens political control? 'In a perfect world the three objectives might be compatible. In the real world public managers usually find themselves facing trade-offs or even downright contradictions' (ibid: 167). We will argue that in most respects, NPM tends to strengthen political control and in doing so undermines rather than promotes democracy in social work.

We will go on to discuss the notion of democratic professionalism (Dzur 2004, 2008) as a way to give citizens more voice, direct professional accountability towards citizens and move accountability from output measurement towards democratic practice. The notion of 'democratic professionalism' is still a rather vague notion but we will try to give it some more flesh and blood on the basis or our empirical data.

As opposed to various other chapters in this volume (Van der Krogt & Hupe; Van der Veen; Tummers, Steijn & Bekkers), our focus is *not* on a possible decline in professional autonomy, as we do not consider professional autonomy as such as something to be cherished. Professional autonomy has been successfully and rightly attacked in the 1970s as paternalistic and undemocratic, and we want to take it from there. Since then, efforts have been made to democratize professional practices, and NPM can be understood as one way of doing so.

Criticism of social work

We focus on the criticism of NPM of public services as undemocratic, although we are conscious of the fact that this term as such is not much used in the NPM movement itself. Moreover, NPM theorists were not particularly interested in social work, but in the public sector more generally. In the 1990s, NPM theorists framed their attacks more broadly in terms of the weaknesses of non-marketized, state-related 'bureaucracy'.

By democratization we do not mean strengthening democratic boards or democratic procedures, but giving more voice and choice and thereby empowering citizens (Newman & Tonkens 2011; Fienieg et al. 2011, Ootes et al. 2011). The first five elements of the seven elements identified by Hood to denote NPM (see chapter 8) can also be seen as democratization in this sense.

It can be argued that NPM built on earlier criticism of the lack of democracy in the public sector (including social work), which was already

EVELIEN TONKENS, MARC HOIJTINK & HUUB GULIKERS

discussed in many western welfare states in the 1970s. We will have a closer look at this critique of social work being undemocratic in four respects: disempowering, self-centred, paternalistic and unaccountable.

First, during the late 1970s the empowering presumptions of social work were under attack. It was argued that the growth of social work was uncontrolled and did not match the needs of citizens, but was an expression of autonomous policy developments regardless of the needs of citizens. It was also argued that social work failed to empower people and merely deepened their independence (Clarke 2004; Clarke & Newman 1997; Tonkens & Duyvendak 2003).

NPM was introduced in the mid-1990s in the public sector, in many Western welfare states. It started off as a criticism of government but was soon more broadly applied to bureaucratic ways of governing in public sector organizations. In their bestselling book *Reinventing Government*, Osborne & Gaebler (1992) echoed the criticism of disempowerment: government was blamed for keeping 'clients' of government passive and denying them choice (p. 169). Bureaucratic state institutions were considered sluggish because of their hierarchical chains of command, and their preoccupation with rules and regulations (Peters & Waterman 1982; Osborne & Gaebler 1992). Government structures had become as historical as dinosaurs and as slow as snails, and thus unresponsive to the needs of their clients.

Secondly, during the 1970s, social work was also criticized for being self-centred (Tonkens & Van Doorn 2001). Sociologists criticized social work for lack of accountability: they were attacked for not serving the needs and demands of citizens but merely being occupied with their own needs, wasting time with endless meetings and not achieving much. If social work wanted to be meaningful at all, it should organize activities that citizens asked for. Professionals were blamed for being solely motivated by self-interest (Clarke & Newman 1997; compare also Van der Veen's description of Illich and Achterhuis' attack on professionals). NPM developed this criticism further, by criticizing the lack of accountability of government and the public sector more broadly (Du Gay 2000).

A third 1970s criticism on social work partly contradicted the second: it was argued that social work was paternalistic and patronizing (Tonkens & Duyvendak, 2003); a criticism that also struck other social professionals such as medical doctors and psychiatrists (Tonkens & Weijers 1999). Not self-centred this time, but rather other-oriented, be it in a problematic manner. Social workers would be 'exercising power over would-be customers, denying choice, through the dubious claim that "professionals know best" and "undermining personal responsibility"' (Clarke & Newman 1997: 15). Of all social professions, this criticism hit social work hardest, because more than nurses, doctors or teachers, social workers claimed to empower and liberate citizens. Therefore, social workers were most seriously struck and silenced by this criticism. Social workers were blamed for having ideas of welfare and well-being, hardly related to the ideas of citizens themselves. The government had 'imposed' social work onto its citizens, it was argued. Social workers were criticized for being authoritarian specialists who came to authoritative judgments on the basis of their expertise without tolerating participation or dispute (Tonkens & Duyvendak 2003). Again, this was taken up by NPM, arguing against the self-centredness of the state and the public sector more generally (Du Gay 2000; Osborne & Gaebler 1992).

Fourthly, the 1970s' critique of social work dismissed its goals as too vague and thus unaccountable to democratic control. Social workers were 'the new exempted'; their work escaped accountability and control (Jordan & Jordan 2000; Tonkens & Van Doorn 2001), a critique again taken up and generalized by NPM (Power 1997; Marquand 2004).

The criticisms summarized above were not answered by a self-assured defence from the side of social work – neither during the 1970s, nor during the 1980s. On the contrary, social workers were baffled, as this criticism hit the core of their work: empowerment was their main reason for existence. The criticism of social work professionals helped to legitimate budget cuts during the 1980s and early 1990s and these in turn further weakened and silenced the sector (Marquand 2004).

NPMS *democratic promise*

NPM reforms offered an alternative to these criticisms by a fourfold promise. The new public sector (including of course social work) would provide service, accountability, choice and voice to citizens, mainly in their role as consumers. The idea was to '"launch a customer revolution", which involved turning organisations and management assumptions upside down (Peters, 1987)' (Clarke & Newman 1997: 107).

To combat disempowerment, NPM promised to empower citizens as clients who would have the power to choose and thus also to dismiss organizations. Just like customers on the market, citizens would have exit options. To combat self-centredness, citizens were redefined as consumers whose wants and needs are to be served. Their demand would force social workers to become client-centred and deliver what citizens ask. Thus, demand-based steering gained popularity in public services and social work in many Western welfare states from the mid-1990s onwards (Clarke & Newman 1997; Rodger 2000; Marquand 2004), including the Netherlands (Tonkens 2011; Van Sambeek et al. 2011; Tonkens & Duyvendak 2003; Tonkens & Van Doorn 2001).

As an alternative for paternalism, NPM promised to refrain from judgment and simply deliver what was asked for (Marquand 2001; Jordan & Jordan 2000). 'To serve rather than patronize', with 'a smile rather than a sermon'. Social workers would be positioned in a serving, client-dependent manner, so that clients' needs, complaints and desires could never again be dismissed: those who would bully clients, would lose their contracts. Clients were setting the rules now by way of 'demand steering' (Pollitt 2003).

Thirdly, NPM also promised citizens voice options. Performance measurement would give citizens both exit and voice options. Performance measurement would provide citizens with the necessary information to see for themselves that a service was failing, and if so, to leave. Indirectly, performance measurement would empower citizens and give them the information to choose between providers (Power 1997).

Fourthly, to make social workers accountable, accountability mechanisms, such as standards, targets and performance measurements, were set up. The efforts moved from input and processes towards output and outcome (Power 1997; Jordan & Jordan 2000). There was also a 'shift towards measurement and quantification, especially in the form of systems of performance indicators and/or explicit standards' (Pollitt 2003: 27). In order to be accountable to external parties, public service organizations should formulate their results in terms of measurable outcomes, understandable to non-experts. Clearer targets and better performance measures would make it easier for politicians to judge if public sector organizations were achieving what they were aiming at (Pollitt 2003).

In summary, NPM promised democratization by strengthening choice, service orientation, voice and accountability. We now turn to our empirical data to see whether and how these promises are visible in the daily practices of Dutch grass roots social work.

NPM in Dutch social work practices

Our research was carried out in seven welfare organizations responsible for social work in the Netherlands. The Netherlands presents an interesting case, because the criticism on social work hit social work particularly hard during the late 1960s and early 1970s, as part of the comparatively successful attack on authoritarian practices during that era in this country. As the American-Dutch historian Kennedy noted, the reigning elite was very receptive to the critique on authorities as it fitted a self-critique that was already (partly latently) present (Kennedy 1995). Today, NPM is firmly rooted in the Dutch welfare sector, with practices such as contracting out and performance measurement. Welfare organizations are responsible for social work, under the authority of local government. Devolution of social work to local government started in the 1980s and was strengthened by a new law, the WMO ('Social Support Act'), introduced in 2007.

We analyzed reports from individual organizations, their umbrella organizations branch and local and central government. We also conducted in-depth interviews with social workers, youth workers, social cultural workers, community workers (total 57), middle and general managers (13), and citizens who work as volunteers (5) between November 2006 and November 2008. In the interviews we discussed their experiences with and views on accountability and client participation in social work. In three organizations we followed efforts to mould performance information to better fit democratic purposes: to reform performance information in such a way that it would be a more informative tool for discussing results with colleagues. What did NPM actually mean for democratization of social work of these organizations? We again discern four themes in which this democratic turn was expected: service, accountability, voice and choice.

Service orientation

In Dutch local social work a major rhetorical shift took place in the 1990s towards service orientation and demand steering and demand orientation (Kremer & Tonkens 2006; De Boer & Duyvendak 2004). Services were redefined in terms of 'products', clients were redefined as 'consumers', the name of the umbrella organization of welfare organizations changed into 'Social Entrepreneurs Group'.

On the level of welfare organizations, however, this shift never really took place. Citizens' demands did not come into view at all, as De Boer & van der Lans (2011) also noted in their essay for the Dutch Council for Social Development. Local governments act in their name. Under the influence of NPM rhetoric local governments now contract social services on behalf of clients. As a consequence, welfare organizations do not adapt their services to the demands of clients, but merely to the demands of local governments. Rather than demand steering we witness government steering. Paternalism is not replaced, but the actor has changed: now the main source of paternalism is government rather than professionals.

As to demand orientations (of professionals, on the individual level), a more ambiguous picture arises. Our respondents argue that they operate in a service- and demand-oriented manner. NPM in a way did stimulate a more attentive attitude to the voices and needs of individual clients, as other research shows as well (Van der Steege & Van Deur 2002). Social workers are more active in figuring out, together with clients, which help and activities they need.

However, it must be stressed that social workers reject the notion of citizens as consumers, and even reject the idea of serving their demands. This, they argue, underestimates the peculiarities of social work. It denies the vulnerability and dependence of a lot of clients who turn to social work. These often fail to have clearly defined demands; they merely have problems and needs. Even if they have demands, social workers consider it part of their professionalism to also make their own judgements. A social worker:

EVELIEN TONKENS, MARC HOIJTINK & HUUB GULIKERS

I also have thoughts of my own. And if I think, based on my expertise of and experiences with the problem, that something else should be done, I bring it up. You have to explain why. Precisely because people come to you in a dependent situation. These people are often vulnerable and have problems; otherwise they would have stayed at home. (Social worker, 16 April 2007)

Welfare clients should also be invited, activated, cared for, corrected or educated, rather than just served. The market discourse of services, products, customers and consumers does not recognize this, social workers claim.

Voice

NPM does reduce social workers' possibilities for voice, but again, it does not give a voice to citizens but to local governments. Local governments contract welfare organizations, and evaluate the performance of social work organizations (De Boer & Duyvendak 2004). One could argue that citizens do get more voice in this manner, but in an indirect, democratic manner: as voters and taxpayers, represented by the local politicians and the government. Social workers complain that local government cannot represent the citizens' voice as it is much too detached from and unfamiliar with social work practice. They feel disempowered. A youth worker:

> The increased power of local government is frustrating. You have to deliver this and that, but they don't know what they are talking about. But you can't ignore them anymore because they may in response contract another organization. [...] So sometimes I feel as powerless as the youngster for whom I'm working. [...] so sometimes I wonder, for whom am I working? (Youth worker, 26 March 2007)

This strengthened voice of local government disempowers not only social workers, but also citizens who receive their support, social workers and managers argue. A middle manager:

> This new Law with the tendering [...] Well, it's really terrible. Today, the top of the organization is only interested in what the local government wants. If we receive signs from clients about demands and problems they experience and we want to formulate a policy in response, there is no space and time. But if a policy-maker of the local government has an idea, we have to implement it tomorrow, regardless of whether it is a good or bad idea. (Middle manager, 10 January 2007)

Citizens as service users should be represented not only by local government but also by client councils. Welfare organizations are obligated to install such councils since the new law (WMO) was introduced, in January

2007. However, none of the organizations involved in our research has a client council. This is no coincidence; client councils in local social work are rare (Tonkens 2010). Considering the traditional mission of social work to empower citizens, it is striking that they keep users silenced concerning their own policy.

One of the explanations of this intriguing contradiction lies in the position of welfare organizations. Welfare organizations are afraid of being squeezed between the demands of the empowered local government and the demands of client, would there be a clients' council. A middle manager:

> Local government wants us to provide a front office where citizens can drop by all day and pose questions. That's consumer friendly, indeed. But we can only organize this with the front office employees who are cheaper than social workers. But clients want to talk directly with social workers. So in these times as social work organization you sometimes really feel you're being squeezed. And if we had a client council, what will it say about it? I mean, can we say something about it ourselves? (Middle manager, 26 March 2007)

We observed the same feelings of powerlessness at the executive level:

> I have to reach a certain amount of customers according to the performance indicators that management arranges with the local government and I have to work in line with some standard procedures. Well, to be honest, that's more than enough; I don't want another party which stands far away from my work to tell me what I should do. (Social worker, 10 January 2007)

A few middle managers have a different view on clients' councils. They see client councils as potential allies who can be useful in countervailing the increased power of the local government:

> The customer-user should take the floor and local government and the top of this organization should take a big step backwards. So it wouldn't be wrong to have some kind of client council that can provide some counterbalance. (Middle manager, 24 January 2007).

Another way users can make their voices heard concerning the way they are treated by professionals is by sending in complaints. Complaint procedures have been introduced in social work over the last few years. However, they are rarely used, as clients feel too vulnerable and dependent on social workers, different respondents explain.

Yet another tool to strengthen the voices of citizens is the introduction of quality management systems to catch the 'perspective of the customer'. When such a system meets certain criteria, an organization gets a certificate, like the HKZ (Harmonisatie Kwaliteitsbeoordeling in de Zorg-sector [Harmonizing Quality Assurance in the Care Sector]), that should guarantee quality. In Dutch local social work (as well as in health and social care) the HKZ certificate has been introduced on a large scale. HKZ is an extensive system that covers many aspects of quality, such as what should be registered, at which moments the service has to be evaluated, etc. The aim of HKZ is 'to stimulate working on quality from the perspective of the consumer' (HKZ website, accessed 10 November 2008). One of the aspects of HKZ that according to respondents are supposed to strengthen citizens' voices is the obligatory evaluations that clients give of the support they have received from social workers. Social workers welcome these standards as contributing to working in a professional manner. Inviting feedback from clients and taking action on the basis of this feedback are part and parcel of a professional attitude.

What they consider to be meaningful are separate evaluation reports by clients. It gives them the opportunity to reflect on and discuss their professional methods used in their work and to learn (see also Hoijtink & Oude Vrielink 2007). However, these reports barely play a role in professional accountability. The main reason for this seems to be a lack of managerial staff. While there is an ongoing debate in the Netherlands about the abundance of managers in the public sector, at the expense of professionals like street-level bureaucrats or front-line workers, in practice social work seems to suffer from a lack of managers, according to some social workers and managers we interviewed. Wiendels et al. (2004) compared the staff of social work organizations with other organizations in the public sector and concluded that the staff is smaller in the social work organizations. Social work lacks the managerial capacity to meet the contradictory terms that welfare organizations are faced with, as Huijben et al. (2003) also found. As a consequence, meaningful accountability in which such evaluations would be discussed is not organized. Secondly, managers tend to be overwhelmed by external demands, particularly from local government.

However, more important than any formal system, social workers argue, are daily informal ways of strengthening citizens' voices. Social workers report putting a lot of effort into giving clients a voice in the support they receive and the activities they organize. Social workers argue that seriously taking the voice of clients into account is at the heart of delivering 'quality':

> It is a process in which both of you participate, you and your client. I am not the only one who defines what the problem is; your client has thoughts about this as well. And very good ones, because he is the one who experiences the problems. Not every client enters the room saying: 'I'd like to talk about this problem.' Some people have a whole bunch of problems. In that case you help them to summarize and to get things straight. And then you ask: 'What is your most urgent problem?' So it is always interaction; you and

your clients collaborate closely to help them overcome their problems. (Social worker, 16 April 2007)

Social workers, community workers, social cultural workers and youth workers report they are continually fine tuning: exploring how clients and client groups experience their analyses, interventions, aid and assistance, and figure out if anything should be omitted, adapted, supplemented, or changed. To this end, clients and client groups are continuously invited, challenged and tempted to voice their experiences.

Summing up, NPM strengthens the voice of local government rather than the voice of citizens as service users. However, there is also an undertow of informal communication, which silently strengthens citizens' voices. But as none of this is documented, it cannot be proved to outsiders. The same counts for the voice of clients at the organizational level. Professionals discuss experiences with policy reforms from clients with their managers and if this gives rise to adjustments, they will try to convince managers and together seek to incorporate the voice of clients (Duyvendak, Hoijtink & Tonkens 2009).

Choice

NPM instruments like contractualization and competition (aimed at providing more choice) are key elements in the new Dutch law, the WMO. But again: for whom? Choice was indeed introduced, but only for local government as the representative of citizens, not for individual citizens directly. Choice is made by a spokesperson; the local government that acts in their name. Citizens who receive support from local social work cannot choose themselves. Their home address determines which organization they should turn to in order to receive support. In health and social care citizens gained consumer power by way of personal budgets, but this never happened in local social work. Organizations now have to compete with each other in order to gain contracts and this has directed the attention from management towards local governments and the performance indicators they set. Social workers complain that what counts is not the quality of their work, but the performance indicators set up by local governments. For example, some youth workers complain that what counts is the number of youngsters they reach, while there is ample attention in the organizations for professionalization and the needs from youngsters themselves.

Accountability

The fourth issue in the democratization of social work by way of NPM was to make local social work more accountable. This democratic promise was the main reason why accountability became so popular in social work. Around the turn of the century, social workers and their managers had high expectations of accountability. They hoped that accountability systems would help to prove that their work was valuable. This would put an end to the persistent suggestion that their work was unprofessional and futile (Tonkens & Van Doorn 2001).

These hopes were not fulfilled at all, our research shows. On the contrary, social workers and their managers experienced accountability systems as a disillusionment. They argue that reports that count are meaningless: not only the evaluations already mentioned but also numerous registrations of work processes, such as the amount of telephone calls. Social workers and their managers experience these as meaningless (see also chapter 8 for meaninglessness):

> I often discussed with my manager why we have to deliver such information. I asked: why on earth is our financier interested in how much telephone acts I have performed in a particular client contact? Or why should I register it because of these quality standards? It has nothing to do with quality, you know. My manager agrees, but she argues we need a certification, because the financier demands this and there are also good standards. Okay, I'll do it, but don't come to me with complaints that I don't see enough clients, because then I will be angry. (Social worker, 21 March 2007)

> In a sense the local government has no idea what is really going on behind the output figures, the amount of customers reached, customer's trajectories that are finished or all those tables with numbers of short contacts. But it has become important, because we make performance agreements, set output goals in this way and are accountable for it. So we have to deliver periodically thick reports full of those tables. But we try to pimp it up with stories and words in order to get it alive because in a sense its, well, you want a feeling it's useful, it make sense. (Middle manager, 20 December 2006)

Some workers argued that registrations were made to match the performance criteria and are also manipulated to meet standard performance agreements, while at the same time upholding professional values. In order to deal with unintended effects – sometimes with the support of their managers – social workers develop different kinds of strategies to meet both the demands and needs of their clients and the accountability demands of the local government. They for instance manipulate registration:

> Some clients take so much time because they have so many problems in different domains, relation, work, debts. Well, for each single demand you create then a new dossier so it counts for two or three, you get it? You have to be a little bit, what I call, creative. (Social worker, 10 January 2007)

Even without manipulation, this performance measurement does not mirror the results of social work. Both social workers and managers argue they want to be held more accountable for the results of their work. Neither service users nor partner organizations play any role in public accountability.

Research indicates that local governments do not use all this information much. 'It seems reasonable to conclude that most aldermen do not consider output-oriented performance information available in the planning and control documents of their organisations very informative and that they use it only infrequently' (Bogt 2006: 241). Politicians gain information mainly by talking to senior officials, other politicians and other influential people, instead of reading reports (Pollitt 2006).

In short, accountability does bring transparency and democracy, but only in relation to local government and also in a problematic way. It not only seems to create new vagueness, but also leads to time-consuming bureaucracy at the expense of accountability to professionals and service users. Opportunities to use forms in a more promising way are neglected because of a lack of managerial capacity and local government steering.

npm's democratic promise

So, what conclusions can we draw on the democratic promise of npm? At the institutional level organizations have become more government-steered rather than demand-oriented. With contracts, standards and performance measurement, npm has strengthened the voice of local government at the expense of the voice of citizens as service users. The fact that there are no clients' councils only adds to this imbalance. npm did not wipe out paternalism, but merely replaced it: now it is local politics that tends to patronize citizens. For ten years Lawton et al. (2000) – reviewing the reforms in the National Health Services in the uk – came to the same conclusion. Citing a health authority manager: 'If they [the employees] have been displaced as the most powerful stakeholder, their place has been taken by the government, not the patient' (Lawton et al. 2000: 17). So choice was indeed introduced, but only for local government as the representative of citizens, not for individual citizens directly. You could call this democracy in the sense of representative democracy, but then it is a very constrained, elitist version of democracy (Hanberger 2006).

At the level of services delivery it seems that npm did stimulate a more attentive attitude to the ideas and needs of individual clients. However, it must be stressed that social workers reject the notion of citizens as consumers, and even reject the idea of serving their demands. This, they argue, underestimates the peculiarities of social work. The npm related

EVELIEN TONKENS, MARC HOIJTINK & HUUB GULIKERS

market discourse of services/products and customers/consumers does not recognize this.

Accountability does bring transparency and democracy, but again only in relation to local government, not to professionals and service users. Moreover, it creates new vagueness, and fuels time-consuming bureaucracy. Social workers try to incorporate accountability norms that fit their professional values and neutralize those that threaten these values. They try to minimize disturbance to their day-to-day activities. Opportunities to use forms in a more promising way are neglected because of a lack of managerial capacity and local government steering.

Democratic professionalism

This somewhat gloomy picture raises the question of whether an alternative way for democratizing local social work can be developed. There is an impressive body of practices as well as research around the notion of *participation* in public service provision (Cawston & Barbour 2003; Cornwall & Gaventa 2001), local democracy (Fung & Wright 2003), including civil initiatives and Asset-Based Community Development (ABCD). Participation tends to start from the perspective of the client; the interaction with professionals is hardly in view. This differs from *civic professionalism* (Sullivan 2004) and *collaboration* (Vigoda 2002), which start from the perspective and tasks of the professional. Civic professionalism departs from a rather traditional idea of professionals as set out by Freidson (2001). Professionals are understood as possessing and maintaining specialized knowledge about their field, and exchanging this knowledge with colleagues, thus expanding the shared knowledge of the profession as a whole. Professionals are expected to be driven by a (possibly secular) calling, rather than by status or money; a calling to serve a transcendental aim, like health, justice or equality. Professionals are expected to engage in democratic exchange with clients as well as with the broader audience (Sullivan 2004). Professionals must 're-engage the public over the nature and value of what they do for the society at large' (Sullivan 2004: 19). Professionals must be 'in real dialogue with their publics and open to public accountability' (ibid.), thereby 'inviting public response and involvement in the profession's effort to clarify its mission and responsibilities' (ibid.).

The most promising perspective in our view starts from neither the client nor the professional but from the *interaction* between professionals, aiming at maximizing the democratic character of this exchange. Albert Dzur coined this *democratic professionalism* (Dzur 2004, 2008). The 'democratic' in democratic professionalism takes shape in face-to-face relations between professionals and clients. Democracy is not just an instrument; it is a value in itself. We will try to sketch the promises of this model by rearticulating it in the terms used above: service orientation, voice, choice and accountability.

Dzur does not explicitly contrast democratic professionalism with NPM's promises such as service orientation, but we can argue that from the perspective of democratic professionalism, service orientation fails to recognize the issue of professional authority. The notion of service orientation even turns the authority relation upside down: by presenting professionals as service providers, the authority lies with the consumer whose demands should be served. Professionals, Dzur argues, cannot and do not function without professional authority. We cannot wipe this out; yet citizens also have authority, based on experiential knowledge. Dzur quotes Dewey who points out that 'the man who wears the shoe knows best that it pinches and where it pinches, even if the expert shoemaker is the best judge of how the trouble is to be remedied' (2004: 10). Democratic professionalism is not about complete equality between professionals and clients. While some theorists of participation argue that 'traditional boundaries between expert and lay become blurred' (Cawston & Barbour 2003: 721), 'democratic professionalism maintains professionals both exercise authority and share it' (Dzur 2004: 12). Professionals must 'be in real dialogue with their publics' (ibid.: 19) but also 'take public leadership in solving perceived public problems' (ibid.: 18). They must 'both exercise authority and share it' (ibid.: 12). This double task is what makes democratic professionalism so complex.

These two sources of authority demand that they are shared by professionals and citizens. Democratic professionalism is about 'sharing authority in public life' by way of dialogue, on the individual, group, and collective level. Knowledge is not only exchanged with colleagues but with clients as well. Professionals explain their views and procedures, acknowledge the knowledge that clients possess themselves and come to a shared view of problems and solutions. Democratic professionals are task sharers, not task monopolists (Dzur 2008: 105).

The voice of citizens is thus crucial, but not primarily on boards or panels. Professional authority and civic authority meet primarily in daily interaction; thus democratic professionalism should take shape exactly there. Informal participation is therefore more important than formal participation, just as the social workers and managers we interviewed claim. This can of course be backed up by formal participation; but this only makes sense if informal participation is well established, because this provides the signs and signals that formal participation builds on (Duyvendak et al. 2009). For professionals, good social work means that they incorporate the client's voice in their support. For social work, this means that the informal democratic practices in social work sketched above deserve recognition and should be linked to formal democratic procedures like clients' councils and accountability systems. Also, the idea of a professional calling should be recognized and cherished within the organizations, because without a firm idea of what the purpose and meaning of their work is, social workers cannot really enter into a dialogue.

Choice, thirdly, is important too, but as a steering mechanism to correct social work organizations, not as something professionals should keep their hands off in the name of citizens' autonomy. Democratic professionals are concerned about the effects of their expertise on the lay public's ability to make self-confident choices, both inside and outside a particular professional domain. As to social work, our interviews make it clear that the provider-purchaser split meant to augment citizen's choice merely augments the choice of politicians. It does not promote citizen's choice nor dialogue between social work and its social surroundings.

There is no less weight attached to accountability in democratic professionalism than is the case in NPM, but this too is a shared task. Accountability is not about external control of professionals who are in turn trying to hide from the public gaze and do their own thing; it also demands something of professionals to begin with. It demands an *inquisitive*, critical attitude from professionals. Dzur builds on Dewey here: 'Dewey's social scientist promotes the growth of critical thinking by challenging common sense views, encouraging abstract thinking, and by embodying certain habits of mind and character' (Dzur 2004: 11). For social work, this demands that knowledge exchange and criticism of colleagues and clients should be welcomed.

For social workers to become democratic professionals, it is necessary that they themselves and their managers leave the self-victimization we can also witness (see also Hoijtink & Van Doorn, 2011). It prevents them from doing what they believe in even though no one forbids them, like discussing individual evaluation reports. Social workers and their managers could show more public leadership. If local social work acts more proactively and innovatively in setting up these dialogues and placing themselves at the heart of the debate on social quality in society – comparable to the way in which housing corporations place themselves at the heart of the debate on social housing and neighbourhoods in the Netherlands today. This might also strengthen their legitimacy in society.

Conclusion

The democratic promise of NPM we reconstructed and analyzed in this chapter was not met in the practice of Dutch social work. We broke this promise down into four elements (service orientation, voice, choice and accountability), and concluded that NPM in Dutch social work strengthens none of these in citizens. It merely strengthens the voice and choice of politicians and policy-makers, and accountability towards them. This kind of accountability does not do justice to their professionalism, social workers argue quite convincingly. However, we also came across self-victimization of social workers and managers. Some of them tend not to take the discretionary space they do seem to have, e.g. to organize ways of accountability that suit them better. On the other hand we also see examples of social workers who do develop a voice among citizens, but more in an informal manner. For professionals good social work means that they incorporate the client's voice in their support.

We also argued that democratic professionalism can serve as an alternative model to develop democratic promises not met by NPM. Democratic professionalism does not negate or try to abolish professional authority. It rather seeks ways to combine professional and civic authority, recognizing the tension involved in both exercising and sharing authority. This ideal could lead the way beyond NPM democratic failure and self-victimization of social workers and their managers.

References

Boer, N. de, & Duyvendak, J.W. (2004). *Welzijn [Well-being]*. In: H. Dijstelbloem, P. Meurs & E.K. Schruijvers, *Maatschappelijke Dienstverlening. Een onderzoek naar vijf sectoren [Social Services. Research into Five Sectors]*. Amsterdam: Amsterdam University Press.

Boer, N. de, & Lans, J. van der, (2011). *Burgerkracht. De toekomst van het sociaal werk in Nederland [Citizen Power. The Future of Social Work in The Netherlands]*. Den Haag: Raad voor Maatschapelijke Ontwikkeling (RMO).

Bogt, H.J. ter (2006). *New Public Management and Management Changes in Dutch Local Government: Some recent experiences and future topics*. Groningen: Universiteit van Groningen.

Cawston, P.G., & Barbour, R.S. (2003). Clients or Citizens? Some considerations for primary care organisations. *British Journal of General Practice, 53*(494), 716-722.

Clarke, J. (2004). *Changing Welfare, Changing States: New directions in social policy*. London: Sage.

Clarke, J., & Newman, J. (1997). *The Managerial State: Power, Politics and Ideology in the Remaking of Social Welfare*. London: Sage.

Cornwall, A., & Gaventa, J. (2001). *From Users and Choosers to Makers and Shapers: Repositioning participation in social policy*. IDS-working paper, Brighton.

Du Gay, P. (2000). *In Praise of Bureaucracy*. London: Sage.

Duyvendak, J.W., Hoijtink, M., & Tonkens, E. (2009). Post-patient Perspectives. User-based logics and the never-ending inequality between users and professionals. In: H. Uwe Otto (Ed.) *Evidence-based Practice: Modernising the Knowledge Base of Social Work?* (pp. 31-47). Opladen & Farmington Hills: Barbara Budrich Publishers.

Dzur, A.W. (2004). Democratic Professionalism: Sharing authority in civic life. *The Good Society, 13*(1), 6-14.

Dzur, A.W. (2008). *Democratic Professionalism, Citizen Participation and the Reconstruction of Professional Ethics, Identity, and Practice*. University Park, PA: Pennsylvania State University Press.

Fienieg, B., Nierkens, V., Tonkens, E., Plochg, T., & Stronks, K. (2011). Why play an active role? A qualitative examination of lay citizens' main motives for participation in health promotion, *Health Promotion International* (Advance Access published September 6, 2011).

Fung, A., & Wright, E.O. (Eds.) (2003). *Deepening Democracy. Institutional Innovations in empowered participatory governance.* London: Verso.

Freidson, E. (2001). *Professionalism: The third logic.* Cambridge: Polity Press.

Hanberger, A. (2006). Evaluation of and for Democracy. *Evaluation, 12*(1), 17-37.

Hoijtink, M., & Doorn, L. van. (2011). Bestuurlijke turbulentie in het sociaal werk. De uitdaging van meervoudige coalitievorming [Administrative Turbulence in Social Work: the Challenge of Pluralist Coalition-formation]. *Journal of Social Intervention, 20*(3), 5-23.

Hoijtink, M., & Oude Vrielink, M. (2007). Managers en Professionals in de Sociale Sector: Ideologische clash of vermenging van waarden? [Managers and Professionals in the Social Sector: Ideological Clash or Mixed Values?]. *Bestuurskunde, 12*(4), 25-33.

Huijben, M., & Geurtsen, A. et al. (2003). *Benchmark overhead 74 welzijnsinstellingen [Benchmark Overhead 74 Welfare Institutions].* Utrecht: Berenschot.

Jordan, B. & Jordan, C. (2000). *Social Work and the Third Way. Tough Love as Social Policy.* London: Sage.

Kennedy, J. (1995). *Building New Babylon: Cultural change in the Netherlands during the 1960s.* Iowa: University of Iowa Press.

Kremer, M. & Tonkens, E. (2006). Authority, Trust, Knowledge and the Public Good in Dissaray. In J.W. Duyvendak, T. Knijn and M. Kremer (Eds.), *Policy, People, and the New Professional. De- and re-professionalization in Care and Welfare.* Amsterdam: Amsterdam University Press.

Lawton, A., McKevitt, D., & Millar, M. (2000). Coping with Ambiguity: Reconciling external legitimacy and organizational implementation. *Performance Measurement Public Money & Management, 20*(3), 13-20.

Marquand, D. (2004). *The Decline of the Public.* Bristol: Polity Press.

Newman, J., & Tonkens, E. (2011). *Participation, Responsibility and Choice. Summoning the active citizen in Western welfare states.* Amsterdam: Amsterdam University Press.

Ootes, S.T.C., Pols, A.J., Tonkens, E.H., & Willems, D.L. (2010). Bridging boundaries; the concept of 'citizenship' as a boundary object in mental healthcare. *Medische Antropologie [Medical Anthropology] special issue 'The body in disability studies', 22* (2), 375-388.

Osborne, D.E., & Gaebler, T. (1992). *Reinventing Government: How the Entrepreneurial Spirit is Transforming the Public Sector.* Reading, MA: Addison-Wesley.

Peters, T.J., & Waterman, R.H. (1982). *In Search of Excellence, Lessons from America's Best-Run Companies.* New York/London: Harper and Row.

Pollitt, C. (2003). *The Essential Public Manager.* Berkshire: Open University Press.

Pollitt, C. (2006). Performance Information for Democracy: The Missing Link? *Evaluation, 12*(1), 38-55.

Pollitt, C., & Bouckaert, G. (2004). *Public Management Reform. A Comparative Analysis.* New York: Oxford University Press.

Power, M. (1997). *The Audit Society: Rituals of verification.* Oxford: Oxford University Press.

Rodger, J.J. (2000). *From a Welfare State to a Welfare Society. The changing context of social policy in a postmodern era.* London: MacMillan Press.

Steege, M. van der, & Deur, H. van (2002). Vraaggericht werken en methodisch handelen. Ruimte voor oprechtheid, intuïtie en flexibiliteit [Working Demand-based and Acting Methodically]. *Maatwerk*, April 2002, 13-17.

Sullivan, W. (2004). Can Professionalism Still be a Viable Ethic? *The Good Society*, 13(1), 15-20.

Tonkens, E. (2010). Civicness and Citizen Participation in Social Services: Conditions for promoting respect and public concern. In T. Bransen, P. Dekker & A. Evers (Eds.), *Civicness in the Governance of Social Services*. Baden-Baden: Nomos.

Tonkens, E. (2011). The embrace of responsibility. Citizenship and governance of social care in the Netherlands. In: Newman and Tonkens, *Participation, Responsibility and Choice. Summoning the active citizen in Western welfare states* (pp. 45-67). Amsterdam: Amsterdam University Press.

Tonkens, E., & Van Doorn, L. (2001). Turning Rough Sleepers into Responsible Citizens. Third Way policies on homelessness in England and the Netherlands. *Renewal: The Journal of Labour Politics*, 3(3), 142-151.

Tonkens, E., & Duyvendak, J.W. (2003). Paternalism, Caught between Rejection and Acceptance: Taking care and taking control in community work. *Community Development Studies*, 38(1), 6-15.

Tonkens, E. & Weijers, I. (1999). Autonomy, Care and Self-realization. Policy views of Dutch Service Providers. *Mental Retardation: The Journal of the American Association on Mental Retardation*, 37(6), 468-476.

Van Sambeek, N., Broer, C., & Tonkens, E. (2011). Sluipend kwaliteitsverlies in de gezondheidszorg. Professionals over de gevolgen van marktwerking [Quality Decline in Health Care. Professionals about the Consequences of Marketization]. *Beleid en Maatschappij (38)*1, 47- 64.

Vigoda, E. (2002). From Responsiveness to Collaboration: Governance, citizens and the next generation of public administration. *Public Administration Review*, 62(5), 527-540.

Wiendels, M., Schulz, M., & Jansen, A. (2004). Doelmatigheid en Doeltreffendheid van Subsidies in het Welzijnswerk [Efficiency and Effectiveness of Subsidies in Welfare Work] . Utrecht: Berenschot.

11 Bounded professionalism

Why self-regulation is part of the problem

Mirjan Oude Vrielink & Jeroen van Bockel

Introduction

In this chapter we analyze what we call 'regulatory pressure'. By this we mean the pressure experienced by individual professionals because they feel encapsulated by rules and standards. As such, it is related to the three general sources of pressures discerned by Hupe & van der Krogt as having an impact on professional work (rule pressure, societal pressure and vocational pressure) and it is related to Tummers et al.'s emphasis on policy pressures and alienation effects. But regulatory pressure has a distinctive meaning referring to the combined effect of different rules and standards (linked to different policies) in daily work practices, encompassing both regulatory and administrative burdens.

In the international literature on regulation, the concept of regulatory pressure disintegrates into a number of component subjects such as bureaucratization, regulatory creep, administrative burden (Van Gestel & Hertogh 2006: 11). To give a general impression of the varying meanings: regulatory pressure refers to the number of regulations imposed by public administration; the inconsistency of regulations; the extent to which the legislator leaves room for behavioral alternatives or private initiatives; the cost of compliance with regulations; a lack of trust in society or in the market; the interactions between government bodies formulating or implementing regulations and those who are required to comply with the regulations; and the way in which compliance is supervised, enforced and sanctioned (Van den Bosch 2005; Van Gestel & Hertogh 2006: 14-17). In this general overview, the emphasis is on public administration actors as the main source of regulatory pressure. This is surprising, as professional conduct – compare Newman's governance narrative – is not only regulated by the state but also by a myriad of non-state actors, including professional organizations and professional associations.

Recently, several explorative studies on regulatory pressure were carried out in various policy areas in the Netherlands, for example by the Ministry of Home Affairs and the Ministry of Education, aiming to identify the most important *hotspots* and causes of regulatory burdens. These types of studies, like previous academic research on regulatory pressure, generally concentrate on the number of rules and the actual amount of administrative burdens involved in regulations and thus the time that is needed to comply (Van Gestel & Hertogh 2006). Though interesting in its own right, the *experience* of regulatory pressure cannot however be explained by the number of rules alone (Van Gestel & Hertogh 2006; Noordegraaf & Sterrenburg 2009a; Dorbeck-Jung et al. 2006). Moreover, in order to understand why professionals feel that regulations put too much pressure on their professional work, we need to look beyond state regulations. An additional focus on the professions' involvement in regulatory pressure is needed.

Professionals in public service typically have a double orientation (cf. Hoijtink & Oude Vrielink 2006; Van Bockel 2009: 64-72): they practise their vocation in an organizational setting, as well as within the institutions of their profession (see also Hupe & Van der Krogt's chapter 4). Consequently, professional regulation is typically taken up, first, by professional associations, 'organized, self-governing social units authorized to represent the profession' (Frankel 1989: 114). Some of these associations have statutory powers or installed regulatory bodies. It is taken up, second, by managers of organizations in which professionals work. As we will contend, self-regulation by professional associations (and professional organizations) might also cause regulatory pressure.

In this chapter we explore what possible effects these multiple sources have on the regulatory pressures experienced by professionals. Drawing on insights from two recent Dutch studies, we will argue that only certain types of rules cause regulatory pressures and that various circumstances within the organizations in which professionals work, as well as their institutional context, may affect the experience of pressure. Against this background, the central question of this chapter is: why does self-regulation fail as a solution to relieve regulatory pressure that professionals experience in day-to-day practices? We start with a description of two empirical studies of regulatory pressure in professional work and focus on three lessons that can be derived. Then (in the fourth paragraph), we highlight the 'rationality' of self-regulation – are (self)regulations of professional work effective and efficient? In the final paragraph, we search for a trust-based alternative to (self)regulation in order to constrain the rise of what we call *bounded professionalism*.

Regulatory pressure and its sources

Regulatory pressure is considered to be a complex phenomenon that defies easy interpretation; lawyers are inclined to define it in terms of 'freedom', economists in terms of 'costs', and experts in public administration in terms of 'performance' (Van den Bosch 2005). In terms of Hupe & Van der Krogt regulatory pressure can be understood as encompassing both rule pressure and vocational pressure.[1] Here we will use the more general concept of regulatory pressure, since work pressure coming from the professions is increasingly interwoven with work pressure stemming from law, policy and management. In this respect it is important to note that next to the self-regulation that has always been a central element of professional work, governments of advanced Western economies are increasingly relying on other forms of (self)regulation as a means to achieve public policy goals. Self-regulation refers to the intentional and goal-oriented process of rulemaking, monitoring and enforcement activities by non-state actors without any special legislative authority (cf. Gunningham & Rees 1997). Empirically, self-regulation – also sought by states – is assumed to have various advantages compared to command-and-control regulation (Baggott 1989; Havinga 2006; Van Boom et al. 2009). It is assumed that self-regulation enhances compliance, since it is based on the expertise of the field. Furthermore, it is believed that self-regulation supports the internalization of norms and improves acceptance of the rules by those who have to comply with them. Also, self-regulation is expected to be a more responsive and flexible regulatory instrument, allowing the organizational field to deal with, for example, rapidly changing technologies and stimulating innovative developments. Because of these potential advantages various Western states have encouraged self-regulation in public contexts. Instead of issuing detailed legal prescriptions (private) organizations are required to engage in self-regulation to meet generally stated policy objectives. Usually this kind of self-regulation is embedded in or invoked by legislation or public policies of central and local government (cf. De Been 2009: 150). Consequently, the rules professionals have to deal with on the workfloor increasingly stem from a hybrid system of legal provisions and self-regulation, not only by professional norms and standards, but also organizational procedures.

Regulatory pressure in professional work explained

Regulatory pressures can be distinguished into two categories, namely a) *regulatory burdens* and b) *administrative burdens*. The first concerns the pressure caused by general compliance costs, for example because regulations are insufficiently attuned to actual practices. Administrative burdens pertain to regulatory pressure that results from administrative and procedural obligations that are imposed by regulations.

Noordegraaf & Sterrenburg (2009a) published an overview of administrative burdens in professional work caused by state regulations. Their chapter was based on empirical studies in the public domains of healthcare and public safety, which explored administrative burdens by measuring time investments and costs of regulations. An explorative study of Dorbeck-Jung et al. (2006) describes the broader category of regulatory burdens caused by legally conditioned self-regulation in the domains of healthcare, higher education and environmental protection. They used the method of qualitative interviews to look into five clusters of factors and circumstances that may explain regulatory pressure. Based on these two studies – in our view – three main explanations for regulatory pressures as experienced by individual professionals in day-to-day practices can be identified.

Meaningless rules

First of all, the studies point to a misfit between regulations and standing professional practice. Professional work is particularly strained by regulations that poorly fit in with norms and routines on the work floor, or by regulations that professionals consider to be meaningless (cf. Dorbeck-Jung & Oude Vrielink 2005). Pressures are felt most strongly when action prescriptions are perceived as useless, unreasonable, impractical or inhibiting a proper treatment of the particulars of a situation. For instance, the findings of Dorbeck-Jung et al. (2006) revealed that a recent policy change in the Dutch higher education sector entailed very detailed action prescriptions regarding the accreditation of vocational schools and universities and severe accountability pressures. Professionals and their managers complain about these prescriptions, which they find hard to reconcile with the particulars of their organizations and the ability to learn from mistakes. In a similar way, Noordegraaf & Sterrenburg (2009b: 248) describe how obligations of registration can lead to annoyance and perceived regulatory pressure. The reason for this reaction is not the regulation itself, but a possible purpose of these registrations in the near future, i.e. a way to hold these professionals to account.

When regulations are meaningful and easily reconciled with standing practice, however, they meet little or no resistance and are sometimes even welcomed by professionals and their managers. Such rules are perceived as an integral part of professional service delivery in contrast to ill-fitting rules that are experienced as external to their core task. The study of Dorbeck-Jung et al. (2006) provides an example. To refine and implement a Dutch legal provision requiring 'responsible care', healthcare centers and domiciliary care organizations both had to engage in self-regulation. In order to establish a quality management system, they were required to adopt internal protocols, procedures, plans, handbooks and the like. Healthcare centers were in the position to organize these regulations around particular types of patients or diseases, whereas domiciliary care organizations had to incorporate them in their quality management systems. Consequently, in the healthcare centers the internal regulations not only easily fitted in with standing practice but even had added value. They cause little if any pressure on the workfloor of the professionals. By contrast, professionals in the domiciliary care organizations complain about the self-imposed internal regulations, which according to them interfere with delivering good quality care on a daily basis.

Costly rules

A second explanation for experienced regulatory pressure that can be derived from both studies deals with the costs of compliance. Professionals who feel that resources required to comply with regulations are not well spent try to ignore the rules or they invest just enough to uphold the impression of compliance (cf. Hoijtink & Oude Vrielink 2007). When regulations cannot be ignored and game playing is no option, the investment of scarce resources to comply with the regulations causes regulatory pressure. Noordegraaf & Sterrenburg (2009a; cf. Algemene Rekenkamer, 2011) point at failing software, as a result of which policemen have to spend more time on filling in ICT forms. Because of numerous bugs in the software, forms have to be completed over and over again. Another example is the administrative burden of family doctors. Family doctors experience administrative burdens in filling out declarations for insurance companies. These companies use different systems; as a result a family doctor's compliance costs increase.

Dorbeck-Jung et al. (2006) found that in situations of scarcity of resources professionals experience quality regulations as more burdensome. The previous example of healthcare centers and domiciliary care organizations may illustrate this once more. Domiciliary care organizations have to invest more time and money in upholding quality management systems than healthcare centers, because of a divergent supervisory approach that results in a difference in the costs of compliance. Both types of organizations are legally obliged to uphold a quality management system. However, when it comes to healthcare centers inspectorates are usually lenient, knowing that it is very difficult to uphold such a system when multiple disciplines co-operate in the delivery of care. By contrast, the inspectorates oblige domiciliary care organizations to comply with the legal requirement of having a quality management system in place. This disparity of the costs of compliance is reflected in the experience of regulatory pressure. Professionals in the domiciliary care centers feel irritated about spending time and money on actions that in their opinion do not directly improve service delivery, whereas the healthcare centers report that their money and time are well spent. Dorbeck-Jung et al. observed a similar reaction to action prescriptions of professional associations. For instance, in the domiciliary care sector a professional association proposed to upgrade the quality norms of a certification scheme (whereby certification is a condition of membership of this association). At the annual meeting the members strongly objected to this plan, arguing that research revealed that stricter norms not necessarily improved the quality of care and that the possible commercial advantages did not outweigh the extra costs and efforts of an upgraded certification scheme.

Regulatory styles

The third explanation that can be drawn from both studies concerns the impact of the regulatory style of the bodies formulating, monitoring or enforcing regulations. The findings of Dorbeck-Jung et al. (2006) show the importance of the regulatory style of professional associations. Professionals and their managers experience fewer regulatory burdens if professional associations give them enough time to implement regulations and support them in terms of blueprint protocols, service desks, informative conferences or information on websites. The experience of regulatory pressures may also result from the style applied by supervisors, as we already indicated when describing the impact of styles of inspectorates on the costs of compliance, and consequently the experience of regulatory pressure. Noordegraaf & Sterrenburg (2009a: 120-121) point to extra compliance costs as a result of various interpretations of what is necessary, according to formal rules, for instance in youth care. The findings show that a strict attitude of supervising or enforcement bodies easily causes regulatory pressures, which is partly caused by the fact that better compliance requires the investment of a greater share of scarce resources. Another factor that enhances regulatory pressures is the feeling that supervisory or enforcement bodies lack expertise or are inattentive to the particulars of the situation and require all sorts of needless registration. Much registration does not result in feedback offering insights into what actually can be added to improve service delivery (cf. Van Gestel & Hertogh 2006).

Lessons

These explanations lead to three possible ways – lessons – to relieve the regulatory pressure on professionals. Those involved in organizing and supervising professional services should be sure that a) regulations are meaningful for those who have to comply with them and easily fit in with standing practices; b) professionals receive financial, administrative and other kinds of support to reduce the costs of compliance to prevent that these costs come at the expense of resources required to perform core tasks; and c) regulations and accountability have to allow enough room for alternative action to ensure that professionals can act upon their knowledge and expertise (cf. Noordegraaf & Sterrenburg 2009b). The second lesson is the easiest one to live up to, as it 'simply' requires the implementation of better support. However, such measures do not get to the bottom of the irritating regulations but only diminish the unpleasantness of having to spend time and money on compliance. Better ways to preempt complaints about regulatory pressure are to make regulations *meaningful* and in line with standing practices with enough room for professionals to act upon the particulars of the situation (lesson 3).

MIRJAN OUDE VRIELINK & JEROEN VAN BOCKEL

These lessons will surprise those who are familiar with the literature on self-regulation since the lessons stress the very reason why self-regulation was promoted in the first place. As we already mentioned before, self-regulation has been stimulated based on the assumption that it improves the quality of regulations, in terms of being in line with professional practice, because the standard setting is the responsibility of actors with detailed knowledge of the industry or sector and with a potential for utilizing peer pressure and for successfully internalizing the responsibility for compliance (Gunningham & Rees 1997: 365). The use of *field knowledge* is expected to result in rules that are more effective, and consequently reduce the experience of regulatory pressure, because of the relatively close relationship between the actors defining the rules and those to whom the rules are addressed (Havinga 2006). What is to be explored, then, is why professional associations and organizations engage in self-regulation but fail to draw up meaningful rules that easily fit in with standing practices. In the next section we will address this question by discussing different rationales of self-regulation to find out whether or not it seems a rational choice to control professional work.

Is self-regulation rational?

Professionals traditionally enjoy their exceptional status on ethical grounds. They exercise control over specialized knowledge and are expected to use this knowledge to serve the public good, rather than their own interests. Professions need to regulate themselves effectively so as to justify their autonomy, while ensuring that their members' clients and the general public benefit from the professions' and individual professionals' actions (Brien 1998: 392). Professionalism is demonstrated by the fostering of ethical behavior backed up by disciplinary procedures (Van Hoy 1993: 91). Professional codes are viewed as the most visible and explicit enunciation of professional norms (Frankel 1989: 110). They often induce internal regulation by member organizations to tailor the general rules and standards to the specifics of the organization, usually through planning and control routines, organizational procedures, feedback mechanisms and administrative actions (cf. Baarsma et al. 2003). Additionally, single organizations may also decide to adopt a corporate code of their own.

Professional control

Internal professional control is both a prerequisite for the delegation of responsibility towards a profession and a necessary condition to protect the autonomy granted to the profession as an institution, as well as its individual members (Frankel 1989: 109, 110; cf. chapter 4 of Hupe & Van der Krogt). Traditionally, codes are intended to shape moral conscience and professional responsibility in order to be recognized as a profession by both related occupations and the general public (Meulenbergs et al. 2004: 333). A similar movement is at the root of the growing ethical guidance in the organizational context. Brooks (1989: 117), for instance, points to the increased regulation of modern organizations giving them a right to pursue their stated objectives in return for accountability through its top management to its shareholders and to the public. Considering the fact that codes and other instruments of self-regulation have always been used to achieve and protect professional autonomy, the question arises why they currently seem to pressure professional work. As Hupe & Van der Krogt (see chapter 4) argue, the answer is to be found in the changed professional contexts. Professionals nowadays are confronted with an increased demand of scarce(r) resources; rising expectations from society; changes in the ideas about what 'good practice' entails, and ongoing specialization. Meulenbergs et al. (2004: 333, 334) discuss similar developments in a nursing context under the terms of growing interdisciplinarity, increasing precedence of economic discourse and an intensified legal framework. They contend that as a result of these changes a different mode of institutionalization operates. Professions can no longer be regarded as the active pole that instigates the regulation of professional practices. Instead of the prevailing power being situated within the professional group, external demands increasingly control professional practices. Codes and other instruments of self-regulation have become, to quote Meulenberg et al. (2004: 334), 'mechanisms of control rather than instruments for the promotion of ethics'.

Professional associations and managers increasingly use self-regulatory instruments to help achieve goals other than enhancing professional ethics. For example, a professional association in the Dutch domiciliary care sector managed to convince its members to agree on the adoption and implementation of quality regulations in a rather short time span. The sector had to deal with a prospect of increased market competition that put the vested interests in a new perspective, creating a sense of urgency among domiciliary care organizations to secure public support by developing a sectoral quality hallmark to distinguish them from commercial providers. This change of professional context even resulted in the acceptance of compliance with the quality regulations as a precondition of membership (Oude Vrielink-Van Heffen, Kraan & Bjørnholt 2006: 15-16).

In the changed context professional associations and managers not only are subject to external demands, they also have to respond to more divergent interests of a wider array of stakeholders. As a code is intended to appeal to many different interests, professional associations and organizations are faced with the difficult task to meet these interests and still fulfill a code's functions for professionals. This thorny situation is further complicated by the fact that various government agencies have awakened to their power to influence or control professions and the or-

MIRJAN OUDE VRIELINK & JEROEN VAN BOCKEL

ganizations they work for. This has made the professional context more *unstable*: policy objectives frequently change, and the widespread use of NPM practices and ideas has also increased the level of competition (cf. Van Boom 2009).

The dynamics of public policies result in shifting policy goals, requiring self-regulatory instruments to change accordingly. Like any other policy instrument, professional associations and managers need to adjust the self-regulation to the policy changes. During this period of time self-regulatory instruments run the risk of being perceived as meaningless by professionals who are required to institute or comply with them. Similarly, professionals may feel pressed by organizational rules that control their behavior to respond to an increased level of competition. Although professionals are part of a wider community, managers sometimes depict their peers as competitors. In situations where the profession and an organization deploy a different view on the right course of action professionals have been found to prefer their profession's code over the code of their organization (Higgs-Kleyn & Kapelianis 1999: 371) in which case the organizational norms and standards are perceived as putting pressures on their professional work.

Control instruments

From the findings presented in section 3 we can learn that rule-compliance is low when professionals consider the rules meaningless or find it hard to reconcile them with standing professional practices. In the absence of enforcement, self-regulation in such situations will be ineffective (Brien 1998: 392). Codes typically provide disciplinary mechanisms and sanctions to signal that the profession or organization is committed to the self-imposed rules. For instance, almost every professional code includes a provision imposing a responsibility on the profession's members to report violation of the code. However, professionals often display a clear reluctance to report infringements or even openly criticize colleagues. Various reasons may explain this reluctance, such as a wish to shield the profession from embarrassment, to avoid increased external control, or to evade legal retaliation (Bird 1998; Frankel 1989: 113). Under these circumstances sanctions are hardly ever effectuated and the accountability of the profession is highly attenuated (Brien 1998: 393).

Responding to the above-mentioned increase of external demands, professional associations and managers have established additional provisions to control professional conduct, such as licensing, peer review, visitation, certification and mandatory reporting. These informative self-regulatory instruments are applied to notify colleagues, clients and the wider public about rule-compliance and professional performances. To the extent that this strategy increases external confidence it helps to protect the autonomy granted to individual professionals and to the profession as a community. Professional associations and managers intend to insulate the profession from threats to its autonomy. However, at the same time they create regulatory pressures through their employment of informative self-regulatory instruments and to a lesser extent through their active enforcement of rule-compliance. They put *pressure* on professionals to comply with rules or to engage in activities that produce information about their performance, even when they know that these rules and performance measurements are meaningless from the professional's point of view and are difficult to reconcile with their standing practices. Professional associations and managers therefore struggle with the difficult task of drawing up regulations that maintain a balance between the interests of professionals and stakeholders. If public demands and values are not properly met, the profession is criticized for being too self-absorbed and serving only private interests. To hold on to professional autonomy, professional associations and managers increasingly use codes as mechanisms of control despite their member's complaints about self-imposed rules and informative instruments.

The use of codes as a means of external control severely impairs its effectiveness. The rule-following orientation that is symptomatic of today's professional context induces a shift from the professional's moral commitment to act upon vocational norms and aspirations to a *legalist* attitude in which the focus is on compliance to the minimum standards required by a code. A strong external orientation runs counter to the exercise of professional discretion, which lies at the core of professional service delivery. Effectiveness is also hampered if regulations are irrelevant for or inconsistent with professional values or objectives. As a result, a professional's skills are subordinate to the public will – i.e. a legalist approach of public service delivery that takes legitimacy and accountability as a starting point. Answering the header of this paragraph, these ways of regulating professional work do *not* seem to be rational at all. In the concluding remarks and the discussion section of this chapter we will elaborate on the rationality and irrationality of modern regulation of professional work by introducing the concept of bounded professionalism.

Conclusion

So far, we have explained the regulatory burdens professionals experience by means of three possible explanations: a) often there is a misfit between regulations and professional practice; b) professionals have problems with the costs of compliance; and c) there is a misfit of regulatory style and professional practice. Based on these three explanations we presented three lessons to relieve the regulatory pressure on professionals, in which meaningfulness of regulation, better support in compliance and allowance of room for action are the core concepts. Various Western economies, among them the Netherlands, encourage *self*-regulation on the assumption that compliance is enhanced if specialized knowledge of the field is used to draw them up. It is believed to support the internalization of norms and lead to a better acceptance of the rules. Professionals, then, would experience less regulatory pressure.

This suggestion, however, is *not* supported by the empirical findings. Professional associations and managers that subsequently tailor professional rules and standards to the specifics of the organizations fail to formulate rules that are meaningful for professionals and that easily fit in with their daily practices. The main reason for this is the changed professional context in which external stakeholders have become active instigators of the regulation of professional practices. Professional associations try hard to defend their professional discretion against exogenous forces – bureaucracy, society and other professions – by using self-regulatory instruments as mechanisms of control rather than instruments for the promotion of moral behavior (cf. Abbott 1987). The interplay of organizational (or bureaucratic) and professional forces which regulate professional practices has paradoxical effects, however.

At the very core, public service bureaucracies are built on the principle of specialization. This implies that only specialized and skilled individuals can work in what is called a professional bureaucracy. At the same time bureaucratic standards regulate professional work. These bureaucratic standards aim to minimize discretion (Weber 1964). Minimizing discretion however also means minimizing professionals' possibilities to carry out their tasks in a way that is best according to their professional judgment. Organizational or bureaucratic standards thus limit the use of professional skills. Hence, professional skills are a prerequisite to enter the organization, but these skills are not fully utilized in daily work. Van Bockel (2009: 215) calls this the *bureaucracy paradox*. Based on the argument of this chapter this also works for professional regulation. It is ironic that attempts to defend professional discretion lead to more regulatory pressure for professionals. In addition to the bureaucracy paradox, we can speak of a *professionalism paradox*.

The sum of these two paradoxes is what we call *bounded professionalism*. This highlights a publicly accepted but theoretically irrational and suboptimal situation, comparable to Simons bounded rationality (1976). On the one hand, the regulation of professional work is bounded by values and codes of the professional community itself, in which legitimacy and responsibility play a key role. On the other hand, society is bounded by a lack of specific professional knowledge. As a result of the second cause, society tries to find ways to comprehend professional work, so that the quality of professional service delivery can be judged. In most cases professionals find these judgments superficial. These reflexes to judge professional work by means of reducing it to generally comprehensible facts and indicators restrict a truly rational approach of regulation of professional practices, in which trust in a professional's abilities would be leading (cf. Fournier 1999).

In previous paragraphs several Dutch examples of professionals' regulatory burdens were mentioned. The Dutch tide seems to be changing, however. Recent publications have indeed emphasized the role of trust in the regulation of professional work (e.g. Tonkens 2008; Jansen et al. 2009). Policy-makers have also started to elaborate the concept of trust (e.g. memo of the Dutch Ministry of Justice, Tweede Kamer, 2008-2009, 31731, no.1). In addition, the possibilities of reducing administrative burdens of – among others – professionals by introducing the concept of trust are being explored (Ministry of Home Affairs 2009). These explorations result in a new challenge; how to conceptualize and implement trust in professional practices.

The two-sidedness of the concept of trust then is of great importance. Professionals demand trust in their work, governments demand trust in government's intentions. As this chapter clearly shows, reducing regulation of professional work as such will not solve the problem of professionals under pressure. Trust implies the acceptance of professional practice, of which incidents will be a part.

Regulatory burdens in professional work also occur in chains of public service delivery, where professionals cooperate to handle problems. When multiple professions are involved, trust can play a key-role in minimizing regulatory burdens that professionals create for each other by asking all sorts of information in formal ways. Professionals themselves thus also have a responsibility to reduce the burdens for professional disciplines.

Trust therefore is more than a policy instrument. Introducing trust in the relation of government, society and professionals implies a cultural shift. Both professionals as well as government have to accept risks and responsibilities. Risk analyses for instance can be used to determine where it is safe to restrain from regulating professional work. Professionals directly face the challenge of a demand for accountability. A professional response then would be to give account of professional standards – values – instead of output or procedures. Professional regulation in this way becomes more *unbounded* and perhaps a bit more rational.

Notes

1. Rule pressure refers to work pressure induced by action prescriptions that are imposed in relationships with a hierarchical nature. Most typically, these actions prescriptions are formal rules that stem from laws, public policies and managerial targets. Vocational pressure pertains to work pressures that are caused by professional norms stemming from the profession involved. Both are presented as objective components of what constitutes work pressure at a specific workfloor, although individual professionals may experience and deal with these pressures in different ways. Hence, rule pressure and vocational pressure add up to a particular amount of work pressure as experienced, in a given setting, by individual professionals.

MIRJAN OUDE VRIELINK & JEROEN VAN BOCKEL

References

Abbott, A. (1987). *The System of Professions: An essay on the division of expert labor.* Chicago/London: The University of Chicago Press.

Algemene Rekenkamer (2011). *ICT Politie 2010.* The Hague: Algemene Rekenkamer.

Baarsma, B., Felsö, F., Van Geffen, S., Mulder, J., & Oostdijk, A. (2003). *Do it Yourself? Stock-taking study of self-regulation instruments.* Study commissioned by the Ministry of Economic Affairs, Amsterdam.

Baggott, R. (1989). Regulatory Reform in Britain: The changing face of self-regulation. *Public Administration, 67*, 435-454.

Bird, S.J. (1998). The Role of Professional Societies: Codes of conduct and their enforcement. *Science & Engineering Ethics, 4*, 315-320.

Brien, A. (1998). Professional Ethics and the Culture of Trust. *Journal of Business Ethics, 17*(4), 391-409.

Brooks, L.J. (1989). Corporate Codes of Ethics. *Journal of Business Ethics 8*, 117-129.

De Been, W. (2009). Regels, marktprikkels en professionele deugden in tegenspraak: over zelfregulering en professionals [Rules, Market Incentives and Professional Virtues in Contradiction: on Self-regulation and Professionals]. In T. Jansen, G. van den Brink & J. Kole (Eds.), *Beroepstrots. Een ongekende kracht [Professional Pride. An Unprecedented Power].* (pp. 150-167). Amsterdam: Boom.

Dorbeck-Jung, B.R., & Oude Vrielink-Van Heffen, M.J. (2005). Do Legal Rules Based on Self-regulation Affect the Behavior of Doctors? The case of Dutch legislation on the contract of medical treatment. In N. Zeegers, W. Witteveen & B. van Klink (Eds.), *Social and Symbolic Effects of Legislation under the Rule of Law* (pp. 203-224). Mellen House, Lampeter, Ceredignion, Wales: The Edwin Mellen Press.

Dorbeck-Jung, B.R., Van Heffen-Oude Vrielink, M.J., & Reussing, G.H. (2006). *Open normen en regeldruk: Een onderzoek naar de kosten en oorzaken van irritaties bij open normen in de kwaliteitszorg [Open Norms and Rule Pressure].* Enschede: Universiteit Twente/IGS.

Fournier, V. (1999). The Appeal to 'Professionalism' as a Disciplinary Mechanism. *Sociological Review, 47*, 280-307.

Frankel, M.S. (1989). Professional Codes: Why, how, and with what impact? *Journal of Business Ethics, 8*, 109-115.

Gunningham, N., & Rees, J. (1997). Industry Self-regulation: An Institutional Perspective. *Law & Policy, 19*(4), 363-414.

Havinga, T. (2006). Private Regulation of Food Safety by Supermarkets. *Law & Policy, 28*(4), 515-533.

Higgs-Kleyn, N., & Kapelianis, D. (1999). The Role of Professional Codes in Regulating Ethical Conduct. *Journal of Business Ethics, 19*, 363-374.

Hoijtink, M., & Oude Vrielink-Van Heffen, M.J. (2006). Dilemma's bij zelfregulering [Dilemmas of self-regulation]. *Bestuurskunde, 15*(4), 23-29.

Hoijtink, M., & Oude Vrielink, M.J. (2007). Managers en professionals in de welzijnssector: Ideologische clash of vermenging van waarden? [Managers and Professionals in the Welfare Sector]. *Bestuurskunde, 4*, 25-32.

Jansen, Th., Van den Brink, G., & Kole, J. (Eds.) (2009). *Beroepstrots. Een ongekende kracht [Professional Pride. An Unprecedented Power].* Amsterdam: Boom.

Meulenbergs, T., Verpeet, E., Schotsmans, P., & Gastmans, C. (2004). Professional Codes in a Changing Nursing Context: Literature review. *Journal of Advanced Nursing, 46*(3), 331-336.

Ministry of Home Affairs (2009). *Nederland regelland, naar merkbare administratieve lastenvermindering van professionals [Rules in the Netherlands, towards a Decrease of the Administrative Burdens for Professionals]*. The Hague: Ministry of Home Affairs.

Noordegraaf, M., & Sterrenburg, J. (2009a). Administratieve lasten voor publieke professionals [Administrative Burdens for Public Professionals]. In: Th. Jansen, G. van den Brink & J. Kole (Eds.), *Beroepstrots, een ongekende kracht [Professional Pride. An Unprecedented Power]* (pp. 115-128). Amsterdam: Boom.

Noordegraaf, M., & Sterrenburg, J. (2009b). Publieke professionals en verantwoordingsdruk [Public Professionals and Accountability Pressure]. In M.A.P. Bovens & Th. Schillemans (Eds.), *Handboek publieke verantwoording [Handbook Public Accountability]* (pp. 231-254). The Hague: Lemma.

Oude Vrielink-Van Heffen, M.J., Van der Kraan, W., & Bjørnholt, B. (2006). The successful implementation of national quality policies: A comparison of Denmark and the Netherlands. In L. Heyse, S. Resodihardjo, T. Lantink & B. Lettinga (Eds.), *Reform in Europe: Breaking the Barriers in Government* (pp. 57-86). Hampshire: Ashgate Publishers.

Simon, H.A. (1976). *Administrative Behavior: A study of decision-making processes in administrative organization*. New York: The Free Press.

Tonkens, E. (2008). *Herwaardering voor professionals, maar hoe? [Recognition for Professionals, but How?]*. ROB lecture, 9 September 2008.

Van Bockel, J.A. (2009). *Gevormde Kaders, bureaucratische en professionele regulering van het werk van ambtenaren in de Republiek der Zeven Verenigde Nederlanden [Embedded constraints, bureaucratic and professional regulation of officials' work in the Dutch Republic]*. Delft: Eburon.

Van Boom, W.H., Faure, M.G., Huls, N.J., & Philipsen, N.J. (2009). *Handelspraktijken, reclame en zelfregulering. Pilotstudy Maatschappelijke Reguleringsinstrumenten [Commercial Practices, Advertising and Self-regulation. Pilot Study Societal Regulation Tools]*. Study by order of the Scientific Center of the Dutch Ministry of Justice (project number 1535).

Van den Bosch, D. (2005). *Regulatory Reform in the Netherlands*. Retrieved from: http://www.dvandenbosch.nl/pages/page_5pag.html.

Van Gestel, R.A.J. & Hertogh, M.L.M. (2006). *What is Regulatory Pressure? An exploratory study of the international literature*. Study by order of the Scientific Research and Documentation Centre (WODC). Tilburg/Groningen: Dutch Ministry of Justice.

Van Hoy, J. (1993). Intraprofessional Politics and Professional Regulation: A Case Study of the ABA Commission on Professionalism. *Work and Occupations: an International Sociological Journal, 20*(1), 90-109.

Weber, M. (1964). *Wirtschaft und Gesellschaft [Economy and Society]*. Köln: Kiepenheuer & Witsch.

MIRJAN OUDE VRIELINK & JEROEN VAN BOCKEL

12 Control of front-line workers in welfare agencies

Towards professionalism?

Rik van Berkel & Paul van der Aa

Local welfare agencies and their workers

Over the past decades, developed welfare states have gone through major reform processes. In the field of employment benefits, one of the main objectives of these reforms was to 'activate' social security arrangements for unemployed people who are able to work and, thus, to promote labour-market participation and reduce welfare dependency (Gilbert 2002). These reforms affected substantive and operational characteristics of welfare states (Borghi & Van Berkel 2007). Not only the entitlements and obligations of unemployed people have changed, but also the ways in which social security arrangements are administered and social services are provided. Many countries introduced forms of marketization in the provision of activation services, changed traditional ways of balancing central regulation and decentralized room for policy-making and policy implementation decisions, established so-called 'one-stop agencies' for the unemployed, and started to make use of New Public Management strategies in managing benefit and public employment services agencies (Kazepov 2010; Van Berkel 2010; Van Berkel et al. 2011).

For benefit and local welfare agencies these reforms have had important consequences: it changed their 'core business' from administering income protection schemes to activation, even though their traditional tasks did not disappear (Van Berkel et al. 2011). The exact nature of these consequences strongly depends on national contexts. The urgency to transform organizations, services and tasks of front-line work in countries with a long tradition in providing employment services to unemployed people, such as the Scandinavian tradition of active labour-market policies (Hvinden & Johansson 2007), will differ from the urgency experienced in countries without such a tradition. Countries where the administration of social insurance and the provision of employment services used to be integrated will experience other problems with coordinating social security and labour-market policy than countries where these tasks were carried out by different agencies. But despite path-dependent reform trajectories and urgencies in individual countries, the transformation of *passive* into *active* welfare states affects the core business of benefit and local welfare agencies in all developed welfare states.

From the perspective of organizational and public management studies, the transformation of welfare states and their impact on the tasks and responsibilities of public agencies and their front-line workers raise some interesting issues. One of these issues concerns the nature, design and management of activation front-line work in the reformed benefit and welfare agencies. Should activation front-line work in these agencies be designed and managed according to the street-level bureaucrat model, and be standardized, in Mintzberg's (1983) terminology, through rules and regulations? Or should activation front-line workers be conceived of as professionals, and should their work as well as standards and management processes be designed accordingly? These questions relate to the previous chapters' reflections on the paradoxes and rationality of (self)regulation. Should front-line workers' room for decision-making in activation be interpreted as an example of discretion, cumbersome but unavoidable, in order to enable them to apply general rules and regulations in individual cases (Lipsky 1980)? Or should it be seen as autonomy, necessary for professional interventions into the lives, behaviour and circumstances of clients? These questions also relate to the chapter by Van der Veen (does deprofessionalization affect discretion or autonomy?) and more indirectly to chapters by Hupe & Van der Krogt (how do front-line workers deal with pressures?) and De Graaf & Van der Wal (where do the loyalties of these front-line workers lie?). This chapter will not only shed more empirical light on these questions by focusing on activation work in local welfare agencies; it will also analyze how the paradoxes of professional work can be organized. Perhaps certain groups of (assumed) professional workers have *not* been so professional after all, and are forced to become professional due to managerial reform.

In the next section, we will elaborate on the nature of front-line work in reformed welfare agencies in more general terms. Then, we will briefly discuss some reforms of Dutch social assistance, in order to contextualize the developments in front-line work in Dutch local welfare agencies. Next, we present our empirical material, which we use to draw conclusions.

Front-line work in reformed welfare agencies

Front-line work in local welfare agencies is often considered to be different from front-line work in agencies administering social insurance schemes such as unemployment benefits or pensions (cf. Brodkin 2007). This is related to the nature and objectives of the social assistance schemes these agencies deliver, which are safety net provisions in developed welfare states. One of the consequences of this is that these schemes are highly selective. Their administration requires that front-line workers scrutinize social assistance claimants' situations in order to be able to apply the relevant rules and regulations (which are often dense and complex) to individual circumstances. Administering social assistance therefore often involves considerable discretion.

Social assistance schemes are characterized by a specific mix of income support and social services (cf. Eardley et al. 1996; Saraceno 2002), and this mix affects the nature of front-line work in local welfare agencies. Front-line work in welfare states that emphasize income provision will be mainly administrative; front-line workers in welfare states that emphasize the provision of social services will resemble social workers rather than benefit administrators. The introduction of activation may take place in a professional or rather bureaucratic tradition of front-line work.

Professional or bureaucratic work

Based on the literature, one could reach the conclusion that 'activation work' should be organized as professional work. Following Hasenfeld's (1983) distinction between people-sustaining, people-processing and people-changing technologies, Meyers et al. (1998) define activation as a type of service that requires people changing technologies. According to Hasenfeld, people-changing technologies are more likely to be found in professional organizations, whereas people-sustaining and people-processing technologies fit with a bureaucratic type of organization. Organizing activation as a professional service would also be in line with Jewell's (2007) observation that activation is usually far less subjected to strict regulation than income provision. Limited regulation and considerable room for decision-making at the front lines of welfare agencies could also be expected on the basis of the literature that studies the effectiveness of activation services. These studies show that services should be de-standardized, flexible, individualized, tailor-made and adapted to local and individual circumstances (e.g. Kluve 2010).

However, organizing activation front-line work in local welfare agencies as a professional activity is not self-evident. In an internationally comparative study, Jewell (2007) found that activation work can be organized as a *professional* function but also as a *bureaucratic* and *administrative* task. As Brodkin (2009) showed for the US, these tasks may be performed under considerable managerial pressures; meeting performance targets rather than serving clients might become front-line workers' first concern. How activation in front-line work is designed and managed, seems to depend on a complex set of contextual factors. The first factor, also mentioned by Jewell, concerns the nature of regulation of activation. In contexts where (national) regulations determine what kind of activation programmes are to be provided for what target groups, local welfare agencies and front-line workers will have less room for manoeuvre than in contexts where activation is deregulated and decentralized. In the former case, a bureaucratic organization of the provision of activation services becomes more feasible, especially when target group definitions are based on relatively objective and transparent criteria (such as age, duration of unemployment or educational level). The second factor concerns the public management of local welfare agencies and how this influences the organization of activation front-line work. Incentive structures as well as financial resources for shaping working conditions of front-line workers may influence decisions regarding the design and management of activation front-line work.

Thirdly, many countries have introduced quasi-markets for the provision of activation services. This offers local welfare agencies the opportunity to export decisions regarding activation services to external providers. Front-line workers in local welfare agencies will then mainly act as referral agents. At the same time, decisions regarding in-house provision or outsourcing are not either/or questions. Local welfare agencies can involve external providers in a variety of ways and for a variety of tasks related to service provision (Van Berkel et al. 2012). But whatever decisions local welfare agencies make regarding the organization of service provision, these decisions will have consequences for the nature of activation front-line work. Finally, despite the fact that national regulations, public management instruments or specific service provision models may restrain the options of local welfare agencies, they do have room to organize activation front-line work in ways they consider fit. In other words, the 'implementation style' (Terpstra & Havinga 2001), or combination of styles, which local welfare agencies adopt in organizing front-line work will at least partly depend on management choices and preferences.

Professionalism, politics and policies

The organization and management of activation front-line work in local welfare agencies are not only interesting from an organizational or public management perspective. Potentially, activation encroaches deeply on the lives of clients, and the decisions of front-line workers may have far-reaching implications for the entitlements and obligations of clients (Handler 2004). The literature on activation suggests that Lipsky's (1980: 4) contention that front-line workers 'hold the keys to a dimension of citizenship' has not lost its relevance in active welfare states; rather the contrary. From this perspective, questions related to the design and management of front-line work, the discretion or autonomy of front-line workers and their accountability (cf. the chapters by Van der Veen and by Hupe & Van der Krogt in this volume) are eventually *political* issues: the ways in which these issues are dealt with and materialize in front-line work practices will affect the nature of welfare state arrangements, the practical meanings of citizenship and the public values underlying the way in which welfare states treat unemployed people and provide services for them.

Before turning to the Dutch case, two final remarks should be made. First, when analyzing activation front-line work from a professional perspective, it should be emphasized that we are talking about a relatively 'new profession'. Activation front-line work often lacks the institutionalized features of classic professions (Freidson 2001; Duyvendak et al. 2006). This means that organizing activation front-line work 'the professional way' will require a strategy to establish the 'activation profession' as such. Secondly, activation is not a service offered to unemployed people voluntarily, but is embedded in rules and regulations concerning the obligations of unemployed people, which are strongly integrated with their entitlements to income support. Even when activation front-line work is organized as a professional function, these rules and regulations will always structure front-line workers' decisions somehow. From this point of view, the policy context in which professional activation front-line workers exercise discretion and autonomy will differ from that of many other public professionals.

Contextualizing the redesign of front-line work in Dutch local welfare agencies

Reforms aimed at activating Dutch social security arrangements started in the late 1980s (Van der Veen & Trommel 1999; Van Berkel 2006). As far as the Dutch safety net provision is concerned, two new social assistance acts have been introduced since then, the first in 1996 and the second in 2004, making 'work before income' the main catchword underlying Dutch social assistance. As a consequence of the emphasis on activation, equity before the law and rightfulness have lost much of their dominance as basic principles underlying social assistance delivery. Instead, providing individualized services and promoting the effectiveness and efficiency of services have become pivotal. This is also reflected in table 1, which shows how Dutch local welfare agencies characterized their organizations in the years following the introduction of the 2004 Social Assistance Act.

Table 1 Characterization of local welfare agencies (2004-2007)

	2004	2005	2006	2007
Mainly oriented at support and rightfulness	49	35	34	22
Mainly oriented at activation and effectiveness	51	65	66	78

Source: Divosa 2008

The 2004 Social Assistance Act brought considerable decentralization and deregulation, especially in the area of activation. Local welfare agencies now have considerable room in decision-making regarding the content of activation programmes they provide for their clients. Hand in hand with decentralization and deregulation, the responsibilities of municipalities in financing social assistance expenses increased, which, among others, should provide incentives to make service provision more efficient and effective. Whereas municipal social assistance expenditures used to be fully reimbursed by the national government, a budget system was introduced in 2004. If municipalities spend less on social assistance payments than the budget they receive from national government, they are free to spend the surplus in whatever way they choose. If they spend more, they will have to find alternative funding resources. Marketization of the provision of activation services is another important reform in this context. Initially, outsourcing activation was obligatory for local welfare agencies, but after the 2004 Social Assistance Act was implemented, this obligation was abolished so that nowadays, local welfare agencies not only have significant decision room concerning the content of activation services, but also concerning the organization of their provision.

In the pre-activation period, front-line work in Dutch local welfare agencies had developed into a highly administrative function. There was a strong emphasis on testing social assistance eligibility and periodical reinvestigations of eligibility, on fraud prevention, etc. This work was strongly rule-guided: extensive manuals existed that should support and guide front-line workers in decision-making processes. Furthermore, front-line workers acted as advisers to senior officials in the agency, who took the actual decisions concerning entitlements, sanctions, etc. This did not mean that the social work function was completely absent in Dutch local welfare agencies, but the enormous increase in the number of social assistance recipients during the 1980s, and the introduction of a more impersonal, business-like approach in dealing with clients eroded it considerably. This also resulted in a shift of the educational profile of front-line workers. Whereas many of them used to have an educational background in social work, a social-legal educational profile became more prominent during the 1990s. By the end of the 1990s, local welfare agencies were often characterized as 'selection bureaucracies' (e.g. Gastelaars 2008) or, more prosaically, 'benefit factories', besides some vestiges of social work and some embryonic forms of activation work.

Methodology

In our study of developments in front-line work, local welfare agencies in two municipalities were investigated. The core issues we were interested in were: how do local welfare agencies reform front-line work against the background of active welfare state reforms and how do front-line workers respond to these reforms? In the study we used various research methods: document analysis, semi-structured interviews with managers and front-line workers in the municipalities, and, in municipality A, observations of client/front-line worker interactions. In case A, data come from an ongoing research project into the organizational and managerial changes that are taking place to adjust to the new policy and governance context. Most data presented here come from 2006 and 2008. In 2006, we conducted group interviews with 35 managers and street-level workers in three out of ten districts of the local welfare agency. In 2008, fifteen group interviews with approximately 80 front-line workers and managers took place. In the smaller municipality, data collection took place in 2007. Here, we conducted a total of 36 interviews with front-line workers, managers and staff personnel.

The local welfare agency in municipality A employs approximately 2,000 fte personnel, the local welfare agency in municipality B about 100 fte personnel. Table 2 presents some core data about the municipalities.

Table 2 Core data of the municipalities, 2006

Municipality	Inhabitants (x 1000)	% of households receiving SA	% SA RECIPIENTS >1 YEAR DEPENDENT ON SA	% deficit/surplus income budget	% deficit/surplus work budget
A	500-600	12	86	-8	23
B	50-100	6	82	-9	9

Source: Kernkaart Werk en Bijstand (http://gemeenteloket.szw.nl/kernkaart/index.cfm)

Activation work in welfare agencies

Activation regulation and local service provision models

As was mentioned before, activation regulation, public management instruments and decisions regarding in-house or outsourced service provision structure activation front-line work in local welfare agencies. The 2004 Social Assistance Act hardly regulates *what* activation services municipalities should provide, although the new financial regime creates strong incentives to reduce the number of social assistance recipients. Local authorities have to make so-called reintegration by-laws, which regulate the activation processes taking place in local welfare agencies (often, the agencies play a significant role in drafting these by-laws). However, these by-laws may still leave a lot of decision room for the agencies. For example, the 2009 reintegration by-law in municipality A defines the kind of activation services that may be offered to clients as follows:

education and training; work experience; participation placements (additional work while receiving social assistance); subsidized jobs; social activation; job mediation; language and civic integration courses. This not only involves a wide variety of quite generally defined services, it also leaves open what kind of services shall be offered to what clients. The reintegration by-law in force during our research in municipality B contained more detailed regulation. It contained five 'activation tracks', each of which represented a certain level of employability of social assistance recipients. Each track was linked to a specific type of activation service (wage subsidies, work experience placements combined with job mediation, work experience placements combined with training courses, etc). Thus, municipal by-laws not only regulate activation in different ways, they also do so to different degrees.

Local political authorities may also exercise influence in a more ad hoc way, for example when sudden urgencies arise, such as an unexpected increase of social assistance claims. Less urgent matters may trigger local politicians to act as well, for example when local politicians want or feel obliged to introduce 'best practices'; or when international visits (various US cities have become popular destinations for these visits during the last decade) stimulate aldermen to experiment with new and 'fashionable' approaches in activation programmes. Both welfare agencies in our research were confronted with these ad hoc interventions by local politicians, which may interfere with 'ongoing' processes of service provision considerably.

As far as organizing the provision of activation services is concerned, both agencies changed their strategies considerably during the years following the new Social Assistance Act of 2004. These changes were facilitated by the abolishment of the obligatory outsourcing of activation services, and stimulated by the dissatisfaction with the quality and effectiveness of activation services provided by external private for-profit providers. Dissatisfaction with privatization was widespread. In 2005, two thirds of municipalities involved in a national study considered it unsuccessful (Divosa 2005). In addition, changes were made possible because local welfare agencies gradually increased their expertise concerning activation, as well as their insight into the market of external providers. During the period of obligatory outsourcing, front-line workers referred clients to external providers on a massive scale and once clients were referred hardly interfered substantially with clients' activation processes. The main development that took place in this period was a diversification of activation programmes and an increase in the number of providers that were contracted. After the abolishment of obligatory outsourcing, the agencies in our study started to strengthen their role in activation. Firstly, more activation services are provided by the agencies' front-line workers themselves, which is in line with national developments (Divosa 2007). Recent cuts in national budgets available for activation seem to accelerate this de-privatization trend. Secondly, front-line

RIK VAN BERKEL & PAUL VAN DER AA

workers play a more active role in determining the nature of the activation offer made to clients. Thirdly, front-line workers monitor clients referred to an external provider more closely than used to be the case in the past. In this way, both agencies try to increase control over individual activation processes and over the services provided by external providers.

Activation in practice

In both agencies, activation and income provision used to be organized in integrated functions. With the changes in the organization of activation elaborated above, both agencies reconsidered the organization of activation work, and separated the income provision and activation functions (in 2005 in municipality B and in 2008 in municipality A). In municipality A, further specialization took place, both in the income provision and the activation area. In the activation area, specialized functions were created for the unemployed who are directly employable, for those who need activation support, and for those with a large labour-market distance. An expert system was used to assign all unemployed to one of these groups, but front-line workers often disagreed with the outcomes of this procedure, which resulted in a quite massive and time-consuming reshuffling of clients between the three specializations. In municipality B, specialization within the domains of income and activation remained limited. In the activation domain, two front-line workers were assigned to design and implement activation services for a group of long-term and vulnerable clients. These front-line workers were given unprecedented room for developing interventions and support for their clients, and for networking with a variety of service providers to organize the support they considered necessary.

Taking into account that most activation front-line workers used to be social assistance administrators, their work has changed considerably over the last few years. Not only in terms of content, but also in terms of management and steering. In general, their *autonomy* in decision-making has increased. First of all, activation front-line workers' decisions are guided by formal rules and regulations to a limited degree compared to what they were used to when administrating social assistance. Secondly, the traditional distinction between 'advisors' (the actual front-line workers) and 'decision makers' (senior officials higher in the organizational hierarchy) no longer exists, partly because of the lack of regulation. Instead, new instruments for quality management and control have been introduced. For example, both agencies started to stimulate fraternal consultation and introduced quality officials who act as coaches of front-line workers – who were not always convinced of the added value of these new officials. Thirdly, increasing diversification of activation services has increased the number of options activation front-line workers need to consider when activating their clients – although in municipality A, the offers available for the unemployed who are considered employable immediately are far more standardized than the offers made to the other groups of unemployed. Fourthly, specifically in municipality A, the definition of target groups of particular activation offers has become increasingly complex, involving a variety of rather difficult to objectify criteria related to clients' willingness to cooperate, their motivation, or the multiplicity of social problems clients are confronted with. This makes the process of diagnosing or assessing cases increasingly difficult and, in the absence of validated tools to assess clients, dependent on front-line workers' judgments.

These changes can be interpreted as an increasing *professionalization* or, at least, strengthened autonomous and expert-based treatment of activation front-line work in the agencies. However, other factors structure front-line work as well. For example, bureaucratic and hierarchical management practices are still present. This was especially the case in municipality A. Partly this can be explained by the different timing of the processes of change in both agencies, and by characteristics of the changes. Municipality B started introducing major changes in a period of economic growth during which the number of social assistance recipients was declining significantly without a corresponding reduction in the number of staff. Municipality A introduced the changes in a period in which the economy started to stagnate, and in which there were signals of a rising number of social assistance recipients. In order to cope with these problems, the agency's management reverted to 'traditional' management strategies: it introduced several new activation programmes that should bring the threat of a rising number of social assistance recipients to a halt. It also obliged front-line workers to select an X number of clients from their caseload for these programmes (so-called 'list work').

Furthermore, the process of task specialization implied that front-line workers were confronted with completely new caseloads. The process of getting to know their clients, together with the reshuffling of clients between specializations, increased their workload considerably (many front-line workers have caseloads of 150-300 clients). In itself, these circumstances slowed down social assistance exits and contributed to the urgency to take emergency measures. And because front-line workers had to select clients for the 'emergency programmes' without having full insight into their caseloads, it is not hard to imagine that this part of their work was reduced to a largely administrative task that left little room for professionalization. As one front-line worker commented: 'I know my lists better than I know my clients'.

Apart from these bureaucratic and administrative tendencies, front-line workers in municipality A were also confronted with performance management. This included a 'guideline' regarding the amount of working time front-line workers should be talking to clients in the consultation room: 80%. Front-line workers considered this target unrealistic, and it was never met, even though front-line workers spend more time with clients nowadays than in the past. In addition, activation front-line workers are expected to place a certain percentage of their caseloads in paid jobs. This element of performance management was not taken very seriously by front-line workers, and some of them talked rather giggly about them. In addition, they were criticized frequently; the performance targets in terms of social assistance exits were seen as undesirable, because they focus on quantity rather than quality. In municipality B, similar kinds of performance targets did not exist. However, front-line workers were asked by their managers what proportion of their clients they had 'in the picture' and how many of them were involved in activation programmes.

All in all, professionalization trends were present in both agencies, but especially in municipality A they were constrained by hierarchical and bureaucratic forms of 'crisis management' and by high work pressure, which partly resulted from the organizational reforms.

Using and justifying decision-making room

Formal decisions regarding the 'freedom to act as granted', to use the terminology of Hupe & Van der Krogt in this volume, reveal little about the 'freedom to act as taken by an actor' and the 'usage of freedom to act'. So how do front-line workers use and justify decision-making room? Many front-line workers in the agencies we investigated do not have an educational background in, nor experience with, activation, providing labour-market guidance and job mediation. Their educational profile matches the 'traditional' rather than the 'new' core business of local welfare agencies. The local welfare agency in municipality B started to send its front-line workers to courses where they were trained in individual job coaching. Front-line workers in municipality A were trained as well, but this training mainly focused on new information systems.

However, as was mentioned before, the challenge that local welfare agencies are confronted with, not merely involves professionalization but also developing the activation profession as such. In this context it was striking to see, that although the agencies' management collects information regarding the effectiveness of activation provided by external providers, this information mainly served management purposes and was not communicated to front-line workers. Therefore, in making decisions regarding individual activation offers, front-line workers mainly rely on their experience. At the same time, one of the municipalities in our study recently became involved in an initiative of six local welfare agencies aimed at making more explicit what 'professional activation work' means, based on an analysis of how activation workers actually 'do' activation and of the theoretical underpinning of the knowledge they use. This initiative exemplifies the growing awareness of the need to develop activation as a profession.

Given the various professional backgrounds of front-line workers and the virtual lack of a shared professional knowledge base or other professional guidelines that could guide their work, it will not come as a surprise that front-line workers use their increased autonomy in a variety of ways. In fact, we can trace the types of public street-level workers as identified by De Graaf & Van der Wal. For example, workers deal differently with the reintegration wishes of their clients. Whereas some front-line workers take the law quite literally by stating that clients are expected to accept any job offer made to them and have 'nothing to choose' (e.g. in terms of De Graaf & Van der Wal they operate as 'objective judges'), others take a more pragmatic approach. They argue that the more a job offer fits with what clients want, the more motivated the client will be to accept the job and the more likely job placements will turn out to be successful and sustainable. In their opinion, taking clients' own wishes into account in activation will help to make activation successful (so they act more as 'neutral intermediaries'). Informal client typologies (Van der Veen 1990) may play a role in this context as well: some front-line workers were inclined to start activation processes themselves (instead of referring clients to external providers) for clients that in their view are motivated and express 'feasible' and 'realistic' wishes regarding their reintegration into the labour market.

These different views concerning how clients should be approached in the activation process were also visible in the encounters front-line workers have with clients, as we observed in municipality A. Whereas in some cases, these encounters can be characterized as monologues in which the front-line worker informs the client about the activation offer he has available, others are more like dialogues in which the front-line worker tries to gain insight into the kind of job clients would like to find. Of course, one could argue that differences in the ways in which front-line workers approach clients reflect the heterogeneity of clients. Front-line workers indeed recognize that a specific client approach is of no avail for certain client groups but may be useful for others. Nevertheless, in line with the findings of de Graaf & Van der Wal, front-line workers also differ in their 'style' in seeing and dealing with clients. Among others, this 'style' is characterized by the value front-line workers attach to giving clients voice and choice. In addition, some front-line workers take a more holistic approach in assessing clients' situations than others, who mainly focus on 'impediments' to labour-market reintegration.

Differences in decision-making

Both local welfare agencies issued mission statements, emphasizing that they want to change from a rule-administrating into a service-centred organization. Values such as client friendliness and client orientation should become guiding principles. For some front-line workers (the 'ob-

RIK VAN BERKEL & PAUL VAN DER AA

jective judges'), client friendliness and client orientation are rather 'empty' concepts; they do not think that the social assistance act requires them to promote client satisfaction. For them, client satisfaction is a feature of 'modern management' rather than part of their public responsibilities. These front-line workers also adopt a rather passive approach when it comes to clients' entitlements to services. They inform clients about these entitlements but consider it the responsibility of clients to actually use and claim entitlements. Others (especially 'objective service providers') adopt a more pro-active approach; they will offer services to clients when they think clients need or are entitled to these services. Similar differences can be found in dealing with sanctions. Some front-line workers apply sanctions immediately when clients do not show up for appointments; others look into the situation of clients before they decide whether clients should be sanctioned.

Differences can also be seen in how front-line workers deal with the groups of clients that are most difficult to employ. Several front-line workers argue that they do not possess the skills to deal with vulnerable clients. Client images may play a role in parking clients; clients' situations are interpreted in terms of 'problems' and 'impediments' standing in the way of participation, so that the best 'solution' is to leave these clients 'in peace'. Large caseloads may have a similar effect. Front-line workers argue that they do not have the time to give vulnerable clients the attention they need. A more bureaucratic argument is that some of these clients are (temporarily) exempted from the work obligation, so that front-line workers do not feel obliged to offer services. In the end, all these practices often imply that these groups of clients are excluded from services. However, not all front-line workers act this way. Some use interviews with clients with a temporary exemption from the work obligation to see if clients need any support and, if they cannot provide that support themselves, to refer them to external providers. Others try to find forms of social participation that fit with these clients' capacities and circumstances. For them, leaving these clients 'in peace' is not a way of meeting their needs but of denying the neediest clients adequate services. All in all, front-line workers hold different opinions on these clients' capacities and needs, on what local welfare agencies should do for them, and on what they as individual front-line workers are capable of offering them.

Front-line workers justify their use of decision-making room in different ways. Some front-line workers are more rule-oriented in their work, whereas others are more service-oriented. The first group justifies their actions and decisions in terms of the core rules of active welfare state arrangements: individual responsibility of the unemployed, their obligation to make every effort to become independent from social assistance, sanctioning in cases of non-compliance. The second group focuses on what clients need and on what makes services effective for clients, and legitimizes actions in terms of 'what works'. These front-line workers may experience tensions between clients' obligations and what they consider to be good for their clients. For example, the law obliges clients to accept any available job, but some front-line workers think that only a job that fits with clients' qualifications and ambitions will result in sustainable labour-market participation.

The first group constructs itself as street-level bureaucrats whose core role it is to administer the law; the second group constructs itself as professionals, and refers to rules and regulations in justifying their conduct in a more instrumental way. Referring to rules and regulations, in turn, allows for a variety of ways of dealing with clients, as policies offer room for various interpretations. For example, even though there is a dominant discourse on 'getting people into a job and out of social assistance as soon as possible', there is also a discourse that emphasizes sustainable labour-market integration. Because of the variety of policy objectives and messages, as well as the ambiguities inherent to them, front-line workers are able to legitimize a variety of activation practices in terms of stated policy objectives.

Front-line workers might also legitimize their actions in terms of what 'professional activation' is about. Based upon their educational background, experience with activating clients, theoretical or common-sense notions of human behaviour, images of clients, etc, they enact practical guidelines for activation decisions. This influences how clients are motivated, what meanings are attached to sanctions and incentives, what roles are attributed to clients' voice and choice in activation processes, how workers deal with 'unwilling' and 'unmotivated' clients, how they assess positive or rather detrimental effects of social participation and work, etc. From the perspective of developing the activation profession, these are crucial issues. However, in the local welfare agencies we studied, there was no tradition to discuss these issues systematically with colleagues in order to develop protocols, professional guidelines or rules of thumb in providing services to clients.

Conclusion

The decision-making room (e.g. discretion) of activation front-line workers is increasing and the agencies' management explicitly promotes this as part of a strategy aimed at professionalizing front-line work. As we saw, the professionalization process is not straightforward and is constrained and conditioned by many factors. But front-line workers leave a considerable mark on what activation looks like in practice, at least in a considerable proportion of cases. The case of front-line workers can be seen as an illustration of Newman's point that change can also imply new spaces of agency for specific occupational groups. Change and the introduction of NPM practices does not always imply deprofessionalization or increasing alienation. These front-line workers appear to be a 'winner' in terms of professionalization, at least for the moment.

Strategies to safeguard the 'professional' use of decision-making room are unclear, however, although there is an awareness that action is needed. Front-line workers are left very much on their own, and their own insights, skills and opinions are often decisive. Bureaucratic management is occasionally used to deal with 'emergencies', but this curbs rather than steers professional work. Performance management is gaining in popularity, but this will mainly hold front-line workers accountable, without facilitating them to find their professionalism in more collective and systematic ways.

This lack of control or steering (which not necessarily implies *managerial* control) also has consequences for clients. For clients, front-line workers' actions and decisions make a difference: they affect job offers, expectations, voice and choice, and the use of sanctions. The more decisions depend on the individual choices and opinions of front-line workers, the more tailor-made service provision becomes problematic. Without professional standards, it is difficult to evaluate the accuracy and reliability of front-line practices.

Professional standards will help to limit too much individual variation in professionals' behaviour towards clients. Certainly, personal characteristics have always played a role in professional practices, as indicated by Hupe & Van der Krogt. But here we see limited professional control over front-line workers' use of decision-making room problematic. Individualized, tailor-made services require considerable autonomy, but may result in arbitrariness and non-transparency in the absence of clear professional criteria that guide decision-making processes. Rules and regulations may be incompatible with tailor-made service provision, but they do provide a certain degree of protection, transparency and predictability for clients.

It is noteworthy that the 'openness' of regulations concerning activation is in no way compensated by strengthening the instruments that clients can use to exercise voice and choice. Accountability vis-à-vis clients where activation is concerned is hardly an issue in the agencies we studied (like in the chapter of Tonkens, Hoijtink & Gulikers with respect to social workers). Formal appeal procedures do exist, but in the absence of rules, rule violation becomes hard to substantiate (cf. Adler 2008). From the point of view of front-line workers, they currently can best be typified as *professionals without a profession* (Van Berkel et al. 2010). Performance management will *not* solve this problem; it assumes that front-line workers know how to diagnose and treat clients in order to realize desired outcomes, but as we have seen, front-line workers' body of knowledge is part of the problem. For the future, building a stronger institutional basis for the profession of activation front-line work could help to mitigate this problem. By taking the professionalization route and by launching an assault on bureaucracy (rather than 'an assault on professionalism', as discussed in Van der Veen's chapter 5), these agencies have started a project that is not only interesting and challenging – it also involves considerable risks.

References

Adler, M. (2008). *Justice Implications of 'Activation Policies' in the UK*. Paper presented at the annual meeting of The Law and Society Association, Montreal, Canada. Downloaded from http://www.allacademic.com/meta/p237074_index.html.

Borghi, V., & Van Berkel, R. (2007). New Modes of Governance in Italy and the Netherlands: The case of activation policies. *Public Administration, 85*(1), 83-101.

Brodkin, E. (2007). Bureaucracy Redux: Management reformism in the welfare state. *Journal of Public Administration Research and Theory, 17*(1): 1-17.

Brodkin, E. (2009). The Politics and Governance of Workfare in the US. In F. Larsen & R. Van Berkel (Eds.), *The New Governance and Implementation of Labour Market Policies* (pp. 139-165). Copenhagen: DJOF Publishing.

Divosa (2005). *WWB monitor. Een jaar Wet Werk en Bijstand [One Year Social Assistance Act]*. Utrecht: Divosa.

Divosa (2007). *Divosa monitor 2007. Verschil maken. Drie jaar Wet Werk en Bijstand [Three Years Social Assistance Act]*. Utrecht: Divosa.

Divosa (2008). *Divosa monitor 2008. Worstelen met invloed. Vier jaar Wet Werk en Bijstand [Four Years Social Assistance Act]*. Utrecht: Divosa.

Duyvendak, J.W., Knijn, T. & Kremer, M. (Eds.) (2006). *Policy, People and the New Professional: De-professionalisation and re-professionalisation in care and welfare*. Amsterdam: Amsterdam University Press.

Eardley, T., Bradshaw, J., Ditch, J., Gough, I., & Whiteford, P. (1996). *Social Assistance in OECD Countries, synthesis report*. London: Department of Social Security, report no. 46.

Freidson, E. (2001). *Professionalism: The third logic*. Cambridge: Polity Press.

Gastelaars, M. (2008). *The Public Services under Reconstruction. Client experiences, professional practices, managerial control*. London: Routledge.

Gilbert, N. (2002). *Transformation of the Welfare State. The silent surrender of public responsibility*. Oxford: Oxford University Press.

Handler, J. (2004). *Social Citizenship and Workfare in the United States and Western Europe*. Cambridge: Cambridge University Press.

Hasenfeld, Y. (1983). *Human Service Organizations*. Englewood Cliffs: Prentice Hall.

Hvinden, B., & Johansson, H. (Eds.) (2007). *Citizenship in Nordic welfare states. Dynamics of choice, duties and participation in a changing Europe*. London: Routledge.

Jewell, C. (2007). *Agents of the Welfare State. How caseworkers respond to need in the United States, Germany and Sweden*. New York: Palgrave/Macmillan.

Kazepov, Y. (Ed.) (2010). *Rescaling Social Policies: towards multilevel governance in Europe*. Farnham: Ashgate.

Kluve, J. (2010). *Active labor market policies in Europe. Performance and perspectives.* Heidelberg: Springer.

Lipsky, M. (1980). *Street-Level Bureaucracy.* New York: Russell Sage Foundation.

Meyers, M., Glaser, B., & MacDonald, K. (1998). On the Front Lines of Welfare Delivery: Are workers implementing policy reforms? *Journal of Policy Analysis and Management, 17*(1), 1-22.

Mintzberg, H. (1983). *Structures in Fives.* London: Palgrave.

Saraceno, C. (Ed.) (2002). *Social Assistance Dynamics in Europe. National and local poverty regimes.* Bristol: Policy Press.

Terpstra, J., & Havinga, T. (2001). Implementation between Tradition and Management: Structuration and styles of implementation. *Law & Policy, 23*(1), 95-117.

Van Berkel, R. (2006). The decentralization of Social Assistance in the Netherlands. *International Journal of Sociology and Social Policy, 26*(1/2), 20-32.

Van Berkel, R. (2010). The Provision of Income Protection and Activation Services for the Unemployed in 'Active' Welfare States. An international comparison. *Journal of Social Policy, 39*(1), 17-34.

Van Berkel, R., Van der Aa, P., & Van Gestel, N. (2010). Professionals without a profession? Redesigning case management in Dutch local welfare agencies. *European Journal of Social Work, 13*(4), 447-463.

Van Berkel, R., De Graaf, W., & Sirovátka, T. (Eds.) (2011). *The Governance of Active Welfare States in Europe.* Houndmills: Palgrave.

Van Berkel, R., Sager, F. & Ehrler, F. (2012). The diversity of activation markets in Europe. *International Journal of Sociology and Social Policy, 32*(5/6), 273-285.

Van der Veen, R. (1990). *De sociale grenzen van beleid. Een onderzoek naar de uitvoering van het stelsel van sociale zekerheid [The Social Limits of Policy: Research into the Execution of the System of Social Security].* Leiden: Stenfert Kroese.

Van der Veen, R., & Trommel, W. (1999). Managed Liberalization of the Dutch Welfare State: A review and analysis of the reform of the Dutch social security system, 1985-1998. *Governance: An International Journal of Policy and Administration, 12*(3), 289-310.

13 Professionalization of (police) leaders

Contested control

Martijn van der Meulen & Mirko Noordegraaf

Introduction

In earlier chapters, we have seen that managers and their management instruments are blamed for exerting pressures on professional organizations and professional work. In this chapter, we will not deal with professionals on workfloors and their relations with managers, but we focus on managers themselves. Increasingly, in sectors like policing, education and healthcare, managers try to become professionals. Not so much as 'managers', but as 'leaders' of organizations that are pressurized by bureaucratic control and performance demands (e.g. Farrell & Morris 2003; Ackroyd et al. 2007).

We do this for two reasons. First and foremost, we show that the managerialization of public domains puts pressures not only on work processes, but on organizational processes as well. It becomes increasingly difficult to organize public service delivery, not so much because of NPM models – which are often straightforward – but because these models are hard to implement, whilst performance expectations have intensified. Instead of seeing managers as the carriers of New Public Management and its models, we show how NPM puts pressures on these very same managers. This explains why public managers want to become 'professional leaders'; they can embrace performance expectations, *and* find the means for meeting them.

Secondly, we show how subsequent professionalization strategies – as coping strategies – imitate classic professionalization strategies. Managers try to build occupational spaces and professional associations that regulate managerial work. Just like traditional professionals who have institutionalized well-known forms of professional work in order to reduce work complexities and strengthen positions. Although this is done to reduce pressures on occupational groups, this in itself creates new pressures. Building spaces and establishing regulatory mechanisms is difficult, partly because managerial work is and remains ambiguous (despite clear NPM models) and partly because public managers will never be 'free' – they are dependent on lots of other parties and stakeholders.

All in all, our basic question is, how do professionalizing public managers cope with the (managerial) pressures that are dominating public domains and their professional services? Empirically, we focus on the development of police leadership, which we see as a professionalization 'project' (cf. Larson 1977; Hodgson 2002; 2005), aimed at improving police organizations and the management of police work. By analyzing police leaders as a professional group, which develops its professionalism by identifying leadership 'competencies', we can understand how and why a profession of police leaders is *made*. Making police leaders, but also the making of other leaders and managers (like healthcare managers), is accompanied by functional desires about 'improving' work. A professionalization project, however, is not only produced by functional actions, like defining work competencies. Other processes are crucial for understanding leadership development, like group formation, legitimation of substance and establishment of control (e.g. Grey 1997; Van der Meulen 2009; Noordegraaf 2012). These processes are not neutral or functional, but strategic and political; they happen in the face of aforementioned ambiguities and dependencies.

In this chapter we analyze how leadership development, as the manifestation of professionalization of public managers, is pursued. We shed light on why the 'project' of improving (Dutch) police leadership has evolved as it has (until 2011, when major reorganizations started to affect the nationwide structuring of Dutch police forces). First, the professionalization of police leaders is briefly introduced. Next we develop a theoretical approach to professionalizing public managers, with particular emphasis on police managers. We then describe the professionalization project of police leaders in more detail, by describing and analyzing how a police leader's profession is construed. We also analyze the 'backstage' processes of professionalization projects, in order to understand why managers focus on leadership and how this might differ in professionalization projects of public managers in different domains. We end this chapter by drawing conclusions and discussing implications for (further) leadership development in the face of managerial pressures on professional services.

Evolution of (Dutch) police leadership

Police leadership receives a lot of attention, both in academic reflection (e.g. Reiner 1992; Adlam & Villiers 2003; Boin et al. 2003; Van der Torre 2007) and practical elaborations (e.g. SPL Yearbook 2004; Nap 2008). In addition, it is a set of even more practical 'competencies' that aspiring police chiefs have to develop if they want to advance their careers in police forces. Police leaders have to possess *leadership competencies* that enable them to be *managerial executives* that *effectively lead* police work amidst societal transformation, changing power relationships and performance requirements (Board of Chief Commissioners 2005). Leadership seems to be the key ingredient for realizing effective police management, but leadership cannot be grasped and defined easily. The attention paid to leadership in police forces is seen as a 'quest' (as e.g. formally stated by the Dutch School for Police Leadership, SPL), an attempt to grasp and define the necessary competencies for realizing effective police management. Schools for Police Leadership search for possibilities for developing leadership skills, together with police chiefs and policy-makers. They search for appropriate activities, programs, work standards and suitable candidates.

In the Dutch police force, leadership development is pursued by means of an extensive competency profile (SPL 2003). For police leaders working at strategic levels of the organization, nine core competencies are applicable. The core competencies form the competence profile: integrity, courage, sociability, empathy, societal orientation, performance drive, creativity, entrepreneurial and political sensitivity (SPL 2003). At other organizational levels, at the levels of group chiefs, unit chiefs and bureau chiefs, work profiles apply and candidates for these positions can develop their operational and tactical leadership competencies. These leaders (working beneath 'strategic leaders') are seen as operational and tactical police leaders. In sum, police leadership consists of matching profiles with different sets of competencies for various managers at different organizational levels.

The current development of police leadership can be better understood by analyzing it against the background of a broader development, namely the professionalization of public and non-profit managers (compare Noordegraaf 2006, 2007). In case of police managers, this is all the more visible: in the last few years, the professionalization of police leaders – which we describe below in more detail – has been linked to the professionalization of Dutch high-ranking civil servants. The Dutch Senior Executive Service (SES, or in Dutch: ABD) has become the institutional shelter for selecting and appointing police leaders.

Such a professionalization perspective makes it possible to go beyond simple and static versions of leadership development (compare Van der Meulen 2009). Leadership development – with its current practice in educational programs, assessments, selection procedures and appointments – is not the only possibility; leadership is a *choice* and the materialization of this choice has a history. It is a 'project' (compare Larson 1977; Hodgson 2005) in which police chiefs, candidates, representatives of educational programs, associations, knowledge institutes and officials of local and state government participate. In addition, the professionalization perspective emphasizes the collective dimension, police leaders developing as an occupational group. Leadership is not so much a personal quality, which some people have or develop, and others lack. Leadership in police forces is also a group profile, and a strategic vehicle for positioning police leaders vis-à-vis subordinates (police men), bosses (mayors, political representatives and policy-makers) and the outside world (other organizations, intermediaries, citizens). Amidst performance pressures, groups of police managers try to shape new organizational and work realities.

Professionalization of public managers

The professional development of police chiefs, who try to become police leaders, must not be seen as a unique activity. It resembles the professionalization of other general managers (e.g. Whitley 1995), including public managers, government administrators, healthcare executives and school leaders (e.g. Noordegraaf 2006; Noordegraaf & Van der Meulen 2008; De Wit & Noordegraaf 2012). These managerial and organizational professionalization processes, in turn, resemble professionalization processes in traditional professional fields, like medicine and law (e.g. Krause 1996; Freidson 2001), as well as the professionalization of other so-called organizational professionals (cf. Larson 1977), like accountants and consultants (see Gross & Kieser 2006; De Sonnavillle 2005; McKenna 2006; Kipping 2011) and also project managers (Hodgson 2002) and interim managers (Maas 2004). But the professionalization of general public managers is unique, in various respects. First of all, managerial work is highly ambiguous and contingent (e.g. Whitley 1989; Mintzberg 2004) and difficult to standardize. It is linked to specific organizational contexts and local circumstances; it is highly informational and relational; it is largely tacit and experiential. Secondly, New Public Management (NPM) – which has become highly influential in the work contexts of general managers – has intensified performance expectations (e.g. Hood 1991; Pollitt & Bouckaert 2004), but it has also intensified performance paradoxes and perverse effects (e.g. De Bruijn 2007). This means that NPM is far less clear than often assumed, especially in organizational practices (see also Diefenbach 2009). Although it sets new standards, e.g. for performance-based managerial practices, its standards turn out to be contradictory (e.g. Hood 1991; Pollitt & Bouckaert 2004) and possibly counterproductive (e.g. De Bruijn 2007).

In all kinds of public and non-profit organizations, such as hospitals, courts, public prosecutor offices, schools, welfare organizations and social services, managers and managerial systems have gained influence (Ackroyd et al. 2007). The increased influence of managers and management systems, such as management information systems and performance management systems, also occurred in the Dutch police sector (Hoogenboom 2006). This was accompanied by the rise of visible and forceful managers and executives who would be 'in charge'. The rise of such managerial fields did not occur smoothly, however. Managerial positions, powers, salaries and behaviors are easily contested. Although scholars like Mintzberg (2004) have argued that management 'will never be a profession', the complexities of managing in managerial times have stimulated a search for managerial professionalism. Most public managers, including police managers, have started attempts to become a profession, or at least to build a recognizable occupational domain, with obvious professional features: an association, educational programs, knowledge transfer, codes of conduct (e.g. Noordegraaf 2006). Interestingly, this resembles professionalization processes of classic professions, like medicine, although managerial professionalism is – paradoxically – often used to control classic professional fields (as we have seen in previous chapters).

From an analytical point of view, this is not surprising. In chapter 4, Hupe & Van der Krogt already showed that professionalization is relevant outside classic and traditional professional fields that mainly included doctors, lawyers, and engineers (Noordegraaf 2007). As suggested by Newman in her chapter, various occupational groups try to reposition themselves by claiming certain organizational bodies of expertise. These bodies of expertise and the mechanisms for regulating them represent professional capital (cf. Noordegraaf & Schinkel 2010) and professionalization has become a 'strategy' for developing organizational strength – for accumulating symbolic and cultural capital.

When we study these professionalization processes, traditional *functional* approaches on professionalization fall short. Although all sorts of functional desires are important for professionalization as such, management is difficult to grasp and appropriate management techniques are difficult to clarify and standardize (Whitley 1989). Attempts to regulate managerial professionalism, by clearly defining and demarcating the occupational boundaries, identifying effective management techniques and educating professional candidates accordingly, will unavoidably be indirect and difficult to sustain (compare Grey 1997; De Sonnaville 2005; Van der Meulen 2009).

At the same time, the professionalization of public managers is more than mere symbolic action. As managers try to acquire legitimacy and status, professionalization processes have *real* (and also functional) implications for how managers shape and control their work. Despite the fact that forming managerial professionalism is complicated, and many attempts to gain control over work and working conditions will fail, public managers are indeed – by trial and error – busy with their profession. This is related to critical events, such as incidents of managerial failure, and institutional changes. Incidents, events and decisions put pressures on organizational action. In addition, new political, economic and social settlements (cf. Clarke & Newman 1997) affect organizational settlements. Social and political forces facilitate the rise of associational and educational mechanisms. Instead of seeing professionalism as a functional fact, we see it as a social and political construct (cf. e.g. Hodgson & Cicmil; 2007). We stress the contextual and socio-political nature of managerial work when we analyze how managers try to improve their work.

Professionalization as socio-political process

A socio-political approach to professionalization (compare Abbott 1988, 1991; Noordegraaf 2008, 2012) starts from the idea that professionalization is an evolutionary process, aimed at getting a grip on work, including a grip on the confused and contested elements of work. In this evolutionary process, managers who try to professionalize 'battle' with others, but not unconditionally. This 'battle' can only be understood within broader societal and institutional contexts. We emphasize three crucial features of such a socio-political approach.

Firstly, building a profession is not an isolated activity. It is a *collective project* (e.g. Hodgson 2002) in which professionalizing managers work together, also with relevant others. Educating managers is a good example. Educational programs do not have clear-cut, standard curricula, but are designed after frequent interactions between representatives of managers' associations, educational institutes and political authorities (for funding and accreditation). During an evolutionary process, experiences of participants and evaluations of the educational programs contribute to programmatic changes and refinements.

Secondly, developing a profession is not unidirectional; there might be setbacks and de-professionalization is possible as well. Professionalization processes consist of moments, *critical moments* (cf. Van der Meulen 2009), at which the development gains momentum, and periods during which not much is happening. Those critical moments are interesting because meaningful distinctions are introduced or serious changes take place. There might be changes in curricula of educational programs, in training requirements, and in selection procedures. These changes might be broadly supported, but they might also be resisted. (Re)designing educational programs, for example, means that certain management definitions and leadership models are selected, and that certain methods are privileged, and all of this might be or become contested. As leadership models are symbolic and have normative aspects, professionalization processes reconfigure power relations. Who profits from the professionalization of public manager is not immediately clear (compare Grey 1997).

Thirdly, a profession consists of *institutions* that have to be organized within an (already) institutionalized structure of a sector (compare the chapter of Hupe & Van der Krogt). Professional groups must have an institutional basis, including a professional association, educational institutes, knowledge organizations and regulative mechanisms. Such (social) structures have (institutionalized) effects on the work and behavior of professionals. These effects are mediated by existing institutional frameworks.

All of this means we must focus on the evolution of professionalization projects *over time*. The current state of affairs cannot be understood without understanding earlier periods and (critical) moments, and in-

MARTIJN VAN DER MEULEN & MIRKO NOORDEGRAAF

tended and unintended choices on definitions, models and standards. *Critical moments* in professionalization projects must be linked to *contexts* that enabled and constrain professionalization processes. We distinguish three formative aspects that determine the nature of (managerial) professionalization: *group formation, substance* and *control* (see Van der Meulen 2009). We analyze how these aspects are institutionalized by associations, educational programs, and knowledge transfer. We especially focus on 'backstage processes' (Van der Meulen 2009). We study the work of police leaders as a critical case for understanding the professionalization of public managers. Ambitions of professional police leaders appear logical and attractive, but are actually contested. Political attempts to influence police work, performance pressures that flow from management systems and longings for professional spaces as workfloors are difficult to align. Developing leadership is seen as a *solution* for improving performance, but it might also be a *threat*, for policemen, for policy-makers or for politicians.

Professionalization of police leaders

In this paragraph we analyze the professionalization project of Dutch police leaders, by unraveling the current state of affairs and by considering the historical development of the profession. We analyze changing contexts and explore how group formation, substance and behavioral control are institutionalized. This rests upon recent (Van der Meulen 2009) as well as earlier studies (Wiarda 1987; Rosenthal et al. 1987; Blouw et al. 1990; Fijnaut et al. 1999; Boin et al. 2003, Hazenberg 2006). We end our analysis in 2011, just before a new nationwide reorganization of the Dutch police starts to take shape (the regionalized Dutch police will be nationalized: one national police force will be established, headed by a police commissioner, who acts as the chair of a board of directors).

State of affairs: Institutional features

High-ranking Dutch police chiefs are part of a selective *group* with exclusive membership. This 'group' is the so-called LMD group, the nationwide 'management development group' for the police force. LMD defines membership of police leaders, administers a file of qualified leaders, facilitates selection and appointment procedures and forms management development policies. Police leaders are members of the LMD if they are appointed to a top-level management position (in terms of salary scales: scale 15+). LMD also selects candidates who are 'interesting' and who qualify for management positions in the longer term. This includes external candidates (from outside the police forces) who are scouted by LMD consultants, as well as candidates presented as 'high potentials' by police commissioners.

Professional *education* for police leaders consists of specifically designed courses and activities, like modules, expert meetings and coaching. The courses are two-year programs specifically geared towards the occupation of police leaders. There are three levels of leadership, and thus three different courses. In addition to the course Strategic Leadership, which is taught at the School for Police Leadership (SPL), the courses on Tactical Leadership and Operational Leadership offer professional education for incumbent and aspiring leaders in the police forces. Police leaders are not obliged to take these courses in order to advance their careers, but there is social and executive pressure. Education elsewhere is possible, but these programs are not specifically designed for the work and challenges of police leadership. Candidates from outside the police force who lack police experience will especially benefit from these police-oriented or 'blue' programs. Some policemen choose not to participate, because they prefer to broaden their capacities with less police-oriented competencies and knowledge.

Most current police executives, by the way, did not attend these courses, because they developed their careers in the period before these courses existed. Predominately, they followed initial training at the Dutch Police Academy or (before that) at the State Institute for the Education of Higher Police Officers, before entering the police force in positions as commissioned and non-commissioned officers (in the municipal police) or chief constables (in the state police) (Boin et al. 2003).

Police leaders do not have to comply with a specific *code of conduct.* This does not mean that police leaders are not behaviorally controlled by law or regulations; it means there is no formal leadership code. Working and career making within the police force presupposes that police leaders conform to (local) authorities and socialize into a police culture (compare Boin et al. 2003). All police chiefs, on every organizational level, have 'bosses' outside the police, such as local authorities (i.e. mayors) and public prosecutor offices (i.e. public prosecutors). Police leaders have to comply with local and national safety policies and the Department of Home Affairs is trying to increase its influence on managerial and administrative issues (e.g. Hoogenboom 2006). Making a career with police forces (and qualifying for LMD) is an administrative issue, which is controlled by the Department of Home Affairs. This is realized by management development policies, most specifically by selecting candidates based on a set of (strategic leadership) *competencies.* The following core competencies form the competency profile: integrity, courage, sociability, empathy, societal orientation, performance drive, creativity, entrepreneurial and political sensitivity (SPL 2003). Another important instrument is the appointment procedure. The Ministry might e.g. promote diversity in the apexes of police forces, while maintaining high levels of competence. This has evoked public discussions on the 'true motives' behind the appointment of women and immigrants in leadership positions.

In short, police chiefs not only have to develop leadership skills and adapt to (local) police cultures, but are also forced to relate to external bosses and nationwide procedures if they want to qualify for leadership and succeed as police leaders. Although there are no explicit professional codes, there are many procedural and implicit codes.

Professionalization in context

The current status of the profession of police leaders can only be understood if we analyze its evolution. The first crucial observation is that the institutional underpinnings of the managers' group and professional education for police leaders were created at the same moment. In 2001, the strategic apex of police forces, new generations of police chiefs and representatives of the Department of Home Affairs participated in a Conference on the Future of Policing. The main topic was the organization and organizational development of the Dutch police force. The Conference led to several conclusions. The regional police forces should set up regional policies for management development and at the same time, management development should be implemented at the national level. Based on an evaluation of an earlier reorganization of the regional police force, the Department of Home Affairs concluded that management development was necessary in order to improve police performance. The department of Home Affairs needed the cooperation of police chiefs, which was assured by granting police chiefs (and local authorities) influence in selection procedures and by setting up regional management development. The idea was that regional management development could profit from the pioneering work of LMD in setting up a competence profile, defining strategic leadership and organizing selection procedures. This compromise made it possible to found a professional association and the School for Police Leadership at the same time.

This evolution of the profession of police leaders, with the establishment of professional structures (association, school and competency profile) cannot be understood without an institutional reflection on the earlier regionalization of the Dutch police force that took place in 1994. The regionalization (e.g. Cachet & Muller 1995) consisted of the dismantling of 148 municipal police forces and 17 districts of state police and the formation of 25 regional police forces and one nationwide police force. This led to a huge reform, resulting in scaling up police organizations. Apart from the political reasons for police reform, the reorganization was necessary, it was argued, because levels of crime increased and crime itself changed. New forms emerged, such as organized crime, environmental crime, financial fraud, cyber crime, calling for more specialized forms of policing that were not possible in a fragmented, decentralized police organization. The reform was considered a success (Cachet &

Muller 1995). Despite that, the police had to take on intensified managerial tasks for which most police chiefs were not trained. The first years after the regionalization were used to make the reform successful (and to facilitate the integration of different police cultures) and the Department of Home Affairs did not want to tighten control or demand management development. Only after the official evaluation (Rosenthal et al. 1998) of the new police law (1993), did the Department of Home Affairs enhance its role in controlling the police and police performance, for instance by defining nationwide priorities for local safety policy. The Department used to finance a course about police leadership (LPL) in order to develop a new generation of police leaders, but this program lacked a structural base. This changed when the aforementioned leadership courses were established many years later. More recently (2011), plans have been made to nationalize the Dutch police even further, as indicated earlier.

Groups

Nevertheless, the first attempt to set up education and form a professional group, directed by the Department of Home Affairs, failed. The reason was not that candidates did not qualify as police leaders, nor that the educational program was inadequate (Koers 2003). Instead, the course received a lot of criticism, including from graduates who did not get the career opportunities they hoped for. The leadership program was seen as the 'spoiled child' of the department, and not yet as a serious vehicle to develop management and leadership within the police force. The program was abolished after three classes and the Department had to continue its search for opportunities to adapt the selection and development of (new generations of) police leaders.

The compromise that enabled the foundation of LMD and SPL in 2001 offered this opportunity. The Department of Home Affairs hoped that it could introduce a more objective way to appoint new leaders based on leadership competencies. Police leaders could take initiative in developing their own work and learning the necessary competencies, through their 'own' school for police leadership. The activities of the SPL were directed at preparing a new generation of chiefs, but these were also interesting for their bosses, who wanted to participate in coaching trajectories or inter-collegial meetings. Police leaders were, of course, not wholly autonomous in the way they developed their profession. The Department was responsible for financing the activities of the School for Police Leadership and it had to determine the so-called 'end terms' for the educational programs, including the 'core competencies' for strategic leadership. Despite this influence of the state, the SPL developed itself as the school of and for police leaders. In addition to accredited educational programs, the SPL organized all sorts of activities that contributed to the development and professionalization of police leaders.

MARTIJN VAN DER MEULEN & MIRKO NOORDEGRAAF

This, together with the regional management development policies, meant that incumbent and aspiring police leaders could take responsibility for their own professional development. From that moment on, the formation of a professional group found its institutional 'hook' in the selection procedure for police chiefs in certain salary scales (scales 15+). This made the professionalization of police leaders 'real'.

Substance

The substantive profile of police leaders was based on a set of competencies, as indicated above. The LMD used this competency profile to assess candidates, plan future appointments and redirect candidates to educational programs if they did not possess the necessary competencies. The SPL used the profile to develop its educational activities, such as programs, courses and meetings. The competencies were 'discovered' after consultations with police forces, former police leaders and external experts, and were 'written down in the back seat of a car'. More than the competencies themselves, it is important to understand how the competencies were embedded. Before the regionalization of the police a 'Profile for Police Leaders' already existed. This leadership profile was used in order to assess and select the new chief commissioners of the newly formed regional police forces, but after the regionalization it had no function any more. In addition, this first Profile was not used to judge the performance of the new chiefs, nor to assess the performance of the new regional police organizations.

The new competence profile with its nine core competencies was explicitly designed to assess candidates and to present a new, 'common language' to talk about management development and strategic police leadership. Individual performance (of chiefs after appointment) was not measured. In 2002, the education for police officers and chiefs was reformed. All programs had to work with competencies. For all (six) levels of policing, with all sorts of subdivisions in those ranks, specific competencies were determined. In addition, educational programs were split into initial and post-initial courses. These changes were also introduced for educating strategic police leaders.

The competencies and the detailed formalizations of these competencies in the educational programs received a lot of criticism from scholars and police leaders. For candidates it is almost impossible to judge what is essential because everything is important. All candidates score 'as average'. It also increased the influence of the Ministry of Home Affairs and the LMD to promote their own (policy-oriented and sometimes external) candidates at the expense of career-oriented police officers. The ambitions of the Department to promote diversity (women and ethnic minorities) in the apexes of police forces conflicted with individual and culturally defined aspirations within the police force. Many appointments turned into small 'battles' between the state and the police sector about who determines who the right candidates are. If newly appointed police leaders focus on management development, policy formulation and external relation, they are not regarded as 'true' police leaders. In traditional police cultures, leadership on workfloors directly involved the primary process, including its action-orientated and crisis-prone nature. In a male-dominated work force and masculine policing cultures, the appointment of (token) women or candidates without experience in the police force in leadership positions led to worries and 'jealousy'.

Control

Finally, the professionalization project is about institutionalizing control. The competency profile defines the skills that aspiring leaders need to possess or have to develop if they want to advance their careers. Assessments, job interviews and individual trajectories are examples of activities by way of which candidates can qualify. But this competency profile does not directly control police leaders. Incumbent chiefs do not have to fulfill all the requirements, because they are not actively pursuing new jobs. They are mainly accountable to their chiefs and local authorities. The professional group of police leaders is thus Janus-faced; police leaders have to meet the nationwide requirements, and police leaders resist centralized procedures. Indeed, in order to show leadership it might be necessary to publicly oppose the trajectories that ground leadership development.

Police leaders are also socialized into resisting centralized attempts to discipline police leaders in other ways. In addition to management development policies and leadership development programs, police forces are disciplined by management techniques, quality models and accounting systems, coming from the New Public Management, as mentioned above. These are implemented but also criticized, as they affect 'professional spaces' and generate 'bureaucracy', it is argued. An example of collective resistance against disciplinary forces was the presentation of a Police View on the core tasks of the police, by the board of chief commissioners (2005). This view stresses the 'serving nature' of police work, but also claims autonomy for developing police professionalism, including a crucial role for professional police leadership. 'Serving with authority' instead of 'serving authority', it was subtly stressed.

Disciplining police leaders by way of leadership development goes hand in hand with autonomy-seeking police leaders who do not want to be disciplined. They do not seek autonomy per se, but autonomous police forces that maintain certain police values, cultures and ways of working. This is happening in times that put pressures on these values, cultures and ways of working, that – more specifically – confuse not only what these values etc. are, but *who* determines, changes and protects them.

Backstage professionalization projects

When we compare police leaders with other groups of professionalizing public managers, such as healthcare executives, we can conclude that the profession of police leaders is less heterogeneous (Van der Meulen 2009). Compared with fragmented executive fields in healthcare, police leaders have clearly defined and demarcated occupational and educational institutions. In healthcare multiple institutions, with diverging philosophies and different educational philosophies, have specialized themselves in developing healthcare executives; there are different 'schools' (Noordegraaf & Van der Meulen 2008). Professionalizing healthcare executives can choose *where* they want to develop themselves, how they *relate* to the profession and which *methods* they see as suitable for their personal development. Police leaders cannot choose a 'school'; their professionalization project is much more coordinated by forces inside and outside of the police domain. In Dutch healthcare, there is more competition between associations and educational institutes. Standardization of managerial and executive work in healthcare is weakly developed, despite attempts to develop codes of behavior and work profiles. Candidates who want to pursue a career in healthcare management do not necessarily participate in professionalization activities.

These differences in professions and professionalization processes can be understood by placing professionalization projects in contexts (Van der Meulen 2009). The role of the *state* in controlling and administrating police forces is much stronger than in sectors like healthcare. The latter sector is traditionally based upon 'private initiatives', especially in countries like the Netherlands (Dijsselbloem et al. 2004). Organizations and leadership are less directly controlled by the state. Governmental policies and public financing are crucial conditions for organizing and managing in those sectors, but managers and administrators have more leeway to make management decisions and strategic choices. In the police sector, the law defines organizational tasks and hierarchies, responsibilities of key players (mayors, police chiefs and public prosecutors), as well as command structures and management systems.

These contextual factors have consequences for how the professionalism of police leaders is developed, compared with other public managers. The 'struggle' over professionalism is different; other issues are at stake. The professionalization of healthcare administrators is geared toward such questions as 'what is good healthcare?' and 'how can effective healthcare be organized?' As governmental policies change, organizations, healthcare administrators, associations and educational institutes respond, e.g. by organizing courses in financial management, introducing consumer-based strategies, and establishing alliances with other parties. When contextual factors change, the professionalization of healthcare administrators receives new impulses.

Police leaders also have to organize effective police strategies and tactics, but their professionalization project is shaped by other influences. Although police leaders take initiatives in determining the future of policing, e.g. by introducing new tasks for police officers and new employers' principles, this is not – yet – the core of the professionalization project. The struggle over professionalism is more geared towards the question 'who controls the police?' and 'how can police leaders claim authority within police forces and within society?' The founding of the LMD and SPL clearly represented a moment at which policy-makers and police leaders reached a compromise over controlling the police, via procedures for appointing and educating police leaders. This compromise paved the way for institutionalizing leadership, most specifically by founding a School for Police Leadership in order to establish management development for top-level police chiefs. Since that moment, appointments were based on leadership development and individual development was framed as 'leadership development'.

Although this compromise ended a longstanding debate about responsibilities for management development and police leadership, and although it 'disciplined' police managers (compare Grey 1997), it enabled the professionalization of police leaders. When police leaders focused too much on central requirements for career-making, they would lose authority in their own forces; when they resisted or ignored national requirements, they would lose their authority in policy and political and arenas. Police chiefs have to cope with these ambivalent constraints. The focus on 'leadership' helped them to uphold the image of 'being in control', in-between political and professional demands, whilst they stressed that they also 'served' other stakeholders. Leadership development of police chiefs cannot be understood without acknowledging its strategic and semantic value.

Conclusion

All in all, leadership development is not a neutral activity, functionally aimed at improving leadership competencies and behaviors, aimed at improving organizational performance. All parties involved – police chiefs, police officers, policy-makers, politicians, political executives, (local) administrators, educators, representatives of intermediaries, citizens – have their own ideas (and ideals) on management and leadership and they have distinctive interests concerning leadership development. Dutch police chiefs are engaged in a professionalization project and they try to develop themselves into professional police leaders. But this project involves choices and struggle, which are heavily dependent on endogenous and exogenous circumstances.

First and foremost, police managers have to find ways to speak about their work and to standardize aspects of it that clarify things, but that do

MARTIJN VAN DER MEULEN & MIRKO NOORDEGRAAF

not really clarify things, as the nature of police work is ambiguous, and as the link between police work and management/leadership is even more ambiguous. Terms like leadership and models like competency models are appropriate, as they must be implemented and leave room for situated judgment. Terms like leadership and competency models can be interpreted in different ways and they can be elaborated in varied ways when they are implemented. In other words, police managers have managed to uphold interpretative spaces when defining their work, which is necessary to defend occupational spaces.

This was supported, in turn, by external relations. There are multiple dependencies when it comes to organizing police work and police management, and these dependencies were used to tighten collective regulative control. Police work and management are clearly *embedded* within state-based systems of work control as well as systems and standards for democratic control, and this means that terms like leadership and competency models can have institutional effects. Much more than in e.g. Dutch healthcare, which is further detached from the state than the Dutch police, police organizations are regulated by outside stakeholders, and this can be used to literally *realize* occupational control. Systems for assessing, selecting and promoting police managers, for example, can really influence careers and organizational development.

This also means that the professionalization is subjected to political struggle. The main question that appears to drive the quest for professional control is 'who controls the police?' (cf. Van der Meulen 2009). The reduction of occupational heterogeneity in the field of police management, much more than in the field of healthcare management, comes at a price: it is much more political in a jurisdictional sense. There is a direct clash of jurisdictions: the field of policing that wants to serve with authority faces policy fields and political authorities that want to be served. Although this is softened by the leadership discourse, terms such as 'leadership' and 'leadership development' have strategic value, not only to substantiate functional desires but also to realize political aspirations. Apparently, the development of jurisdictional *spaces*, aimed at improving work and buffering work against outside interference, presupposes certain institutional *constraints* that enable professional development.

All in all, professionalization is 'imposed' upon police managers by circumstances, but how it materializes can be strategically manipulated. Occupational development is construed by managers, in interaction with many other parties, institutional settings and expectations about results and responsibilities. The search for better police leadership, then, is not so much about defining police competencies, but much more about organizing spaces for leadership and its development, despite societal demands for safety and political struggles over control over police performance. In terms of pressures on work, the theme of this book, as well as the starting point for this chapter, this implies that there are many opportunities to alleviate work pressures, both for managers and workers, but also that managerial pressures will always *indirectly* affect professional work. Occupational spaces are far from absolute and they can all the more be used to control police work. Although the rhetoric of leadership and competencies hides struggles, professional control within police circles is actually controlled by others in order to control police work.

References

Abbott, A. (1988). *The System of Professions*. Chicago: The University of Chicago Press.

Abbott, A. (1991). The Order of Professionalization: An empirical analysis. *Work and Occupations, 18*(4): 355-384.

Ackroyd, S., Kirkpatrick, I. & Walker, R.M. (2007). Public Management Reform in the UK and its Consequences for Professional Organization. *Public Administration, 85*(1): 9-26.

Adlam, R. & Villiers, P. (2003). *Police Leadership in the Twenty-First Century*. Hampshire: Waterside Press.

Blouw, H. de, Copini, F., & Van Lochem, P. (1990). *Professie, Macht en Dienstbaarheid: 40 Jaar politieleiding aan het woord [Profession, Power and Service]*. Arnhem: Gouda Quint.

Board of Chief Commissioners (2005). *The Vision on Police: The Police in Evolution*. The Hague: NPI.

Boin, A., Van der Torre, E., & 't Hart, P. (2003). *Blauwe Bazen: Het leiderschap van korpschefs [The Leadership of Police Chiefs]*. Zeist: Kerckebosch.

Bruijn, J.A. de (2007). *Managing Performance in the Public Sector* (2nd ed.). London: Routledge.

Cachet, A., & Muller, E. (1995). De Reorganisatie van de Politie. *Bestuurskunde, 4* (2): 71-79.

Clarke, J., & Newman, J. (1997). *The Managerial State*. London: SAGE.

Diefenbach, T. (2009). New Public Management in Public Sector Organizations: The Dark Side of Managerialistic 'Enlightenment'. *Public Administration, 87* (4), 892-909.

Dijsselbloem et al. (2004). *Maatschappelijke Dienstverlening [Social Service]*. Amsterdam: Amsterdam University Press.

Exworthy, M., & Halford, S. (1999). *Professionals and the New Managerialism in the Public Sector*. Buckingham: Oxford University Press.

Farrell. C., & Morris, J. (2003). 'The Neo-Bureaucratic' State: Professionals, Managers and Professional Managers in Schools. General Practices and Social Work. *Organization, 10*(1): 129-156.

Fijnaut, C., Muller, E.R., Rosenthal, E., & Van der Torre, E.J. (1999). *Politie: Studie over haar Werking en Organisatie [Research into the Organization of the Police]*. Alphen aan den Rijn: Samsom.

Freidson, E. (2001). *Professionalism: The Third Logic*. Cambridge: Polity Press.

Grey, C. (1997). Management as a Technical Practice: Professionalization or responsibilization? *Systems Practice, 10*(6): 703-726.

Gross, C. & Kieser, A. (2006). Are Consultants Moving Towards Professionalization? In R. Greenwood & R. Suddaby (Eds.), *Professional Service Firms (Re-*

search in the Sociology of Organizations, Volume 24), pp. 69-100. Bingley: Emerald Group Publishing Limited.

Hazenberg, A. (2006). Politiebiografie Aanknopingspunt voor Leren Leren [Police Biography: Starting Point to Learn Learning]. *Tijdschrift voor de Politie, 68* (12): 17-22.

Hodgson, D. (2002). Disciplining the Professional: The case of project management. *Journal of Management Studies, 39*, 803-821.

Hodgson, D. (2005). Putting on a Professional Performance: Performativity, subversion and project management. *Organization, 12*(1): 51-68.

Hodgson, D., & Cicmil, S. (2007). The Politics of Standards in Modern Management: Making 'the Project' a Reality. *Journal of Management Studies, 44*(3), 431-450.

Hood, C. (1991). A Public Management for All Seasons? *Public Administration, 69*(1): 3-19.

Hoogenboom, B. (2006). *Operationele Betrokkenheid: Prestatiesturing en bedrijfsvoering Nederlandse politie [Performance management and Operational Management in the Dutch Police]*. Den Haag: Reed Business.

Kipping, M. (2011). Hollow from the Start? Image Professionalism in Management Consulting. *Current Sociology, 59*(4), 530-550.

Koers, A. (2003). Exit Leergang Politie Leiderschap [Exit Course for Police Leadership]. *Tijdschrift voor de Politie, 5*, 16-18.

Krause, E.A. (1996). *Death of the Guilds. Professions, States and the Advance of Capitalism*. New Haven: Yale University Press.

Larson, M. (1977). *The Rise of Professionalism*. Berkeley: University of California Press.

Maas, A. (2004). *Op Weg naar Professionalisering: Spiegel voor Interim managers [Towards Professionalization for Interim Managers]*. Assen: Van Gorcum.

MacDonald, K. (1995). *The Sociology of Professions*. London: SAGE.

McKenna, C.D. (2006). *The World's Newest Profession: Management Consulting in the Twentieth Century*. New York: Cambridge University Press.

Mintzberg, H. (2004). *Managers, Not MBAs*. London: Financial Times Prentice Hall.

Nap, J. (2008). *Stil Staan bij Politieleiderschap [Police Leadership]*. Warnsveld: SPL.

Noordegraaf, M. (2006). Professional Management of Professionals: Hybrid Organisations and Professional Management in Care and Welfare. In J.W. Duyvendak, T. Knijn, & M. Kremer (Eds.). *Policy, People, and the New Professional*, pp. 181-193. Amsterdam: Amsterdam University Press.

Noordegraaf, M. (2007). 'From 'Pure' to Hybrid' Professionalism: Present-Day Professionalism in Ambiguous Public Domains. *Administration & Society, 39* (6): 761-785.

Noordegraaf, M. (2008). *Professioneel Bestuur [Professional Governance]*. Den Haag: Lemma.

Noordegraaf, M. (2012). The Making of Professional Public Leaders. In M. Dent, E. Ferlie, & C. Teelken (Eds.). *Leadership in the Public Sector: Promises and Pitfalls*. London: Routledge.

Noordegraaf, M., & Van der Meulen, M. (2008). Professional Power Play: Organizing management in health care. *Public Administration, 86*(4): 1055-1069.

Noordegraaf, M., & Schinkel, W. (2010). Professional Capital Contested. A Bourdieusian Analysis of Conflicts between Professionalism and Managers. *Comparative Sociology, 10*(1), 97-125.

Pollitt, C., & Bouckaert, G. (2004). *Public Management Reform*. Oxford: Oxford University Press.

Reiner, R. (1992). *Chief Constables*. Oxford: Oxford University Press.

Rosenthal, U., 't Hart, P., & Cachet, A. (1987). *Politie-Management: Een politiek-bestuurlijke visie [Police Management]*. Arnhem: Gouda Quint.

Rosenthal, U., Bruinsma, G. & Muller, E. (1998). *Evaluatie Politiewet 1993: Diepte-onderzoek [Evaluation Police Act 1993]*. Den Haag: VUGA.

Sonnaville, H. de (2005). *Retorische Aspecten van Professionaliseren: Een zoektocht naar beroepsvorming bij organisatieadviseurs [Rhetoric Aspects of Professionalizing]*. Amsterdam: Dutch University Press.

SPL (2003). *Kerncompetenties voor Strategisch Politieleiderschap [Core Competences for Strategic Police Leadership]*. Den Haag: BZK.

SPL (2004). *Publiek leiderschap [Public Leadership]*. Apeldoorn: School voor Politieleiderschap.

Van der Meulen, M. (2009). *Achter de Schermen: Professionalisering en vakontwikkeling van publieke managers in de zorg en bij de politie [Behind the scenes: The professionalization of public managers in healthcare and policing.]* Delft: Eburon.

Van der Torre, E. (2007). *Lokale Politiechefs [Local Police Chiefs]*. Den Haag: Elsevier.

Whitley, R. (1989). On the Nature of Managerial Tasks and Skills: Their distinguishing characteristics and organization. *Journal of Management Studies, 3,* 209-224.

Whitley, R. (1995). Academic Knowledge and Work Jurisdiction in Management. *Organisation Studies, 16*(1), 81-105.

Wiarda, J. (1987). *Als het Donker Genoeg is, Worden de Sterren Zichtbaar: Management development bij de politie [Management Development at the Police]*. Warnsveld: Politiestudiecentrum.

Wilensky, H. (1964). The Professionalization of Everyone? *American Journal of Sociology, 70*(2): 137-158.

Wit, B. de, & Noordegraaf, M. (2012). Reform Responses: How Management Reforms Affect Managerial Relations and Loyalties in Education. *Public Administration,* to be published.

14 Conclusions and ways forward

Mirko Noordegraaf & Bram Steijn

Introduction

In the previous chapters, pressures on professionals have been analyzed from multiple angles, based upon different conceptual and empirical analyses. It is now time to draw conclusions and propose ways forward. In doing so, we will explore the 'state of professionalism' with critical and political points of view that transgress Dutch borders. We will do this by returning to the various themes or parts that made up this book: *I. Professionals and (managerial) pressures, II. Controlling professional practices,* and *III. Organizing professionalism.* After a short summary of the main findings we will outline the main points of our own perspective on 'pressured professionals' in which the concept of ownership plays an important role. The chapter ends with a research agenda for the near future.

Professionals and (managerial) pressures

In chapter 3 Janet Newman has set the scene: there is *no* such thing as 'the' pressures on 'the' professional. This was reiterated by other authors, especially in part I (chapters 4, 5 and 6). With respect to professions we have seen that professions differ structurally and practically. Structurally, in terms of institutionalization, organizational connections, educational backgrounds and demographical make-up. Practically, in terms of the extent to which professions themselves are contested when it comes to client or case treatment (chapter 4), and the extent to which professionals have autonomy and discretionary spaces (chapter 5).

Professional forms and the pressures they undergo, moreover, are never static. With respect to this change, three observations can be made. Firstly, changes affect different relations (between, in Newman's terms, government, organizations, associations and the public) and these relations generate multiple 'sites of contestation' that might hinder professionals, but might also help them to develop resistance and conflict. Professionals themselves have various coping strategies to deal with pressures (Hupe & Van der Krogt, chapter 4). They might individualize work (*coping*), seek stronger associational control (*networking*), or politicize professional fields (*activism*).

Secondly, with respect to professional work there is no such thing as linear change, with ever increasing pressures. Professionals have always been pressured (chapter 3) and new changes do *not* automatically increase pressures. However, various types of pressure can be discerned. In this respect, Hupe & Van der Krogt (chapter 4) discern three types of pressure (rule, vocational and societal pressures) stemming from three different sources: public administration, the profession, and society at large.

Thirdly, these changes do not exert clear pressures, which *increasingly* harm or obstruct professional behaviors. 'Multiple forces and pressures are assembled in specific contexts,' Newman argues in chapter 3. This suggests that we have to focus not only on the pressures themselves, but more importantly on how they are (re)assembled. For instance, professional associations might have *capacities* to counter managerial pressures, but they might also assist politicians and policy-makers in reforming service sectors, and as we have seen thereby assist in fueling pressures on professionals. This is illustrated in later chapters, when the introduction of DBCs in (mental) healthcare is explored (chapter 7) and the policy alienation in healthcare and education is studied (chapter 8). All of this does not contradict the fact that professionals may *experience* pressures, burdens and bureaucracy, *perceive* 'assaults' on professionalism (cf. chapter 5), are *experiencing* 'bounded professionalism' (chapter 11) or *feel* 'alienated' on workfloors (chapter 8). Indeed, these very same chapters show that certain undeniable forces, especially those of managerial reform, *are* indeed affecting professional work. This – almost literally – forces professionals to be clear about and account for their performances. However, several chapters, especially in part I, have put these forces into the perspectives we already outlined in the introduction: perceived and experienced pressures do not have to be taken literally; they signify 'bigger' struggles over public services, which are not merely about professional work, but also about changing socio-economic and organizational 'settlements' (cf. chapters 2 and 3). Taken together, these chapters show that:
- The restructuring of public services induces certain forces that constrain service sectors, not in the least because they call upon professionals to clarify their performances, which contrasts with professional values and beliefs that were developed in previous periods.

They also show that:
- These forces and new service realities have no 'immediate' and 'objective' consequences; their effects are moderated by experiential, strategic and practical conditions.
- Effects differ, because some professionals might feel powerless, but others are not; because professional associations and professionals might resist managerial forces, or not; and because professionals

MIRKO NOORDEGRAAF & BRAM STEIJN

might still possess discretionary powers, and know how to cope with change.

Controlling professional practices

This brings us to part II, in which new control forms are explored, and in which these experiential, strategic and practical conditions are analyzed in more detail. In fact, it is analyzed where these conditions come from – why do professionals feel powerless, or not? Why do associations resist change, or not? Why do professionals possess discretionary space, or not? The chapters in part II elaborate on the argument that it is far too simple to blame the so-called *New Public Management* (NPM) as responsible for the increase in work pressure felt by professionals (chapter 4) or 'deprofessionalization' of public service delivery (chapter 5). In this way, Ackroyd's observations (chapter 2) are elaborated; the effects of NPM-like reforms are not universal, but depend on 'the existing condition of the profession and how it perceived opportunities and threats constituted by the introduction of new policies'. We can work this out by distinguishing between several types of moderation.

Firstly, there is *cognitive* moderation within specific professional fields. Tummers et al. show that professionals react differently to pressures (chapter 8) and De Graaf & Van der Wal (chapter 9) highlight the importance of *loyalties* for understanding how professionals respond to pressures. Because loyalties vary, professional responses vary. This means there are important *subjective* and *relational* sides to pressures on professionals, which underscore the previous part's emphasis on acknowledging the varieties of professional work.

Secondly, there is *political* moderation within professional fields. Smullen (chapter 7) shows how a new financing system (DBCS), which was originally supported by medical doctors (outside mental healthcare), fuels controversies within a professional field. How these controversies are played out has far-reaching consequences. Later, chapter 11 on professional self-regulation takes this argument one step further by showing 'how attempts to defend professional discretion lead to regulatory pressure for professionals'.

Finally, there is *institutional* moderation. Tummers et al. (chapter 8) show how feelings of policy alienation are affected by interactions within the specific field, shaped by professional associations and groups. When associations are strong and act as 'advocates' for professional fields, and when groups have 'higher status', it is easier to maintain discretion and feel less policy pressures. Whereas part I mainly focused on connections between managerial reform, 'objective' pressures on professionals, and varied professional responses, part II elaborates on and explains these responses. The chapters in part II show that:

- Connections between reforms, pressures and work are moderated: loyalties, strength of associations and group status explain how pressures reach workfloors, and why professionals respond as they do.

They also show that:
- These moderated responses influence the nature of reform and subsequent pressures.

Organizing professionalism

The third part of the book on Organizing Professionalism remains close to the previous themes, but adds a few other insights as these chapters take a more organizational point of view. This is important in itself as we have seen that professionals are becoming more and more entrenched in organizations (chapters 4 and 5). They either analyze how organizations (and the professionals inside them) are reconfigured, such as welfare organizations (chapter 12), or they explore how the resettling of professional services affects managers, such as police managers (chapter 13). There is a contradictory logic here. Whereas people on work floors experience increasing 'bureaucracy', those who are at the helms of bureaucratic organizations – i.e. managers – experience increasing 'professionalization'. Of course, as shown in chapter 11, these two logics must *not* be seen as wholly contradictory; professionals need bureaucratic standards in order to be and act professional. Empirically, this is illustrated in chapter 12: welfare workers who must 'reintegrate' clients without clear professional standards are 'professionals without a profession'. All in all, the chapters in part III show that:
- Organizing professionalism is no strict 'organizational' affair; it depends on the organizational capacities of professionals and their fields to develop and apply standards.

In addition, they show that:
- It depends on the abilities of managers to develop 'professional' standards that are not merely functional, but meaningful and 'trustworthy' in the light of more fundamental service-related controversies.

A perspective on public professionalism

Taken together, the three parts of this book and their respective chapters enable us to develop a perspective on public professionalism that builds upon earlier studies (such as Exworthy & Halford 1999; Kirkpatrick et al. 2005; Noordegraaf 2007, 2011; Muzio & Kirkpatrick 2011; Faulconbridge & Muzio 2012; see also chapter 1) but also adds a few things. First and foremost, this perspective does not limit its focus on well-known dichotomies, such as managerialism versus professionalism or organizational versus professional control. It highlights the *intersections* between apparently opposing or contradictory logics, which can also be found in studies with emphases on hybrid professionalism (e.g. Noordegraaf 2007; Faulconbridge & Muzio 2008; Kuhlmann & Saks 2008; Kirkpatrick et al. 2009). For example, the chapters in this book show that professionals are not passive victims of outside developments; they might be real 'reflective' practitioners who can actively shape their own situation (Noordegraaf 2007).

In addition, it highlights managerial and organizational *transitions within* professional fields (compare Waring & Currie 2009; Noordegraaf 2011). It shows how professionals and professional groups might adopt organizational mechanisms and managerial techniques, not only to defend themselves, but to (re)organize their work. This means we need to understand intersections and transitions from more *institutional* and *political* points of view. New Public Management reform represents more than organizational forms and techniques and values like efficiency; it is about a more fundamental reordering of professional services, against the background of shifting societal values. What *is* effective care or education nowadays?

Professionalism as ownership

This book underscores these points of view by portraying public service delivery not as a neutral endeavor, but as layered and controversial. Service transactions cannot be detached from organizational and policy contexts, which set service parameters and – more importantly – which determine who *owns* these parameters.

To begin with, many authors have shown that public professional work is never (and never has been) 'free'. Professionals do not 'have' (and never had) individual autonomy; their autonomy was governed by professional fields, which established strict mechanisms for controlling their members. In fact, the most classic professional fields, such as medicine, have always been tightly controlled by selection procedures, educational standards, ethical codes and codes of conduct, sanctioning procedures, etc.

Furthermore, many authors have shown that professional service transactions are double-edged. First and foremost, private wishes must be reconciled with public concerns; but at the same time, these public concerns have become increasingly paradoxical in themselves. Values like solidarity might be at odds with economic values like efficiency, especially in periods of fiscal stress and neoliberal economic policies. In short, efficiency gains which are valued by the so-called New Public Management are not only private or business-like values; efficiency gains can represent public values as well. Like some earlier studies (Larson 1977; Burrage & Thorstendahl 1990), the chapters also stress the processes through which these dynamics are played out. Politicians, policy-makers, professional associations, organizations and their managers, and professional workers themselves – they all have to be taken into account to get a well-rounded picture of pressured professionals in public services.

Lastly and perhaps most importantly, this book stressed the political aspects of such dynamic processes, especially in terms of searches for *ownership*. The reorganization and reconfiguring of public services professionalism, amidst various relations (knowledge/power knots and the like), changing standards (objectification etc.) and paradoxical values (private values that are public values as well), are mainly redefining the ownership of professional services and their added societal value. Concerns over pressured professionalism are not necessarily about pressures on autonomy and work-related freedoms, or about changing rules and standards – more organizational and less professional. Pressures symbolize the fact that *others* are determining workspaces and standards, and are thereby affecting the nature of the services rendered. The question thus becomes: *are these services still owned by professionals* (assuming they ever were owned by them), *or do managers, organizations, clients, policy-makers and/or politicians 'rightfully' determine who gets which service in what way?*

Socio-political perspective

When we take these elements together, we can summarize the perspective developed in this book. We can develop *a socio-political image of public professionalism as 1) configured, 2) moderated and 3) experiential.* There are evident pressures on professionals and professional work, but what these pressures represent and whether these pressures are really felt as 'pressures', is ambiguous. They might symbolize shifts in ownership in dynamic webs of relations, with governmental, occupational, professional and organizational actors. How they are played out depends on specific sectors, contexts and organizations in which pressures and professionals come together, as well as on how distinctive agents behave. Even when strong patterns arise, like some of the patterns described in the previous chapters (increasing problems in education, the normalization of psychiatry, and the like), these are not unavoidable and predetermined. Apparently, there are *strategic spaces* in and around pressures on professionals that can be used to influence how pressures work out.

Unavoidably, micro-practices have to be linked to macro-processes in order to understand pressured professionalism. Objective or structural forces have to be linked to subjective experiences and feelings. Functional concerns over services have to be linked to political agendas. The mechanisms through which bigger structural and political forces are connected to organizational and behavioral surroundings are becoming

MIRKO NOORDEGRAAF & BRAM STEIJN

crucial then. As we have shown, there are several mechanisms that determine how pressures are seen and played out, also in the longer term. There are *cognitive* mechanisms, i.e. orientations, ways of thought, loyalties and identifications, which determine how pressures are perceived. There are *institutional* mechanisms, i.e. roles of associations and status perceptions, which affect the relation between policy pressures and workfloor responses. Managerial acts, including the degree of support given to professionals, can be seen as a part of such institutional moderation. Finally, there are *political* mechanisms, i.e. interactions and negotiations that determine whether new and 'normalized' occupational patterns come into existence.

Instead of 'complaining' about pressures, associations, organizations and professionals might develop strategies to *respond* to more structural and political changes. Of course, complaints might be a resource for this, but more is needed to reshape professional services. Professional associations might be careful when critical negotiations occur, e.g. with politicians or policy-makers. Organizations might find ways to reform professional work in meaningful ways. And professionals might find ways to adapt to change, but also retain certain feelings of professionalism. In other words, the searches for new forms of professionalism in public services call for new capacities to guide and implement these searches. Merely ignoring or resisting changes is as unwise as merely accepting and complying with change. *Public professionalism calls for capacities to shape the reconfiguration of public professionalism, aimed at reducing negative or destructive experiences.* This is not only the task of policy-makers.

Further research

Although the previous chapters show many things about the reconfiguring of public services and the consequences for professional work – related to earlier studies that already showed a lot – the chapters also clarify what is (still) less clear. On the one hand, they highlight certain *aspects* of public service reconfigurations, which might in the future be analyzed in more detail.

Firstly, the (changing) roles and status of professional *associations* should be clarified. They are important moderated forces, but their acts and interactions with other actors seem to be under-studied. And when they are studied, they remain black boxes. Not many (recent) studies focus on the ways in which associations respond to changing and increasingly critical environments, and on how they (re)establish relations with their members who will be less willing to passively comply with occupational rules and regulations.

Secondly, the *capacities of professionals* to cope with change should be studied more. This will not only be a matter of personal loyalties and orientations, but of cognitive features that are developed over time, partly influenced by professional associations – including schooling and training – and partly influenced by (earlier) organizational experiences. Capacities in other words cannot be decoupled from demographic and cultural developments. How professionals are educated and socialized will influence how they perceive changing environments and whether they are able to cope with the reconfigurations that have been highlighted.

Thirdly, the role and relevance of professional *standards* should be analyzed more. Instead of seeking oppositions between organizations and professionals, related to appealing oppositions between bureaucracy and professionalism and bureaucratic and professional control, we need more in-depth understandings of how policies, organizations *and* professional practices depend on standards when services are delivered. In fact, in many ways our socio-political perspective rests upon a sensitivity for standards:

– What standards are set, by whom? (ownership)
– How are these standards perceived and experienced? (experience)
– How are standards applied, used and/or resisted? (strategic response)

On the other hand, the previous chapters also indicate that certain research *approaches* might be valuable in order to develop more refined understandings of professionals under pressure, in resettled public services.

Firstly, we need *comparative* approaches. Of course, comparative approaches are always relevant, but in the case of pressured professionalism there seems to be all the more reason to compare public service sectors and (national) contexts. Although the reconfiguration of professional public services is a generic phenomenon, the actual resettling of service relations and practices, and the consequences seem to be tied to *contexts* in several important ways.

– Institutional parameters influence which structural forces are unleashed, and how resettlements evolve. The extent to which service sectors are controlled by the state, for example, will influence which policy plans are developed and how they are implemented.
– Patterns of professionalization will influence how moderating mechanisms work out. Professionalism might have been developed from 'the bottom up' or from 'the top down' (e.g. Burrage & Torstendahl 1990), and this influences how associations interact with other actors. The strength and status of professional fields, also based upon the strength of schooling and socialization, will be relevant as well for understanding how pressures develop.
– Service contexts will influence spaces for action. They will not only determine how actors (policy-makers, managers, professionals, and the like) interact, but also how these various actors act. The number

MIRKO NOORDEGRAAF & BRAM STEIJN

and size of service organizations, the services they render, the size of clienteles they reach – this will all determine how pressures develop when services are resettled. In addition, distinctive cases and incidents will influence the (media) attention paid to certain sectors, and subsequent responses.

Secondly, we need *longitudinal* approaches. Although we can not necessarily generalize every element of Ackroyd's description of what happened with UK professions (chapter 2) to other contexts and countries, his account of thirty years of research of 'new' government policies does of course provide such an approach. Looking at the Netherlands, pressures on professionals have suddenly become a new topic of public and academic debate, representing working conditions inside public services and symbolizing struggles over public service delivery. We must be careful with accepting such a tempting but also possibly misleading anachronistic stance. As we have seen, professionalism has never come naturally and professionals have always been pressured. Moreover, merely highlighting pressures in current service surroundings and ignoring patterns of change that develop over time, runs the risk of missing certain formative influences. Pressures might be generated by certain time-bound factors:

— *Contrasts* between past and present. If things were 'different' or 'better' in previous times, pressures might be felt.
— *Generational* changes. Pressures might be linked to generational effects. When new generations of professionals are trained differently or have different (organizational) experiences, they feel less (or more) pressured.
— Changes in *ownership* might fuel feelings of loss and powerlessness. When resettlements change incentive and ownership structures, professionals do not need to be pressured more, in order to complain about work pressures.

This – as a final remark – also underscores the need for more *empirical* research in those various contexts-in-transition. What pressures are we talking about, where do they come from, and how do they manifest themselves in day-to-day work? We need both quantitative and qualitative empirical research. Quantitative studies will be helpful to find out the degree of pressures felt by professionals, the differences between several groups, and (objective) factors influencing these. Qualitative studies are needed to get an understanding of the way professionals *actually* experience and cope with pressures, and to understand the mechanism driving (diverging) professional behaviors.

Pressured professionalism thus contains many pressures for more systematic academic research and more refined practical interventions in and around professional service practices. The resettling of public services and its unsettling effects will also resettle academic and practical action. Research traditions in the field of professionalism are both reinforced *and* renewed; practical interventions are both real and realized.

References

Burrage, M., & Torstendahl, R. (1990). *Professions in Theory and History: Rethinking the study of the professions*. London: Sage Publications.

Exworthy, M., & Halford, S. (Eds.). (1999). *Professionals and the New Managerialism in the Public Sector*. Buckingham: Open University Press.

Faulconbridge, J. & Muzio, D. (2008). Organizational professionalism in globalizing law firms. *Work, Employment & Society, 22*(1), 7-25.

Faulconbridge, J., & Muzio, D. (2012). Professions in a globalizing world: Towards a transnational sociology of the professions. *International Sociology, 27* (1), 136-152.

Kirkpatrick, I., Ackroyd, S., & Walker, R. (2005). *The New Managerialism and Public Service Professions*. Basingstoke: Palgrave Macmillan.

Kirkpatrick, I., Kragh Jespersen, P., Dent, M., & Neogy, I. (2009). Medicine and management in a comparative perspective: The cases of England and Denmark. *Sociology of Health and Illness, 31*(5), 642-658.

Kuhlmann, E., & Saks, M. (Eds.). (2008). *Rethinking Professional Governance: International directions in healthcare*. Bristol: Policy Press.

Larson, M.S. (1977). *The Rise of Professionalism: A sociological analysis*. Berkeley: University of California Press.

Muzio, D., & Kirkpatrick, I. (2011). Introduction: Professions and organizations – a conceptual framework. *Current Sociology, 59*(4), 389-405.

Noordegraaf, M. (2007). From pure to hybrid professionalism: Present-day professionalism in ambiguous public domains. *Administration & Society, 39*(6), 761-785.

Noordegraaf, M. (2011). Risky business. How professionals and professionals fields (must) deal with organizational issues. *Organization Studies, 32*(10), 1349-1371.

Waring, J., & Currie, G. (2009). Managing expert knowledge: Organizational challenges and managerial futures for the UK medical profession. *Organization Studies, 30*(7), 755-778.

About the editors and authors

Editors

Prof.dr **Mirko Noordegraaf** is full professor of Public Management at the Utrecht School of Governance, Utrecht University. He studies public management, managerial behavior, organizational reform and public professionalism, and focuses on the reconfiguration of professional work. He has published in *Organization Studies, Public Administration, Administration & Society, Public Management Review, Current Sociology, Comparative Sociology, Journal of Management Studies* and *International Journal of Public Sector Management*. He is editor of *Public Administration Review* (PAR).

Prof.dr **Bram Steijn** is full professor of HRM in the public sector at Erasmus University Rotterdam. He has published about strategic HR, labor market issues, quality of work, motivation of employees, public service motivation and policy alienation of public professionals in *Public Management Review, Public Administration, International Review of Administrative Sciences, Review of Public Personnel Administration, International Public Management Journal, New Technology, Work and Employment*, and *Work, Employment and Society*. He is a member of the *Dutch HRM network* and of the editorial board of *Review of Public Personnel Administration*.

Authors

Dr **Paul van der Aa** is evaluation researcher for the Municipality of Rotterdam. He studies the organization, delivery and outcomes of local social policies, with a particular focus on local unemployment policies. In 2012 he published his PhD thesis, aimed at understanding the delivery of activation services. Together with Rik van Berkel he has published in the *European Journal of Social Work* and the *Journal of European Social Policy*.

Prof. **Stephen Ackroyd** is emeritus professor of organizational analysis at Lancaster University Management School in the UK. He is honorary professor at Cardiff Business School and visiting professor at Bristol School of Management (UWE) and elsewhere. His research interests concern the boundaries between formal and informal organization, including organizational misbehavior, the organization of professional groups and group agency in organizational innovation. He has published in a variety of journals and written or edited 10 books including *The New Managerialism and The Public Service Professions* (Palgrave 2005, with I. Kirkpatrick) and *Redirections in the Study of Expert Labour* (Palgrave 2008, edited with D. Muzio and J.-F. Chanlat).

Prof.dr **Victor Bekkers** is professor of public administration and public policy at the Department of Public Administration of the Erasmus University Rotterdam. He has published on the role of policy alienation in the implementation of public policies, on social innovation in the public sector and on the role of ICT and social media in the shaping of public policy processes. His work has appeared in *Public Management Review, Public Administration, The Information Society, Information Policy* and *International Revue of Administrative Science*. Recently, he edited a book on *Innovation in the Public Sector: Linking capacity and Leadership* (Palgrave Macmillan, 2011).

Dr **Rik van Berkel** is associate professor at the Utrecht School of Governance, Utrecht University. His research interests include welfare state transformations, new models for the provision of social services, and the implementation of social policy and governance reforms by frontline workers. His work focuses particularly on activation and welfare-to-work reforms and their implementation. He published in *Journal of European Social Policy, Public Management, Journal of Social Policy* and *Social Policy & Society*.

Dr **Jeroen van Bockel** is a senior policy advisor at the Dutch Advisory Board on Administrative Burden (Actal) since 2009. He finished his PhD thesis at the Utrecht School of Governance, Utrecht University, in 2009: *Embedded constraints; Bureaucratic and professional regulation of officials' work in the Dutch Republic* (1648-1795) (published in Dutch, with a summary in English, Eburon, Delft). For Actal, he prepared several reports, including reports on red tape of police officers and regulatory burdens in the construction industry. More broadly, he focuses on mechanisms for reducing regulatory burdens so that people, businesses and professionals actually notice differences. His chapter in this book does not necessarily reflect Actal policy views.

Dr **Gjalt de Graaf** is associate professor Public Governance at the Department of Governance Studies of the VU University Amsterdam. He studies conflicting values in governance, governing dilemmas, public values, integrity of governance and public management. He published in *Journal of Public Administration Research and Theory, Public Administration Review, Social Sciences & Medicine, Public Administration, American Review of*

Public Administration, Public Management Review, Perspectives on European Politics and Society, Public Integrity, Journal of Business Ethics, Public Administration Quarterly, Administration & Society, and *Health Policy.* He guest-edited Symposium issues of *Public Management Review, American Review of Public Administration, Public Integrity,* and *Public Administration Review.*

Drs **Huub Gulikers** is teacher and researcher at Social Studies of HAN University of Applied Science. As a PhD student he studies accountability in the social work sector, supervised by Professor Evelien Tonkens, Amsterdam University. He has been chairman of the counsel of Cultural Social Work Educations in the Netherlands and has published on the role of the market and marketization in the field of (cultural) social work.

Drs **Marc Hoijtink** is sociologist and researcher at the Research & Development Centre for Society and Law and lecturer for the Master programme Social Work at the Amsterdam University of Applied Sciences. He studies reforms in social policy and social work practices in urban areas. He has published about professionalism, new public management, labor issues in social work in *Journal of Social Intervention, Tijdschrift voor Beleid en Maatschappij, Sociétés et Jeunesses en Difficultée* and *Bestuurskunde.*

Dr **Peter L. Hupe** teaches Public Administration at Erasmus University Rotterdam. Currently he is a Visiting Fellow at All Souls College, Oxford. His research regards the theoretical and empirical study of the public policy process, particularly policy implementation and street-level bureaucracy. He has published articles in *Public Administration, Public Management Review* and *Policy and Politics.* With Michael Hill he wrote *Implementing Public Policy: An introduction to the study of operational governance* (2nd ed. 2009).

Dr **Theo van der Krogt** is emeritus associate professor of Public Management at the School of Management and Governance, University of Twente. He studied sociology of organizations, public personnel management, and professionalization processes, and published about these issues. For fifteen years he was the director of the executive master in public management program at his university. He still is the secretary-general of the European Association of Public Administration Accreditation (EAPAA).

Mr dr **Arie-Jan Kwak** is assistant professor at Faculty of Law (Encyclopedia and Philosophy of Law) of Leiden University. He studies and teaches on the subjects of legal professionalism, legal ethics and the methodology of legal scientific research. He has published *in Sociologische Gids, Trema, The Netherlands Journal of Legal Philosophy, Justitiële Verkenningen,*

Rechtstreeks and *Bestuurskunde*. In 2009 he edited *Holy Writ, Interpretation in Law and Religion* (Ashgate 2009).

Dr **Martijn van der Meulen** studied Political Science and Public Administration at Leiden University. In 2009, he received his PhD from Utrecht University, for his study on the professionalization of public managers. Martijn van der Meulen is assistant professor at the Utrecht University School of Governance; he teaches courses on public administration, policy implementation and public management. He also participated in advisory and research projects, e.g. on the professionalization strategy of the School for Police Leadership, implementation strategies of the Department of Education and Sciences and violence against public authorities.

Prof. **Janet Newman** is emeritus professor in the Faculty of Social Science at the Open University, UK. Her research interests include questions of governance, politics and power, with a particular focus on publics and publicness. Recent publications have focused on activist engagements with governance (Bloomsbury Press, 2012), on the politics of austerity (*Critical Social Policy*, 2012), public leadership as public-making (*Public Money and Management*, 2011) and working across the academic/ practitioner boundary (*Policy and Politics*, 2010). She is the author or editor of twelve books and has papers in journals such as *Sociology, Journal of Social Policy, Public Administration, Critical Social Policy, Critical Policy Studies* and *Cultural Studies.*

Dr **Mirjan Oude Vrielink** is senior researcher at the Department of Public Administration of the University of Twente. She studies issues of governance and regulation and public sector innovation. Currently she is involved in a two-year project that examines new forms of management that large Dutch cities have implemented to deal with multi-problem households. She published in *Regulation and Governance*, the *International Encyclopedia of Civil Society, Handbook of the Politics of Regulation, Law and Philosophy*. She is a member of the editorial board of two Dutch journals, *Bestuurskunde* and *Recht der Werkelijkheid.*

Dr **Amanda Smullen** is senior lecturer of Policy & Governance in the Crawford School of Public Policy at the Australian National University (ANU). She is also deputy director of the Menzies Centre for Health Policy at the ANU. Previously she was assistant professor at the University of Amsterdam. She focuses on comparative public management, institutions and argumentation. She has published in *Public Administration, Critical Policy Studies* and *Comparative Policy Analysis* and is also the author of books on agency reform and performance measurement. More recently, she entered the field of comparative mental healthcare policy and reform.

Prof.dr **Evelien Tonkens** is professor of Active Citizenship at the Department of Sociology at the University of Amsterdam. Her research concerns sociological analysis of changing ideals and practices of citizenship and professionalism. She has published in *Social Politics, Citizenship Studies, Sociology, Health Promotion International, Social Policy and Society, Culture, Renewal, Medicine and Psychiatry, Social History of Medicine, Community Development Studies*, and *Mental Retardation*. With J. Newman she edited the book *Participation, Responsibility and Choice. Summoning the Active Citizen* (Amsterdam University Press 2011) and with M. Hurenkamp and J.W. Duyvendak she wrote *Crafting Citizenship. Understanding Tensions in Modern Societies* (Palgrave 2012).

Dr **Lars Tummers** is assistant professor of Public Management and Policy Processes at Erasmus University Rotterdam. He studies public management, policy implementation, policy alienation, professional behavior, leadership and HR, especially in health care organizations. He has published in *Public Administration, Public Administration Review, Public Management Review, International Review of Administrative Sciences, Administration & Society* and *Health Policy*. He is co-chair of the research colloquium Reframing public professionalism, supported by the Netherlands Institute of Government (NIG).

Prof.dr **Romke van der Veen** is professor of Sociology of Work and Organization at Erasmus University, Rotterdam. His research focuses on the administration and organization of social policies and on processes of policy implementation. He has published on social security and social welfare, on health care and on (activating) labor market policies. Recently he published (with Peter Achterberg and Mara Yerkes) *The transformation of Solidarity. Changing Risks and the Future of the Welfare State* (AUP 2012).

Dr **Zeger van der Wal** is associate professor at the Lee Kuan Yew School of Public Policy, National University of Singapore, and research fellow at the VU University Amsterdam. He studies government elites, public values, public versus private management, public service motivation, and public professionalism. He has published in *Public Administration Review, Public Administration, Administration & Society, American Review of Public Administration, Public Management Review, Public Personnel Management, Journal of Business Ethics*, and *Public Integrity*. He is founder and chair of the NIG research colloquium Good Governance and editorial board member of *Bestuurskunde*.

Printed in Great Britain
by Amazon